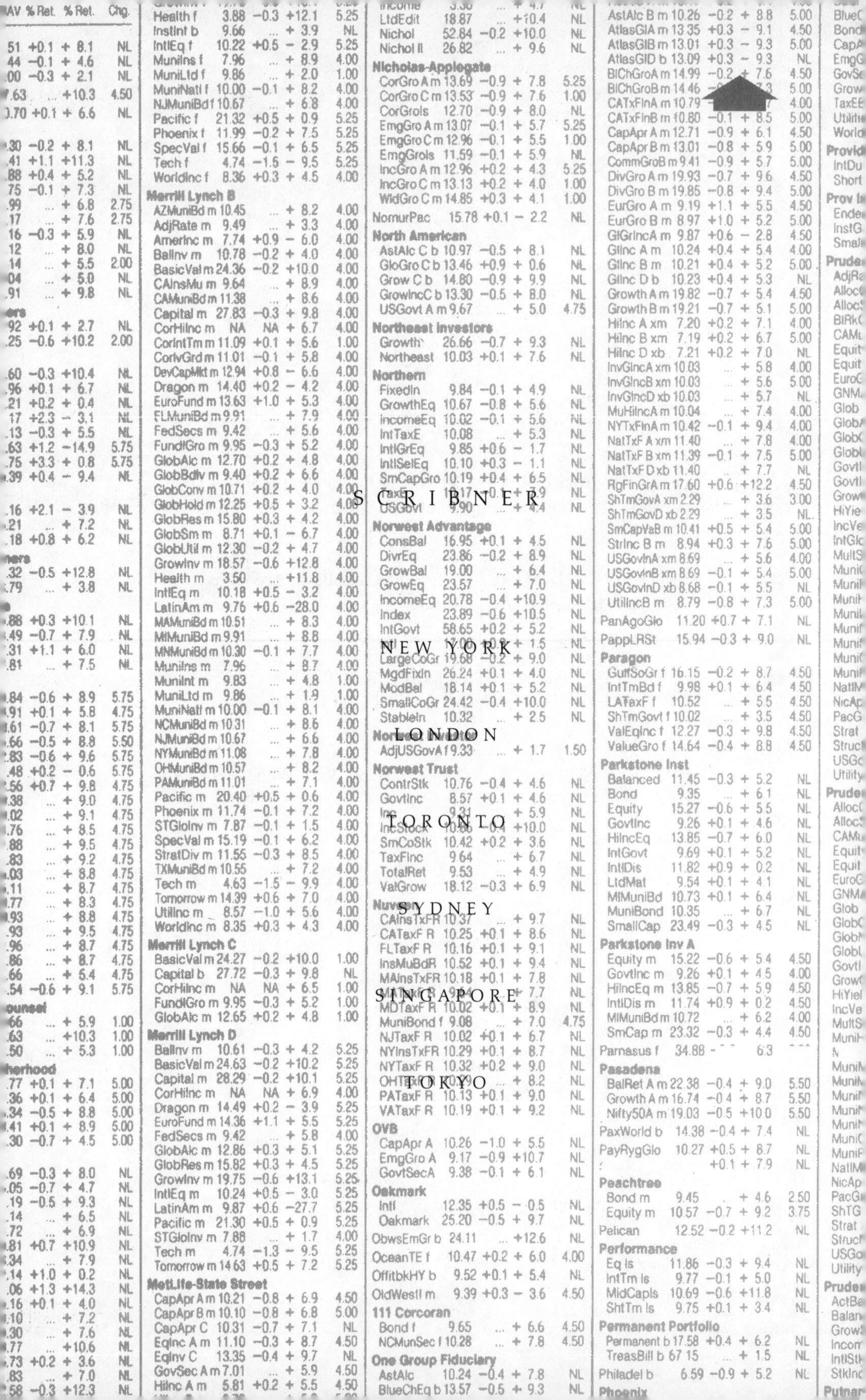

NAV	% Ret.	% Ret.	Chg.
.51	+0.1	+ 8.1	NL
.44	−0.1	+ 4.6	NL
.00	−0.3	+ 2.1	NL
7.63		+10.3	4.50
0.70	+0.1	+ 6.6	NL
.30	−0.2	+ 8.1	NL
.41	+1.1	+11.3	NL
.88	+0.4	+ 5.2	NL
.75	−0.1	+ 7.3	NL
.99		+ 6.8	2.75
.17		+ 7.6	2.75
.16	−0.3	+ 5.9	NL
.12		+ 8.0	NL
.14		+ 5.5	2.00
.04		+ 5.0	NL
.91		+ 9.8	NL
.92	+0.1	+ 2.7	NL
.25	−0.6	+10.2	2.00
.60	−0.3	+10.4	NL
.96	+0.1	+ 6.7	NL
.21	+0.2	+ 0.4	NL
.17	+2.3	− 3.1	NL
.13	−0.3	+ 5.5	NL
.63	+1.2	−14.9	5.75
.75	+3.3	+ 0.8	5.75
.39	+0.4	− 9.4	NL
.16	+2.1	− 3.9	NL
.21		+ 7.2	NL
.18	+0.8	+ 4.7	NL
.32	−0.5	+12.8	NL
.79		+ 3.8	NL
.88	+0.3	+10.1	NL
.49	−0.7	+ 7.9	NL
.31	+1.1	+ 6.0	NL
.81		+ 7.5	NL
.84	−0.6	+ 8.9	5.75
.91	+1.1	+ 5.8	4.75
.61	−0.7	+ 8.1	5.75
.66	−0.5	+ 8.8	5.50
.83	−0.6	+ 9.6	5.75
.48	+0.2	− 0.6	5.75
.56	+0.7	+ 9.8	4.75
.38		+ 9.0	4.75
.02		+ 9.1	4.75
.76		+ 8.5	4.75
.88		+ 9.2	4.75
.83		+ 8.8	4.75
.03		+ 8.7	4.75
.11		+ 8.3	4.75
.77		+ 8.8	4.75
.93		+ 9.5	4.75
.96		+ 8.7	4.75
.86		+ 8.7	4.75
.66		+ 5.4	4.75
.54	−0.6	+ 9.1	5.75
.66		+ 5.9	1.00
.63		+10.3	1.00
.50		+ 5.3	NL
.77	+0.1	+ 7.1	5.00
.36	+0.1	+ 6.4	5.00
.34	−0.5	+ 4.8	5.00
.41	+0.1	+ 8.9	5.00
.30	−0.7	+ 4.5	5.00
.69	−0.3	+ 8.0	NL
.05	−0.7	+ 4.7	NL
.19	−0.5	+ 9.3	NL
.14		+ 6.5	NL
.72		+ 6.9	NL
.81	+0.7	+10.9	NL
.34		+ 7.9	NL
.14	+1.9	+ 0.2	NL
.06	+1.3	+14.3	NL
.16	+0.1	+ 4.9	NL
.10		+ 7.2	NL
.30		+ 7.6	NL
.77		+10.6	NL
.73	+0.2	+ 3.6	NL
.83		+ 7.0	NL
.58	−0.3	+12.3	NL

	NAV	Chg.	% Ret.	
Health f	3.88	−0.3	+12.1	5.25
InstInt b	9.66		+ 3.9	NL
IntlEq f	10.22	+0.5	− 2.9	5.25
MuniIns f	7.96		+ 8.9	4.00
MuniLtd f	9.86		+ 2.0	1.00
MuniNatl f	10.00	−0.1	+ 8.2	4.00
NJMuniBd f	10.67		+ 6.8	4.00
Pacific f	21.32	+0.5	+ 0.9	5.25
Phoenix f	11.99	−0.2	+ 7.5	5.25
SpecVal f	15.66	−0.1	+ 6.5	5.25
Tech f	4.74	−1.5	− 9.5	5.25
WorldInc f	8.36	+0.3	+ 4.5	4.00

Merrill Lynch B

	NAV	Chg.	% Ret.	
AZMuniBd m	10.45		+ 8.2	4.00
AdjRate m	9.49		+ 3.3	4.00
AmerInc m	7.74	+0.9	− 6.0	4.00
BalInv m	10.78	−0.2	+ 4.0	4.00
BasicVal m	24.36	−0.2	+10.0	4.00
CAInsMu m	9.64		+ 8.9	4.00
CAMuniBd m	11.38		+ 8.6	4.00
Capital m	27.83	−0.3	+ 8.9	4.00
CorHiInc m	NA	NA	+ 6.7	4.00
CorIntTm m	11.09	+0.1	+ 5.6	1.00
CorIvGrd m	11.01	−0.1	+ 5.8	4.00
DevCapMkt m	12.94	+0.8	− 6.6	4.00
Dragon m	14.40	+0.2	− 4.2	4.00
EuroFund m	13.63	+1.0	+ 5.3	4.00
FLMuniBd m	9.91		+ 7.9	4.00
FedSecs m	9.42		+ 5.6	4.00
FundIGro m	9.95	−0.3	+ 5.2	4.00
GlobAlc m	12.70	−0.2	+ 4.8	4.00
GlobBdIv m	9.40	+0.2	+ 6.6	4.00
GlobConv m	10.71	+0.2	+ 4.0	4.00
GlobHold m	12.25	−0.3	+ 3.2	4.00
GlobRes m	15.80	+0.3	+ 4.2	4.00
GlobSm m	8.71	+0.1	− 6.7	4.00
GlobUtil m	12.30	−0.2	+ 4.7	4.00
GrowInv m	18.57	−0.6	+12.8	4.00
Health m	3.50		+11.8	4.00
IntlEq m	10.18	+0.5	− 3.2	4.00
LatinAm m	9.76	+0.6	−28.0	4.00
MAMuniBd m	10.51		+ 8.3	4.00
MIMuniBd m	9.91		+ 8.8	4.00
MNMuniBd m	10.30	−0.1	+ 7.7	4.00
MuniIns m	7.96		+ 8.7	4.00
MuniInt m	9.83		+ 4.8	1.00
MuniLtd m	9.86		+ 1.9	1.00
MuniNatl m	10.00	−0.1	+ 8.1	4.00
NCMuniBd m	10.31		+ 8.6	4.00
NJMuniBd m	10.67		+ 6.6	4.00
NYMuniBd m	11.08		+ 7.8	4.00
OHMuniBd m	10.57		+ 8.2	4.00
PAMuniBd m	11.01		+ 7.1	4.00
Pacific m	20.40	+0.5	+ 0.6	4.00
Phoenix m	11.74	−0.1	+ 7.2	4.00
STGloInv m	7.87	−0.1	+ 1.5	4.00
SpecVal m	15.19	−0.1	+ 6.2	4.00
StratDiv m	11.55	−0.3	+ 8.5	4.00
TXMuniBd m	10.55		+ 7.2	4.00
Tech m	4.63	−1.5	− 9.9	4.00
Tomorrow m	14.39	+0.6	+ 7.0	4.00
UtilInc m	8.57	−1.0	+ 5.6	4.00
WorldInc m	8.35	+0.3	+ 4.3	4.00

Merrill Lynch C

	NAV	Chg.	% Ret.	
BasicVal m	24.27	−0.2	+10.0	1.00
Capital b	27.72	−0.3	+ 9.8	NL
CorHiInc m	NA	NA	+ 6.5	1.00
FundIGro m	9.95	−0.3	+ 5.2	1.00
GlobAlc m	12.65	+0.2	+ 4.8	1.00

Merrill Lynch D

	NAV	Chg.	% Ret.	
BalInv m	10.61	−0.3	+ 4.2	5.25
BasicVal m	24.63	−0.2	+10.2	5.25
Capital m	28.29	−0.2	+10.1	5.25
CorHiInc m	NA	NA	+ 6.9	4.00
Dragon m	14.49	+0.2	− 3.9	5.25
EuroFund m	14.36	+1.1	+ 5.5	5.25
FedSecs m	9.42		+ 5.8	4.00
GlobAlc m	12.86	+0.3	+ 5.1	5.25
GlobRes m	15.82	+0.3	+ 4.5	5.25
GrowInv m	19.75	−0.6	+13.1	5.25
IntlEq m	10.24	+0.5	− 3.0	5.25
LatinAm m	9.87	+0.6	−27.7	5.25
Pacific m	21.30	+0.5	+ 0.9	5.25
STGloInv m	7.88		+ 1.7	4.00
Tech m	4.74	−1.3	− 9.5	5.25
Tomorrow m	14.63	+0.4	+ 7.2	5.25

MetLife-State Street

	NAV	Chg.	% Ret.	
CapAppr A m	10.21	−0.8	+ 6.9	4.50
CapApr B m	10.10	−0.8	+ 6.8	5.00
CapApr C	10.31	−0.7	+ 7.1	NL
EqInc A m	11.10	−0.3	+ 8.7	4.50
EqInv C	13.35	−0.4	+ 9.7	NL
GovSec A m	7.01		+ 4.9	4.50
HiInc A m	5.81	+0.2	+ 5.5	4.50

	NAV	Chg.	% Ret.	
Income	3.36		+ 4.7	NL
LtdEdit	18.87		+10.4	NL
Nichol	52.84	−0.2	+10.0	NL
Nichol II	26.82		+ 9.6	NL

Nicholas-Applegate

	NAV	Chg.	% Ret.	
CorGro A m	13.69	−0.9	+ 7.8	5.25
CorGro C m	13.53	−0.9	+ 7.6	1.00
CorGroIs	12.70	−0.9	+ 8.0	NL
EmgGro A m	13.07	−0.1	+ 5.7	5.25
EmgGro C m	12.96	−0.1	+ 5.5	1.00
EmgGroIs	11.59	−0.1	+ 5.9	NL
IncGro A m	12.96	+0.2	+ 4.3	5.25
IncGro C m	13.13	+0.2	+ 4.0	1.00
WidGro C m	14.85	+0.3	+ 4.1	1.00
NomurPac	15.78	+0.1	− 2.2	NL

North American

	NAV	Chg.	% Ret.	
AstAlc C b	10.97	−0.5	+ 8.1	NL
GloGro C b	13.46	−0.9	+ 0.6	NL
Grow C b	14.80	−0.9	+ 9.9	NL
GrowIncC b	13.30	−0.5	+ 8.0	NL
USGovt A m	9.67		+ 5.0	4.75

Northeast Investors

	NAV	Chg.	% Ret.	
Growth	26.66	−0.7	+ 9.3	NL
Northeast	10.03	+0.1	+ 7.6	NL

Northern

	NAV	Chg.	% Ret.	
FixedIn	9.84	−0.1	+ 4.9	NL
GrowthEq	10.67	−0.8	+ 5.6	NL
IncomeEq	10.02	−0.1	+ 5.6	NL
IntTaxE	10.08		+ 5.3	NL
IntlGrEq	9.85	+0.6	− 1.7	NL
IntlSelEq	10.10	−0.3	− 1.1	NL
SmCapGro	10.19	+0.4	+ 6.5	NL
USGovt	9.90		+ 4.4	NL

Norwest Advantage

	NAV	Chg.	% Ret.	
ConsBal	16.95	+0.1	+ 4.5	NL
DivrEq	23.86	−0.2	+ 8.9	NL
GrowBal	19.00		+ 6.4	NL
GrowEq	23.57		+ 7.0	NL
IncomeEq	20.78	−0.4	+10.9	NL
Index	23.89	−0.6	+10.5	NL
IntGovt	58.65	+0.2	+ 5.2	NL
LargeCoGr	19.68	−0.2	+ 9.0	NL
MgdFixIn	26.24	+0.1	+ 4.0	NL
ModBal	18.14	−0.1	+ 5.2	NL
SmallCoGr	24.42	−0.4	+10.0	NL
StableIn	10.32		+ 2.5	NL

Norwest Institutional

	NAV	Chg.	% Ret.	
AdjUSGovA	9.33		+ 1.7	1.50

Norwest Trust

	NAV	Chg.	% Ret.	
ContrStk	10.76	−0.4	+ 4.6	NL
GovInc	8.57	+0.1	+ 4.6	NL
Inc	9.31		+ 5.9	NL
IntStock	11.05	+0.9	+10.0	NL
SmCoStk	10.42	+0.2	+ 3.6	NL
TaxFInc	9.64		+ 6.7	NL
TotalRet	9.53		+ 4.9	NL
ValGrow	18.12	−0.3	+ 6.9	NL

Nuveen

	NAV	Chg.	% Ret.	
CAInsTxFR	10.37		+ 9.7	NL
CATaxF R	10.25	+0.1	+ 8.6	NL
FLTaxF R	10.16	+0.1	+ 9.1	NL
InsMuBdR	10.52	+0.1	+ 9.4	NL
MAInsTxFR	10.18	−0.1	+ 7.8	NL
MDTaxF R	10.02	+0.1	+ 8.9	NL
MuniBond f	9.08		+ 7.0	4.75
NJTaxF R	10.02	+0.1	+ 6.7	NL
NYInsTxFR	10.29	+0.1	+ 8.7	NL
NYTaxF R	10.32	+0.2	+ 9.0	NL
OHTaxF R	10.13	+0.1	+ 8.2	NL
PATaxF R	10.13	+0.1	+ 9.0	NL
VATaxF R	10.19	+0.1	+ 9.2	NL

OVB

	NAV	Chg.	% Ret.	
CapAppr A	10.26	−1.0	+ 5.5	NL
EmgGro A	9.17	−0.9	+10.7	NL
GovtSecA	9.38	−0.1	+ 6.1	NL

Oakmark

	NAV	Chg.	% Ret.	
Intl	12.35	+0.5	− 0.5	NL
Oakmark	25.20	−0.5	+ 9.7	NL
ObwsEmGr b	24.11		+12.6	NL
OceanTE f	10.47	+0.2	+ 6.0	4.00
OffitbkHY b	9.52	+0.1	+ 5.4	NL
OldWestl m	9.39	+0.3	− 3.6	4.50

111 Corcoran

	NAV	Chg.	% Ret.	
Bond f	9.65		+ 6.6	4.50
NCMunSec f	10.19		+ 7.8	4.50

One Group Fiduciary

	NAV	Chg.	% Ret.	
AstAlc	10.24	−0.4	+ 7.8	NL
BlueChEq b	13.57	−0.5	+ 9.3	NL

	NAV	Chg.	% Ret.	
AstAlc B m	10.26	−0.2	+ 8.8	5.00
AtlasGIA m	13.35	+0.3	− 9.1	4.50
AtlasGIB m	13.01	+0.3	− 9.3	5.00
AtlasGID b	13.09	+0.3	− 9.3	4.50
BlChGrinA m	14.99	−0.2	+ 7.6	4.50
BlChGroB m	14.46	−0.2	+ 7.5	5.00
CATxFinA m	10.79		+ 8.2	4.00
CATxFinB m	10.80	−0.1	+ 8.5	5.00
CapApr A m	12.71	−0.9	+ 6.1	4.50
CapApr B m	13.01	−0.8	+ 5.9	5.00
CommGroB m	9.41	−0.9	+ 5.7	5.00
DivGro A m	19.93	−0.7	+ 9.6	4.50
DivGro B m	19.85	−0.8	+ 9.4	5.00
EurGro A m	9.19	+1.1	+ 5.5	4.50
EurGro B m	8.97	+1.0	+ 5.2	5.00
GlGrincA m	9.87	+0.6	− 2.8	4.50
GInc A m	10.24	+0.4	+ 5.4	4.00
GInc B m	10.21	+0.4	+ 5.2	5.00
GInc D b	10.23	+0.4	+ 5.3	NL
Growth A m	19.82	−0.7	+ 5.4	4.50
Growth B m	19.21	−0.7	+ 5.1	5.00
HiInc A xm	7.20	+0.2	+ 7.1	4.00
HiInc B xm	7.19	+0.2	+ 6.7	5.00
HiInc D xb	7.21	+0.2	+ 7.0	NL
InvGincA xm	10.03		+ 5.8	4.00
InvGIncB xm	10.03		+ 5.6	5.00
InvGIncD xb	10.03		+ 5.7	NL
MuHiIncA m	10.04		+ 7.4	4.00
NYTxFinA m	10.42	−0.1	+ 9.4	4.00
NatTxF A m	11.40		+ 7.8	4.00
NatTxF B m	11.39	−0.1	+ 7.5	5.00
NatTxF D xb	11.40		+ 7.7	NL
RgFinGrA m	17.60	+0.6	+12.2	4.50
ShTmGovA xm	2.29		+ 3.6	3.00
ShTmGovD xb	2.29		+ 3.5	NL
SmCapVaB m	10.41	+0.5	+ 5.4	5.00
StrInc B m	8.94	+0.3	+ 7.6	5.00
USGovA m	8.69		+ 5.6	4.00
USGovnB xm	8.69	−0.1	+ 5.4	5.00
USGovnD xb	8.68	−0.1	+ 5.5	NL
UtilIncB m	8.79	−0.8	+ 7.3	5.00
PanAgoGlo	11.20	+0.7	+ 7.1	NL
PapplLRSt	15.94	−0.3	+ 9.0	NL

Paragon

	NAV	Chg.	% Ret.	
GulfSoGr f	16.15	−0.2	+ 8.7	4.50
IntTmBd f	9.98	+0.1	+ 6.4	4.50
LATaxF f	10.52		+ 5.5	4.50
ShTmGovt f	10.02		+ 3.5	4.50
ValEqInc f	12.27	−0.3	+ 9.8	4.50
ValueGro f	14.64	−0.4	+ 8.8	4.50

Parkstone Inst

	NAV	Chg.	% Ret.	
Balanced	11.45	−0.3	+ 5.2	NL
Bond	9.35		+ 6.1	NL
Equity	15.27	−0.6	+ 5.5	NL
GovtInc	9.26	+0.1	+ 4.6	NL
HiIncEq	13.85	−0.7	+ 6.0	NL
IntGovt	9.69	+0.1	+ 5.2	NL
IntlDis	11.82	+0.9	+ 6.2	NL
LtdMat	9.54	+0.1	+ 4.1	NL
MIMuniBd	10.73	+0.1	+ 6.4	NL
MuniBond	10.35		+ 6.7	NL
SmallCap	23.49	−0.3	+ 4.5	NL

Parkstone Inv A

	NAV	Chg.	% Ret.	
Equity m	15.22	−0.6	+ 5.4	4.50
GovtInc m	9.26	+0.1	+ 4.5	4.00
HiIncEq m	13.85	−0.7	+ 5.9	4.50
IntlDis m	11.74	+0.9	+ 6.2	4.50
MIMuniBd m	10.72		+ 6.2	4.00
SmCap m	23.32	−0.3	+ 4.4	4.50
Parnasus f	34.88	− −	6.3	− − −

Pasadena

	NAV	Chg.	% Ret.	
BalRet A m	22.38	−0.4	+ 9.0	5.50
Growth A m	16.74	−0.4	+ 8.7	5.50
Nifty50A m	19.03	−0.5	+10.0	5.50
PaxWorld b	14.38	−0.4	+ 7.4	NL
PayRygGlo	10.27	+0.5	+ 8.7	NL
			+0.1	+ 7.9	NL

Peachtree

	NAV	Chg.	% Ret.	
Bond m	9.45		+ 4.6	2.50
Equity m	10.57	−0.7	+ 9.2	3.75
Pelican	12.52	−0.2	+11.2	NL

Performance

	NAV	Chg.	% Ret.	
Eq Is	11.86	−0.3	+ 9.4	NL
IntTm Is	9.77	−0.1	+ 5.5	NL
MidCapIs	10.69	−0.6	+11.8	NL
ShtTm Is	9.75	+0.1	+ 3.4	NL

Permanent Portfolio

	NAV	Chg.	% Ret.	
Permanent b	17.58	+0.4	+ 4.2	NL
TreasBill b	67.15		+ 1.5	NL
Philadel b	6.59	−0.9	+ 5.2	NL

Phoenix

RISKY BUSINESS

An

Insider's

Account

of the

Disaster at

Lloyd's of London

Elizabeth Luessenhop

Martin Mayer

SCRIBNER
1230 Avenue of the Americas
New York, NY 10020

SCRIBNER and design are
trademarks of Simon & Schuster Inc.

Designed by SONGHEE KIM
Manufactured in the United States of America

1 3 5 7 9 10 8 6 4 2

Library of Congress Cataloging-in-Publication Data
Risky Business : an insider's account of the disaster at Lloyd's of
London / Elizabeth Luessenhop, Martin Mayer.
p.   cm.
Includes bibliographical references and index.
1. Lloyd's (Firm) 2. Insurance companies—England—London—
History. I. Mayer, Martin, date. II. Title.
HG8039.L93 1995
368'.012'0604212—dc20   95-35469
CIP

ISBN 0-684-19739-1

WITH LOVE TO CYNTHIA AND MIKE,

CONSEY AND TOMMY,

JOHN AND CHARLES,

LOUISE, CHARLOTTE, McCREA,

AND HARRIET

ACKNOWLEDGMENTS

I called Edward T. Chase in the spring of 1993 to ask if he liked the idea of doing a book about Lloyd's of London. He agreed after ten minutes. Within the next half hour he'd contacted Martin Mayer to collaborate with me.

That was my second lucky phone call. A novice is extremely fortunate to work with a successful author on her first book. Martin has taught me much more than I can describe here.

After our contracts were signed, Edward Chase told me, "Betsy, the best thing a publisher earns is not his check but the opportunity to meet interesting people." He and his lovely wife, Lynn, lead my list. From our first conversation, their wise counsel and encouragement have been constant. I've made dear friends in England and the United States. The generous support of new and longtime friends has been overwhelming. The people who work at One Lime Street are among the most polite I know. Everyone I've asked to see has given freely of his time, made useful suggestions, even searched out papers and photographs. I am grateful to all of them, but most especially to Nick Doak and the entire executive staff of the press office. Without their very professional help there would be no book. It is easy to talk about a business when the profits are flooding in. It takes strong character to do so when things go wrong. Nick is always knowledgeable and forthright, and fun, too.

Lloyd's is a beautiful place, a tragic place. It's been a great experience to study it.

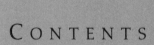

CONTENTS

INTRODUCTION

This book is Elizabeth Luessenhop's first, and—counting four books that I wrote for someone else's signature—my thirty-sixth, half of them about business subjects. Both our names are on the cover, and correctly so. Where not neutral, the voice of the book is Betsy's voice—as Betsy's voice sounded toward the end of long conversations with me. The experiences that inform the book are Betsy's experiences. A few of the interviews quoted here were mine without her participation, and some involved both of us, but by far the bulk of the interviewing was hers alone. She has a gift for it: People who answer others in monosyllables will spill their guts for Betsy. She also has the reporter's instinct for picking up and squirreling away for later use any document that happens to be lying around loose.

What follows is a personal *and* analytic account of the wreck of one of the world's most romantic and longest-lived business institutions—Lloyd's of London—and the $13 *billion* that disaster took from the private resources of twenty thousand mostly upper-middle-class professional people and business people and their spouses in England and America. This is a great story, one of the most interesting and infuriating business stories of our time, and it's been great fun to tell it.

One technical detail: American readers not being interested in British pounds, I have in all contexts except direct quotation converted pounds to dollars. Over the years of this story, the value of the pound in dollars fluctuated from little less than two to one to little more than one to one. But it kept returning to $1.50. For convenience's sake, pounds have been converted to dollars throughout the book at the rate of $1.50 per pound, regardless of the year in which the gains or losses occurred.

Most terms of art from the insurance business or Lloyd's are explained—one hopes, adequately—at their first use, but readers may occasionally find it helpful to consult the Glossary that begins on page 341.

MARTIN MAYER

CHAPTER 1

A SENTIMENTAL
BUSINESS EDUCATION

Thirteen billion dollars is the latest estimate of liabilities which I and 33,000 other people owe for insurance claims, mostly from U.S. companies. I, along with others, have unlimited liability for my losses. Our names are on policies written by syndicates at Lloyd's of London. Through Lloyd's, we as *individuals* are accepted as alien reinsurers and nonaccredited surplus line insurers in forty-eight states and accredited in two.

It is amazing to me now that I should have taken such an enormous risk. But it may be even harder to believe that American companies would place their coverage with syndicates that are supported by people like me and expect to be paid millions without a worry.

Victims of asbestosis, prosperous yacht owners, businesses large and small depend to a greater or lesser extent on prompt payments. Lloyd's can boast that its syndicates have done so for three hundred years, but can it continue to pay all claims? Although I passed a means test for admission to the Society of Lloyd's, my net worth is not audited and the truth is that Lloyd's doesn't know how much I could pay.

I made my first trip to Europe in 1965, when my husband took me to what was his first International Congress of Neurosurgeons in Denmark. We spent a week in London before the conference and a week afterward in Paris at a beautiful apartment on the rue de Mexico, red geraniums in the boxes on the terrace. Our hostess was the daughter of our neighbor in McLean, Virginia, General Leon Johnson, who had been the U.S. representative to SHAFE (Supreme Headquarters Allied Forces in Europe) in the years right after the war. Sally had been brought up in Paris and she was very chic. She was married to a former fighter pilot who represented General Dynamics in France, and they knew everybody. The dollar was still strong, and expense accounts for American businessmen were flowing. We were up late partying every night with NATO officers and B. J. Cutler, publisher of the *Paris Herald Tribune,* whose evenings out began at eleven, after the paper went to bed. We usually wound up at a place called Los Calvados, headquarters for the 1960s expatriate Americans, with a black jazz pianist in the basement. Porfirio Rubirosa and Aly Khan were among the habitués; both later died in automobile accidents in the Bois de Boulogne after an evening at Los Calvados.

Three weeks and I was hooked on Europe for life. All that beauty, history, and style excite me still. I wanted to live abroad for a long period, not just visit as a tourist.

My involvement with the rich, traditional, complex, and sometimes horrifying business of insurance began in 1983. My wish was going to come true.

Imagine being a divorcee with four grown children, previous commercial experience limited to the grocery store and Saks Fifth Avenue, and a modest amount of cash. Longtime friends from East Hampton decide to help by offering an opportunity to join Lloyd's of London. You're told it's a safe and glamorous way to increase your income, if they accept you. You don't simply invest, you become a member of a society, a "Name." You can keep your assets plus any interest or dividends they earn. You merely pledge them and after the initial three years you will receive a check each June. While you will be asked if you understand the concept of unlimited liability, you are assured that three hundred years of success are proof against financial distress. No U.S. company has such an illustrious record. I said yes. I was accepted.

"Never trust a Frenchman in love, and never trust an Englishman in business." Baron Alain de La Cam gave me that advice during the wonderful week in Paris in 1965. A love affair with a Frenchman might have been fun, but instead I became a Member of Lloyd's. A very expensive choice. Thousands of Americans and Canadians, and many more thousands of British gentry who were well-off a few years ago are less well-to-do now. Many are impoverished, and some say at least thirty are suspected of suicide because they listened to the siren song from a London market.

I was easy to convince. My family on both sides goes back to Colonial times. Mother firmly believed the United States should never have separated from the mother country. In our home it was a given that the English set the standards of good taste and integrity for the world. Most people I knew in Boston and Philadelphia would have agreed. The heroes of our family were the cousins who volunteered in World War II. One died flying in the Canadian Royal Air Force. Another was wounded badly in France.

In the optimistic years of the booming eighties, placing my stocks in the hands of English gentlemen seemed perfectly reasonable. Besides, Russell Tandy of the giant California insurance brokerage agency Marsh and McLennan had proposed my sponsor. I would use the same agents. Walking in Russell's footsteps was all I needed to do. I blush now to admit that I've spent more time selecting dresses than I did in learning about the institution I intended to join.

However, I did caution my agent, charming Rupert Brett, "I don't want to make a fortune. I want the smallest percentage of gain because I want to run the least risk." This plea brings a laugh at so many Names meetings these days because so many of us asked the same thing. I don't believe our agents intended to put us in jeopardy. They didn't know where danger awaited in many cases. My members' agents, Ken Sanders and Rupert Brett, had placed themselves on Merrett 418 before putting my name on the syndicate. We sat together at meetings of our action group, which is suing to recover our losses.

The way the system worked, my agent explained, was that insurance underwriters calculated the premiums they charged their policyholders in such a way that the premiums and the income the underwriters made by investing them more than covered the losses that they expected would have to be paid to the policyholders. But the people and companies who bought the policies needed assurance that the underwriter had the resources to pay off if his losses were greater than he expected.

Lloyd's custom was that this underlying "capital" was not provided permanently by investors in the insurance business but separately for each year's insurance contracts, by individuals, "Names," who pledged their assets and their credit to paying out the insured losses that might be incurred by the "syndicates" of which they became "members." Each syndicate was a little insurance company that in effect wrote its own insurance policies. The word "Names" traces back almost three centuries, to a time when one or a few individuals signified their guarantees by personally signing the policies they underwrote; people paid the premiums for the policy because they trusted these Names. Now most syndicates have hundreds or even thousands of members, whose contract is with a Names' agency rather than with the underwriters they back or the insured themselves, but they're still called "Names."

In form and in law, the premiums paid for the policies went not to the syndicates, but to the Names individually—though of course they didn't get the money, which was credited to a trust account opened on their behalf. The total amount of premiums a Name could receive was a function of the size of the deposit the Name left with Lloyd's to establish his credit. Each Name was a "sole trader," and if there were losses, he would be responsible only for that share of the losses by the syndicate represented by his share of the total premium income the syndicate had accepted.

The words "each for his own part and not for any other" were printed on every Lloyd's insurance policy. By the same token, each Name would get a proportion of the syndicate's profits (after expenses) equal to his share of the syndicate's total premiums.

"Profits." The English have a way of saying the word "profits" that is just divine. At an "Annual General Meeting" of thousands and thousands of Lloyd's Names in spring 1993 at London's Royal Albert Hall (the largest concert hall in the country), Lloyd's chairman David Rowland, looking ahead, kept insisting that the future would be a world of "profits," and even knowing all I had learned about Lloyd's, I felt I could listen forever to his voice as he said the word "profits." It's so much nicer a sound than "making money." The "business plan" for the future published by Lloyd's in April 1993, when Lloyd's was near the edge and scrambling for salvation but still trying to coax more money out of its Names, was called *Planning for Profit.*

The beauty of the system was that you didn't have to *invest* any money to receive your share of these profits. You simply *pledged* assets. Your deposit at Lloyd's was like your deposit at a bank (though not always so easy to take out); you still owned it. This was a perfect way for Englishmen who had inherited property to hold on to their families' land even though that land didn't yield much (or any) income. By pledging their property to the fulfillment of insurance contracts written at Lloyd's, and collecting a share of the profits of the insurance syndicates, the Names could live in style while trying to make money from their estates. Others pledged their "gilts"—British government bonds—to increase their income from these (also often inherited) investments.

Lloyd's itself sometimes looked like a collection of family businesses. The institution called Lloyd's was a marketplace, not an insurance company—the original Edward Lloyd had been a man who owned a coffeehouse where people in the shipping business, sea captains and merchant princes, congregated, and arranged to spread the risks that ships and cargoes might be lost at sea. Resplendent in red tailcoats with brass buttons and luscious black velvet–trimmed collars and cuffs, the liveried attendants who guard the doors and make themselves useful on the Lloyd's floor are still called "Waiters" as a kind of tribute to the origins of the market. The Waiters are about the only people at Lloyd's who have maintained a wholly positive attitude about the place. I always look forward to a wave and sunny smile, a "Good morning, Madam," as I walk up the steps to be checked at the door by some harder types in black suits asking to see my gold Lloyd's membership card. In 1994, I had lunch at the Ship and Turtle, an ancient City pub, with Mr. McDonnell, a very genial, big man who stands in the little guardhouse at the entrance to the trading floor and checks people's credentials before they enter. "We don't realize how lucky we are," he said, "to work at this wonderful place, where the ladies are ladies and the gentlemen are *gents.*"

Many of the leading brokers and agents and managers of the insurance syndicates that were housed at Lloyd's were the children of the people who had run Lloyd's in the past, and their friends' children. Lloyd's was as much a club as it was a business. Every afternoon at five o'clock, one of the Waiters, reverting to the old function, would bring glasses and a bottle of champagne on a silver tray to the chairman's office. Rebuking an upstart broker and manager who was making huge profits on the insurance of the first wide-bodied jet aircraft, an old-timer said grimly, "First generation don't even speak in this place." In the years before World War II, virtually all the few thousand Names were English, and most of them knew one another. It wasn't until 1969 that Lloyd's accepted Names who were not citizens of a British Commonwealth country—or who were female.

American and Canadian Names came from a different social stratum; they were mostly professional and retired people who were trying to build an estate with investments. (The Canadians, middle-class specialists, most of them recruited from the area around Hamilton, Ontario, were known at Lloyd's as "the medics.") Lloyd's asked American Names to deposit a bank letter of credit for a minimum of $150,000, and to give evidence of an additional $400,000 of "net worth." The more money you put up in your "deposit" or your letter of credit, the higher the premium income you would be permitted to receive under Lloyd's rules. For $150,000, you would get a premium limit of $450,000. All the arrangements associated with the letter of credit would be made for you by your agent at Lloyd's. The largest number of Americans got their "l/c" from Bank of Boston, as I did. The only requirement was that you deposit at the bank, as security, stocks and bonds with a face value large enough to guarantee that if Lloyd's demanded money from the l/c to pay out the losses of a syndicate, the bank could sell the collateral and meet the demand.

In this way, Lloyd's apparently gave everybody something for nothing. Bank of Boston put out no money and ran no risks, and charged you a 1 percent commission each year on the face value of the letter of credit. The new Name very visibly got something for nothing. You, not the bank and not Lloyd's, continued to own the stocks and bonds or CDs you had deposited as collateral for the letter of credit. You continued to receive the dividends and interest on your securities, and if their price went up, you got the benefit. You kept your investments, and you made something extra by using them as collateral at the same time. "Your money worked twice" was the usual expression. And for some of the Names it could be a lot of income: The more successful syndicates could boast years when the profits they paid to their Names were greater than the Names' earnings on the securities they had deposited to back the letter of credit—and the Names got the earnings from the securities, too.

It took almost ten years for me to learn that becoming a Name on these smaller, specialty syndicates required more contacts than newcomers like myself would ever have; the syndicates available to us have proved to be more dangerous. John Trulett, a friendly British Name, told me that he once asked his Name's agent to put him on a syndicate he'd heard good things about, and the agent said, "You can't get on *that*. My chairman can't get on *that*." Syndicate 45 had a ten-year waiting list—though "working Names," people actually engaged in Lloyd's business, however young, might be jumped to the head of the queue. When David Coleridge was chairman of Lloyd's and was criticized because his wife had been put on three of the most popular syndicates without waiting her turn, he found the "line of questioning so unattractive and unbecoming that I am considering asking my wife to resign as a member of Lloyd's. I shall take up all her underwriting commitments myself. . . ."[1]

And, of course, becoming a Name was not just a business proposition: It was a membership in the club, a kind of recognition that only the English landed gentry can give. Only a Name could propose someone for a membership in Lloyd's, and the new member was not "accepted," he was *"elected."* The banker George Moore, who was also president of the Metropolitan Opera, became a Name after he retired as chairman of Citicorp, which is trustee for Lloyd's American investments. "The first reason to be a 'name' at Lloyd's," he wrote in his memoirs, "is the honor of it, the world's knowledge that you have met all the responsibility requirements and passed a strenuous interview. It beats any 'gold card' or 'platinum card' any consumer-credit organization ever issued."[2] Actually, you weren't supposed to talk about being a Name, because it was such a restricted privilege. But it gave a certain self-confidence.

When I signed on, there were only a little more than twenty thousand Names worldwide, and only about one thousand of them were Americans. As late as 1958, there had been only four thousand Names, all of them British, and when the first Americans signed on in 1969 there were fewer than seven thousand Names. Between my "election" in 1983 and 1989, another ten thousand Names—more than fifteen hundred of them Americans—would be added. Though the material was not presented this way, a little conversion to real numbers of the percentage figures in Sir David Walker's report on reinsurance at Lloyd's (commissioned by Lloyd's itself) shows that over the period 1983–90, Names who worked at Lloyd's made a *profit* of about $150,000 on

$600,000 of premiums accepted (about the average risk in the market), while Names from North America showed a *loss* of about $55,000.[3] And this, remember, was *before* crediting these insiders with their "profit percentage" on those syndicates that did make a profit, their dividends from their stock in the incorporated agencies, or their capital gains on that stock, which kept rising in the markets through the years when in reality Lloyd's was accumulating losses for its "external" Names.

Though we didn't know it at the time, many of the "members' agents" who put the Names into the underwriting syndicates were paying commissions to recruiters who brought in new candidates. James Deely, who first became a Name when he was a senior vice president of Citibank handling insurance industry accounts, was introduced to Lloyd's by the firm of Wilcox and Barringer, the British subsidiary of the big American insurance broker Johnson and Higgins, a good customer of both his bank and Lloyd's. A few years later, to his astonishment, his Name's agent, Colin Murray, told him in an irritated way that "we're getting tired of paying Barringer a subagent's commission on you every year." The American Names Association estimates that approximately one third of Americans and Canadians were recruited by agents who paid commissions for the referrals. It says a lot about the English ability to sustain myths that the mystique of the exclusive club was somehow maintained. Of course, it was not until 1991 that Lloyd's, for the first time since 1961, reported a losing year (which was 1988: Lloyd's has always reported results after three years).

Everybody who dealt with Names and proposed Names was terribly cheerful about Lloyd's. They still are. John Robson is an extraordinarily suave, articulate, and handsome man in his forties who could charm the paint off the walls, a Name's agent who told me he had persuaded seven very rich men to accept $1.5 million of "capacity" to underwrite insurance in 1994, after the huge losses of the previous three years. In October 1993, Robson made a speech to the Insurance Institute of London, and reminisced about the life of a members' agent in the early 1980s: "It was a happy ten years. Santos and May [the chief Waiters in the Captain's Room] became part of the family as I entertained Names every day. The profits flowed and a regular cheque of account on January 1st to assist in paying the previous year's tax liabilities was the norm."[4]

For me, becoming a Name at Lloyd's was part of my love affair with England. And the love affair is still there, with London and with country weekends—and with many of the people I have come to know at Lloyd's. A few of them of course are real snakes, but even the snakes are at least interesting. They still do a lot of things just right at Lloyd's. The most gorgeous lunch I've ever had was in Boston in July 1993, at an angry meeting of *seven hundred* American Names, when the Bank of Scotland was my host. Bagpipes took us into lunch, the salmon had been flown in that morning, there was a pound note at each place as a party favor, a different wine was served with each course, and there was a scrumptious strawberry dessert with Scotch shortbread cookies. It was really heaven—just to sell the services of the bank as the writer of your letter of credit to Lloyd's!

Bernie Daenzer, an American insurance man who was the first U.S. Name at Lloyd's, recruited scores of Floridians to membership in Lloyd's with parties at the Ocean Reef Club and the Coronado Hotel. He became a director of the Alexander Howden agency in London, and when Howden blew up, I'm told, it turned out he was the most highly paid director at the place, probably as a reward for all his American Names. One of them, Carl Aronson, also an insurance man, remembered being met at Heathrow with a Rolls-Royce whenever he visited London, and being ferried to a luxurious Howden apartment where he would stay "free of charge," he says, "except that really, of course, it wasn't."

When I came to London in 1983 for my interview at Lloyd's, I didn't worry about whether I was doing something commercially wise. It was almost as though I wondered whether I was worthy. On previous trips to London I had stayed at the Dorchester House, but somehow Park Lane seemed too touristy for this visit. I knew that when royalty came to London they stayed at Brown's; so for the occasion of my Lloyd's interview, I stayed at Brown's. Before packing my bag to depart, I consulted with my friend Betty Loughead, who had "proposed" me for membership, about what would be the proper attire for an interview at Lloyd's, and finally I decided on a dark suit as the most dignified choice.

Following the meeting with the Rota Committee, I returned to Brett's office at the firm of Bland-Welch and signed a membership agreement designating the firm to be my Name's agent. I could make requests for placement on various syndicates under the contract, but like most Names I relied on my agent's choice, being too ignorant of the market to make a decision myself. Choosing syndicates for their Names is the principal responsibility of a member's agent. Names receive a general overview of their syndicate's performance from both their Name's agent and the managing agents of the syndicates under their control. Only the underwriters on the trading floor could know details of the risks they insured because syndicates write hundreds or thousands of policies in a single year. Names were free to talk to their agents and underwriters at any time. However, a majority of Names, like me, did not seem to have the basic knowledge of insurance to ask meaningful questions.

The payments which I made to agents for expenses and a share of my profits would go automatically out of my premium trust funds to them. I would know what salaries the syndicate managers and underwriters paid themselves after a bylaw change, but not the cost of bonuses and perks.

Though there was a new syndicate every year for the purpose of writing new insurance, each syndicate would remain in existence for three years, and then wind up its affairs, reinsuring what risks might remain from the contracts on its books. In the spring of the year following those three years, my Name's agent would send a report telling me how much money my syndicate had made (or—of course there was always the possibility—lost) and what my share of the profits was. Again, that pretty word.

In this atmosphere, everybody enjoying everybody else's company, even bankers like George Moore didn't ask the kinds of questions that businessmen would normally pose before assuming the risks that it turned out we had assumed.

The ranks of American Names include many apparently sophisticated businessmen. Charles Schwab, founder and proprietor of the nation's largest discount brokerage firm, was a Name at Lloyd's, and a loser. So was James Harvey, chairman of Transamerica Corporation. And George Gould, former undersecretary of the treasury. And James Patton, senior partner of the famous Washington law firm of Patton Boggs, movers and shakers in the American political world. Supreme Court justice Stephen Breyer was a Name, on the same syndicate that tortures me.

Like me, the businessmen never learned until it was much too late that the agents who represented them were really as much in the dark as they were. What was really happening was gaily described by John Robson in his 1993 speech: "As the pressure grew from Names wanting to increase their underwriting and the number of new Names coming to us quickened, so we expanded the number of syndicates which we supported. It was extraordinarily unsophisticated and relied almost entirely on personalities and relationships with little regard for business plans which were unheard of, reinsurance résumés which were definitely not available, or regular meetings off the golf course with the managing agency, which usually meant meeting the underwriter over lunch or coffee once or twice a year."[5]

Under the Lloyd's system it was only the *brokers,* not the underwriters, who really knew who was insuring what, because only the brokers had complete copies of the policies and all the "slips" the underwriters had stamped to signal their acceptance of this risk. "Because they do not have filing space to maintain voluminous documents," the American insurance lawyer Seth B. Schafler explained in 1993, "Lloyd's syndicates generally rely on Lloyd's brokers to maintain essential underwriting and claims records on their behalf."[6] One of the reasons Lloyd's can't close the books on many older syndicates is that the records are so confused nobody knows what the underwriters for some of the now defunct Lloyd's managing agencies had or had not insured. A whole new profession of insurance archaeologist has developed to search through old warehouses for policies written years ago with claims for today. And they will find big ones.

Joseph Wechsberg, the Czech-American journalist who wrote about the Rothschilds but most often about music and food and travel, found at Lloyd's a "relaxed, schoolboy atmosphere," and noted in an article in the London *Times* in the late 1950s that "no man at Lloyd's (as in any well run, discreet organization) knows exactly what the other fellow is doing, and no one in its marble-filled headquarters in Lime Street knows everything about the entire operation." But in an insurance business, it is desperately important to know what other people are doing, and what information they may have that you don't have. It was, after all, other people's money—the Names' money, my money—that the Lloyd's brokers and underwriters were shepherding. That's not work to be done in a relaxed, schoolboy atmosphere.

I went to see Stephen Merrett, then deputy chairman of Lloyd's. He was the son of Roy Merrett, who had been a folk hero in the market—an imaginative but diligent underwriter who had risen from the equivalent of office boy to become proprietor of one of the largest managing agencies at Lloyd's (and who told Joseph Wechsberg that his hours in the Lloyd's trading room had been the happiest of his life). Stephen Merrett's syndicate 418 for the year 1985, in which I was a Name, was maybe one of the biggest losers at Lloyd's. I told Merrett I was writing a book. "Oh, dear," he said. "I imagine you will make me look even more stupid than others have made me look." In our three interviews, Mr. Merrett was extremely gracious and forthcoming in his answers, even adding a bit of humor the last time. The politeness of the British is remarkable. After all, I am suing the man for a lot of pounds.

Merrett resigned from his position as deputy chairman in summer 1993, and in late autumn his managing agency was dissolved and his syndicates placed in other hands. I've been told when he was riding high, there was no one more arrogant than this casual, handsome man with a great mop of white hair. Once, I heard, when he didn't like the premium a broker was offering to pay, he took the man's papers and threw them half the length of the trading room, scattering them under the tables of other syndicates. As negotiator for the companies that would have to pay out the equivalent of malpractice insurance after Outhwaite 317, one of the first of the big cases Names brought against a Lloyd's underwriter, had come to settlement talks, Stephen Merrett was scheduled for a meeting with the lawyers for late in the afternoon. He kept everybody waiting until after midnight—half a dozen lawyers billing hundreds of dollars an hour while they waited. Merrett finally showed up, dressed in white tie, with the excuse that he'd been at the opera, and had to stay for a reception for the queen afterwards.

Talking with Englishmen can be deceptive for an American, because here when anyone speaks well, he's well educated, and that's not necessarily true there. Frequently they have attended a prestigious private preparatory school (four years of high school) and then enlisted for two years in a socially prominent military regiment. Sometimes you can't understand, anyway, because they have that public school accent where they choke to death on every word they say.

Among the worst losers were Devonshire 216 and 833/834, which concentrated on reinsuring other syndicates so they could close and pay off their members. The "active underwriter" for those syndicates told a committee appointed by Lloyd's to investigate their losses that he set the premium for such business by "gut feeling," adding that "whatever gut feelings you might have had, shall we say, in the late eighties have gone out the window because they have been displaced by so adverse a market experience the like of which we have never encountered." Some of the worst losses, he said, had come as the result of decisions by a subordinate "who had actually forgotten what my instructions were to rearrange the business."[7] This was not a gentleman's business but no business at all.

As I now know, some of what was happening at Lloyd's in the 1980s appears a lot worse than just ignorance. The drive to recruit new Names to Lloyd's had begun for other reasons, but by the time Russell Tandy came to Betty Loughead, who in turn came to me, the Lloyd's membership machine was being fueled by fear. Insiders at Lloyd's knew they had huge losses coming down the pike, and they were bringing in new Names from different countries and different social strata to help the old Names carry the burden. David Rowland, who would later be chairman of Lloyd's but was then a senior Lloyd's broker chairing a task force on the future of the market, admitted the real reason for growth in his 1992 report entitled *Lloyd's: A Route Forward.* "The market has to be able to grow," he argued, "if it is to trade through the overhang of old years claims. . . . A contracting base could place the entire burden of all old years claims on a diminishing pool of capital providers for whom there would be an increasing incentive to leave."[8] In the United States, we call that a Ponzi scheme, named after the Boston postman who stole millions of dollars from people in the 1920s by promising them extravagant returns on their money, paying the early subscribers with the deposits of later subscribers until the machine exploded.

The reason to recruit new Names, Lloyd's kept telling the world, was to increase the "capacity" of the insurers who worked in the Lloyd's trading room and needed more backing to underwrite more risks. But that "capacity" was not used to increase the total amount of Lloyd's insurance of real customers. Instead, the newcomers, guided by agents who theoretically represented their interests, were put in syndicates that were reinsuring the risks a few older Lloyd's members had insured against during the postwar years—risks that were soon going to generate horrendous losses as unlimited as the liability of those who would have to meet them.

By 1995, the admitted losses in the Lloyd's syndicates—all to be borne, keep in mind, by individuals like me, who had pledged all their wealth to the insured—totaled more than $14 billion, with more to come. The 1985 year of Mr. Merrett's syndicate 418 had taken the risks of loss from asbestosis and toxic waste off the shoulders of his earlier syndicates. Between the 1984 year (which paid out a small profit to its Names) and the 1985 year (which will be bleeding its Names for a long, long time, if the courts permit), the number of members of the syndicate rose from less than three thousand to more than four thousand. Mr. Merrett himself when I first spoke with him, in 1993, was launching a new insurance operation in Bermuda, which was designed to keep him well afloat whatever happened at Lloyd's. In 1994, in cooperation with J. P. Morgan and Company and Marsh and McLennan, he expected to open a new insurance business in London itself, outside Lloyd's. When we met in early 1995, he was ensconced in a palatial office with two glass walls high above the City of London. But his deal with the Americans had fallen through.

After the losses began, Names started trying to find out what was happening as cash calls commenced. An older Name at Lloyd's, Alan Smallbone, remembers that Lord Cromer, head of Barings Bank and later of the Bank of England, conducted an investigation of Lloyd's in 1969, and gave the agents and managers his report in 1970. "I asked my agent," Smallbone told a meeting of Names, ". . . 'Could I see it?' My agent said to me, 'You may not see it.' I said, 'Why not?' He said, 'The Committee have told me not to show it to you.' I wrote to the Chairman. In those days, I was younger and I was palmed off with a Deputy Chairman. He told me that they were not going to show it to me. I said to him, 'Sir'—as I was very respectful—'it has been settled English law since the 18th century that no agent may conceal from his principal matters of interest to him. Clearly the *Cromer Report* is such a matter.' He said, 'Do not be impudent.' "[9] Some years later, it became common knowledge that Lord Cromer had criticized the high salaries and bonuses the Lloyd's insiders paid themselves whether or not their Names made money.

One of the good things about the situation in 1983, Mr. Brett advised me, was that Lloyd's had just been exempted from government regulation under the forthcoming Financial Services Act.

Instead, under the new Lloyd's Act, Lloyd's would be an entirely self-regulating body, setting the standards for the brokers and underwriters who worked there. That meant, Mr. Brett informed me, that regulation would be done by people who really understood insurance, not by government bureaucrats who could impose rules that might diminish the profits of the syndicates.

The exemption had been fought through the House of Commons by Lloyd's chairman Peter Green, who would be knighted for his services to Lloyd's, and would receive the precious, rarely awarded Lloyd's Medal from his peers. Later he got in trouble and was fined by the Council; cynics noted that if Lloyd's had been covered by the Financial Services Act instead of by its own precious Lloyd's Act, he might have been sent to jail. Lloyd's let him keep his medal, but replaced the marble on which had been incised the names of Lloyd's Medal–winners (including the Queen Mother) with a new panel that eliminated Sir Peter. As a punishment for stealing money from his Names, which is what he had done, it was like fifty lashes with a wet noodle.

Walking over to the building where I was to be interviewed for membership in Lloyd's, Mr. Brett did speak about the risk of loss that Names carried when they became members of the syndicates that wrote the insurance policies. Lloyd's itself didn't run the risks—Lloyd's was just a marketplace. Mr. Brett and Bland-Welch were very knowledgeable about which syndicates took larger risks, and would make sure not to endanger me, but by their nature Lloyd's policies were subject to acts of God. Stories of possible but improbable catastrophes circulate in the Lloyd's community. For example, when the Italian liner *Andrea Doria* sank in 1956, a Name had told me, its cargo included a number of valuable paintings. The "cash calls" on the letters of credit deposited by members of the Lloyd's syndicates that had insured the *Andrea Doria* had been as much as $8,500 each. Mr. Brett heard this story with some amusement.

This sort of thing was not uncommon. Testifying to a Lloyd's committee of inquiry on Gooda Walker 299, a syndicate that reinsured other insurers and then bought reinsurance for itself presumably to protect its Names, Anthony Willard, the underwriter in charge, said that Names' agents had at one time or another let him speak to about one hundred of the people who were backing his policies. "Agents would tend to try and highlight the effect of one major loss on the syndicate. They delighted in asking, if the QE II sank, 'Mr. Willard, what would your loss net of insurance be?' and I would say, '£25,000.' The Name would then be told, 'There you are. You have only 0.1% of that, so it is nothing, is it?'"[10] However, Sir Peter Green was bluntly honest to his newcomers. "Give me a blank check with your signature. That's the risk you are undertaking as a Name at Lloyd's."

Still, I was daunted by the sheer number of papers they were asking me to sign. I asked Mr. Brett whether it might not be wise for me, as a very inexperienced businesswoman, to ask my lawyer to look at the papers. I was dating a lawyer at the time. Mr. Brett thought that would be a waste of his time, because he was an American lawyer, and these were English legal papers. So I went to what was then the marble-encrusted Lloyd's building in the City, a very dignified Edwardian temple of commerce, for my interview; and then I signed my papers.

Prospective Names are interviewed by the Rota Committee in the grand boardroom of Lloyd's, a Robert Adam creation that was originally the dining foyer of the Marques of Lansdowne's country mansion, Bowood. It has been kept intact, moved from building to building as Lloyd's has built itself new homes in the twentieth century. Now the room sits in its eighteenth-century glory, two stories high, inside the new third-millennium Lloyd's building. And before I entered the Adam Room I waited in another room that was kept as it had been in the early years of the nineteenth century—the Nelson Room, with souvenirs of the life of the great British admiral. The Empire takes care of you. . . . Then the doors sprang open, and I was ushered into this wonderful creation with nautical paintings on the walls, built around the largest table I had ever seen in my life.

Two rather serious men in dark suits, members of the Lloyd's Council, sat across the enormous table. There was no "arduous interview." They asked, indeed, only one question: "Do you understand that by becoming a member of Lloyd's you have accepted *unlimited liability*?"

Mr. Moore described this scene very jauntily, shortly before the roof fell in. "A new 'name' must appear before members of the 'committee' of Lloyd's," he wrote, "and acknowledge that all his worldly goods are 'on the line,' if necessary, to pay the obligations."[11] But of course nobody really does understand that—really believes that simply by accepting election as a Name at Lloyd's one risks everything one holds dear. My friend in East Hampton who had first told me about Lloyd's remembers that in her own way she *did* understand, and when they explained that she was risking all she had, she said, "No. I don't want to do that." At which point Rupert Brett, her Name's agent as well as mine, interrupted the proceedings briefly to take her into the hall and tell her not to be frightened. Not knowing what risks your name has insured, you never know which of the ravages you read about in the news are about to cost you money.

I became concerned about Lloyd's only four years after I joined—for no special reason, just because I felt the checks I was getting were not as large as I'd hoped they would be. Agents were holding back some of the profits they said I had made, to build reserves for me. I realized I didn't know enough about insurance to understand the reports agents sent me. I wasn't at all sure I was doing the right thing. I called Dick Otto, the man at Bank of Boston who handled the letters of credit for Lloyd's Names. I asked him point-blank what he thought I should do, and he told me he couldn't advise me, he had a duty to the Names, but he also did a lot of business with Lloyd's, he had a conflict of interest. When I called back I announced I was going to quit; I had decided that 1987 would be the last year for which I would let my assets be used as the backing for Lloyd's policies. He then told me that he thought I had done the right thing.

The next year, I heard the words "open year" for the first time and found that I couldn't just get out: One syndicate, Merrett 418 for the year 1985, could not "close" its accounts. Like all the Lloyd's syndicates launched in 1985, Merrett 418 was supposed to be wound up in 1988, three-plus years after its origination, distributing its profits or billing Names for its losses, reinsuring the surviving risks into Merrett 418 for 1986, which was still alive, awaiting the anniversary that would end it. But I received an announcement that my syndicate could not be closed, because the auditors could not come to a decision about the size of the premium the 1986 year would have to be paid to assume the continuing liabilities of the 1985 year. I called London and asked Mr. Brett, "Why doesn't my syndicate close?" and he said, "We don't know."

I got exasperated. "How do you get your information?" I asked.

He said, "Well, we talk with people on the floor, we hear the rumors."

It was like *Alice in Wonderland.*

By then Mr. Brett and his agency had been absorbed into Sedgwick Holdings, a giant financial services conglomerate that included a Names' agency as well as the second-largest insurance brokerage in the world and a real estate house. My usual contact with him was at the annual New York meeting of the American Lloyd's Names, where the Sedgwick Lloyd's men made gallant speeches and gave elaborate cocktail parties at the Pierre Hotel for their Names and their Names' spouses. Mr. Brett said I shouldn't be concerned about my involvement with Merrett 418, if there were any losses they would be minimal, and Mr. Merrett would clean it all up in 1989. Nevertheless, Brett offered to get me a quote for my own personal reinsurance to take me out of Merrett 418, because once I had decided to leave, I wanted to go. There was a syndicate at Lloyd's that took such risks. The price was $100,000. Mr. Brett said that was off the wall, the losses wouldn't be anything like that at worst. Another 418 Name and I agreed with Rupert. We were probably wrong.

Merrett 418 still hadn't closed in 1990, but I wasn't in New York for the meeting of Names. I was in England, where I had been invited to my first-ever proper English country wedding, an experience every woman should have. The women wear wonderful enormous hats, and all the men are in morning clothes, striped pants and jackets with tails. There are no groomsmen, only scads of beautifully dressed little girls, who attend both bride and groom. So I was very cheerful, still thinking of flowers and romance, when I made a visit to Sedgwick and, in the absence of Mr. Brett, who was in America, was escorted to meet a young assistant whose name was David Shepherd.

Mr. Shepherd was very open and frank. He had recently come to Sedgwick, he said, because he couldn't stand the disorganized practices at Lime Street, another Names' agents' establishment, run by Robin Kingsley, who specialized in recruiting new Names from Canada and New Zealand as well as England. When I asked Shepherd about Merrett 418, he said, without emotion, "That syndicate will never close. You have incurred asbestos and pollution liabilities, and your only way out will be to sue Sedgwick." He suggested that I talk with Richards Butler, a law firm that was handling a similar case for the Names on the Outhwaite 317 syndicate. He won't discuss it now, and years later when I called him for an appointment and told him I was working on a book, he insisted that he bring with him "one of my colleagues, who knows much more than I do." The colleague said very little at lunch, but kept his eyes fixed on Shepherd.

The bad news comes in the spring of the year, in a letter from your agent announcing that some syndicate to which he had pledged your assets would have to make a cash call on its Names to pay its obligations under insurance contracts, and your share would be roughly this number of thousands or tens of thousands or hundreds of thousands of pounds. You should get ready to make the payment when the bill came. (If you've been paying British taxes on prior years' profits, you may get the news from the government in the form of a tax refund before your agent tells you.

You know you're in trouble at Lloyd's when the Inland Revenue sends you a check and you don't know why.) Then in late May or early June another letter arrives with the precise number you owe this year, and a warning that if the payment isn't made by July 31, your agent will begin charging you interest on it at 2 percent over bank rates. And the cash call may be for more money than all your worldly goods are worth.

Most ruined Names will never have the chance to rebuild their lives: There is no time. The average Name is fifty-eight years old. Recently, longevity of Names has been lower than average for their age range, perhaps reduced by the trauma of unlimited liability. Several hundred Names died in 1991–93, maybe thirty of them by suicide, though Lloyd's, commenting on the undoubted suicide of Admiral Sir Richard Fitch, a hero of World War II who hooked up a rubber tube to the exhaust pipe of his car, said in a statement that only "seven deaths . . . have been attributed, by other, in whole or in part to the deceased's membership of Lloyd's."[12] At a recent Annual General Meeting, a Name called for a moment's silence for the thirty-four people who had committed suicide as a result of their losses at Lloyd's. David Rowland presided over the somber remembrance. Literally thousands of people have much less to live for and much more to regret.

I first encountered these human tragedies at a small dinner given by Lady Rona Delves Broughton, an unusually ambitious, attractive blond lady with sharply drawn, regular features. Rona revels in her position on Lloyd's Council, takes her duties seriously, and produces a well-written monthly column first entitled "Rona's Mailbag" and now "Viewpoint" for the Lloyd's publication *One Lime Street*. Herself a Name who has suffered losses in the millions of dollars, she ran for election to the Council "to help the external Names," those who do not work in the market. Rona is most proud of the amendment that she sponsored with underwriters. She is closely allied with the High Premium Names group, which she founded and heads. These approximately seven hundred members supplied about one-fourth of the total capacity underwritten in 1995 when the rules were changed to allow the really rich to accept more insurance business than the merely well-to-do. The lady has become the fiercest opponent of Names who don't pay cash calls. "I paid my losses, they should pay theirs."

Well known too in London social circles, Lady Broughton can be a lot of fun, especially at her most assertive. She makes good copy for journalists. Her lawsuit claiming $75 million from the estate of longtime friend and business associate Eric Hoptner was described in detail in the press.

At her dinner, I was seated next to Anthony Kinsman, a pleasant man who never changed the rhythm of his spoon in the soup as he told me how he had paid his share: Lloyd's had just taken the country house that had been in his family for more than two hundred years. Nor was this any sort of record: In 1992, Christie's auctioned off the home of a Lloyd's Name with the laconic comment that it was the first time the property had come on the market in more than five hundred years.

And suicide is not an escape. Dead Names' estates are tied up because the ultimate losses under the policies they backed are still unknown, and the obligation to pay the Lloyd's policyholder survives death. A briefing in June 1994 by the Association of Lloyd's Members, an organization typically friendly to the management of Lloyd's, warned Names not to violate Section 423 of the Insolvency Act, which prohibits "transactions defrauding creditors." Still, the ALM advised, "the more that can be done to minimise the Name's personal asset worth, the better. Above all, it should not be increased. Family members should therefore be discouraged from

- making an outright gift to the Name; or
- settling assets on trust (either in their lifetime or under their will) in such a way that the Name has an interest in possession (i.e., the right to the income from the assets) . . ."[13]

One of those who most serenely told me not to be upset about Lloyd's in 1993 was an aviation underwriter named Jimmy Houston, an athletic man who loved trout fishing. He died in a fishing accident with some years on syndicates he had backed still "open." His wife is now distraught, and unless his syndicates are closed, his estate cannot be settled for twenty-one years.

An elderly widow living in a pretty cottage in Hampshire, was, on ninety days' notice, forced to sell two paintings that were her reserve in case of ill health. She fears her house will have to go next. Her only child rages at her for joining Lloyd's and at the Lloyd's agents for destroying her mother's final years and her own inheritance. London is full of young people who once had what Dickens called great expectations and now find themselves in limbo, because their parents' estates have been frozen by Lloyd's to pay unknown losses.

In 1993, Sotheby's and Christie's started new divisions of their auction houses to specialize in helping Names sell their belongings to meet cash calls. The Sotheby's advertising leaflet for this purpose posits a cash call for $180,000 (and suggests that the client's lawyer is the firm of Jarndyce and Jarndyce, Dickens's masters of legal delay: The English have not lost their sense of humor). One way to raise the money would be to sell the family Gainsborough. Another might be to borrow against the security of the family silver, which is kept in a bank vault anyway. Some fraction of the Lloyd's victims can manage their losses that way—not enough, it turned out, to sustain separate departments of an auction house. But there are many, many others who are literally ruined, people of ordinary means in England and America and especially Canada. The British writer Anthony Sampson, himself a burned but not incinerated Name, says he knows a widow whose only interest is in what she calls "the DFG"—Distance From the Gutter.

People in Hamilton, Ontario, and then Toronto often met the Lloyd's wealth qualification only by pledging their homes to the bank, up front. At least two of Robin Kingsley's Canadian Names have become suicides. Russell Bailey, facing cash calls from Lloyd's for several times his net worth, hanged himself in his living room while his wife was shopping for groceries. Fred Yeo hanged himself in his barn. They died in early 1992, but as of late 1994 they still had not been released from Lloyd's, and their widows face this financial nightmare alone.

I now know that many of the Lloyd's syndicates were managed by people who had no understanding of the responsibilities *they* were supposed to have assumed when, in effect, they asked people who knew nothing of insurance to co-sign their notes. It seems to me that *they* were the ones who had a truly unlimited *moral* liability, to the Names whose fortunes had been entrusted to their care. They bought us excellent lunches and dinners to show us their goodwill and the prosperity in which we would participate, and increasingly they lived it up elsewhere, too, at our expense.

At the Annual General Meeting in London in 1993, Martin de Laszlo spoke up as a Name and a cousin of Robin Kingsley by marriage. He said his father had died from concern about the family's plight because of his deep involvement at Lloyd's. The de Laszlos, descended from a famous family of portrait painters, were travel agents, and had arranged Kingsley's trips to America, where he lured hundreds of Americans and (especially) Canadians into backing some of the worst syndicates at Lloyd's. When Kingsley was first recruiting, de Laszlo recalled, he traveled in economy class, but "the more money he lost for his members, the more expensively he travelled, culminating finally in plans to travel to America in Concorde." At an Extraordinary General Meeting a month earlier, a corporate restructuring expert who had joined the Council of Lloyd's delicately identified its problem as the excess profitability of previous years, which "encouraged so many levels of intermediate profit to come before the names themselves who are the ultimate investors."

Many of the Lloyd's agents and underwriters are decent people who are themselves caught in this tragedy. B. Q. Adams, managing director of Sturge Marine Syndicate 206, wrote to his Names in the Annual Report of 1992 that "it is desperately dispiriting to be an underwriter at Lloyd's in today's environment. To have presided over a loss-making syndicate is depressing enough. To be done so at a time when financial ruin is being inflicted upon many names within the community is totally demoralizing. Regardless of which syndicates have generated the worst losses, it is impossible for any underwriter to dissociate himself and his syndicate from the collective responsibility we all have within the market to maintain it in good order." This is a minority view: The openly proclaimed position of Lloyd's, in its new business plan, was that the losses from older syndicates shall be "ring-fenced" and left with the Names who were unlucky enough to be put into them, while everyone else walks on to a bright future of "profits." But we are Banquo's ghost, and we will be seen.

It's impossible for an American not to feel that there was especially little concern for the "wogs" (originally, they tell me, among some of the underwriters the letters stood for "worthy Oriental gentleman"). But I have learned from speaking with people at Lloyd's that many of them did not realize that they were behaving foolishly. And the biggest losers, of course, have been the English Names. One of them said at the 1993 Annual General Meeting that he "had been mugged over eighteen months ago and was nearly killed and I am still having medical treatment for the eye I nearly lost. I was able to come to terms with that mugging much more easily than the mugging which I received at Lloyd's."[14]

Americans, moreover, have had the sympathetic support of their friends, because losses at Lloyd's appear from far away as a misfortune. In England, the Names were like lepers. The common attitude was that these were people who had made a lot of money out of Lloyd's in years past, and now that they've had some losses, they're whining. But the truth is that for Lloyd's as a whole the underwriting years 1988–92 have more than wiped out all the profits since World War II—and that most of the worst losers are relative newcomers who never participated in the better years. Half the Names, moreover, have been in syndicates that have shown profits or small losses through these awful years, and they fear contagion from the victimized Names who wish to compel their luckier colleagues to accept some of their losses.

There wasn't much sympathy even for the "Members of the Royal Household" who were, as the enraged losing Name who compiled the list put it, "victims of Lloyd's robbery": seven members of the royal family, including the duchess of Kent and her two princesses, Sir Angus Ogilvy KCVO, and the earl of Lichfield; Mrs. K. E. H. Dugdale DCVO JP, a Woman of the Bedchamber; the duchess of Argyll, wife of the Hereditary Keeper of Dunstaffnage, the Hereditary Bearer of the Royal Standard of Scotland; the personal secretary and treasurer to Prince Charles; the queen's vet in Windsor and his wife and son. . . .

This attitude was completely reversed by the judge's opinion in the case against Gooda Walker's agents, which placed the blame squarely on the negligence of the underwriters. Both the public and the newspapers pity the burned Names today. Still, the governments, the corporations that bought the insurance, and the beneficiaries of the claims under those policies care only about the policyholders. The Names are an embarrassment: Their failure to pay will cause losses to those who have sued the makers of their miseries, to the insured companies that were the cause of those miseries, to other insurance companies in jurisdictions like the states in America where a guarantee pool has been established to make up the defaults of bankrupt insurers, and, if it gets bad enough, to the governments themselves and their taxpayers. When the authorities look at insurers, they inquire about their "solvency," their ability to pay claims, which in the case of Lloyd's means their ability to take ever more money from the battered Names. The governments want Lloyd's to beat the money out of the Names. When we turned to our elected representatives, we found human sympathy but nothing more. We were definitely part of the problem, not part of the solution.

Lloyd's charter calls for the Society to promote the interests of the Names. To protect the integrity of the disciplinary proceedings that are required by the Society's role as self-regulator, however, the Lloyd's Act of 1982 specifically protected the Society from suits brought by insiders. Names are "members" of the Society, and therefore "insiders." Lloyd's successfully maintained in the British courts that it did not even owe its Names a duty of good faith and fair dealing.

Fortunately, the agents who placed us into the syndicates and the managers of those syndicates were not protected by the Lloyd's Act, and the British commercial courts in the end will follow the banner first waved by their great eighteenth-century leader Lord Mansfield: *Fiat justitia*—let justice be done, though the heavens tremble. In 1994, the judgments began to pour from the courts, proclaiming the agents' liability for the Names' losses, and Lloyd's could no longer maintain the fantasy that its business would continue as usual with new sources of capital to replace the bankrupted Names.

Beyond the woes of the Names and the sheer drama of the possible collapse of a three-hundred-year-old institution, the Lloyd's story raises important questions of economic impact and public policy in both Britain and the United States. "Unlicensed" insurance companies—companies not subject to regulation in the states where the risks against which they insure are located—write about $8 billion a year of reinsurance premiums in the United States, and about $3 billion of that goes to Lloyd's. Some 12 percent of all reinsurance in the United States used to be at Lloyd's, and the percentage was much higher in the reinsurance of catastrophe risks. Many of the larger American property/casualty insurers claim reinsurance protection from Lloyd's as a large part of the assets assuring their own solvency. American homes and businesses are protected by Lloyd's policies their owners and employees do not know exist—but they could find out, very unhappily.

Vincent L. Lorenzano, the New York State Deputy Insurance Commissioner, says that if Lloyd's continues to pay claims, he isn't going to concern himself with questions of "solvency." If Lloyd's syndicates fail to pay reinsurance claims there are "a number" of New York insurance companies that he could no longer permit to operate. Lloyd's deputy chairman Robert Hiscox commented in 1993 that if Lloyd's stopped paying claims, "all I can say is the American insurance industry would be dead."[15]

If Lloyd's ceases to operate, there may be no place for a multitude of asbestosis victims to look for satisfaction of their claims. Insurance against damage from hurricanes and earthquakes may become much more costly and much harder to find; AllState has already decided to run from Florida because there's no reinsurance. The stockholders in companies that run risks would find it much more expensive to share those risks. The costs of cleaning up sites carelessly polluted by manufacturers of toxic substances might fall on the taxpayer. Worldwide, Lloyd's accounts for only about 2 percent of all the insurance written, but its social function has been to take the risks conventional insurers shun, a category that includes important activities like oil rigs and commercial aviation, and its economic function has been to set prices that other, often larger insurance companies will adopt when writing reinsurance.

Virtually everyone would pay some part of the enormous costs that will be imposed on the commercial world if this keystone of the insurance industry falls. Political leadership will have to deal with the failure of the American legal system to think through the practical consequences of judicial decision, and with the refusal to date of the British government to accept responsibility for the regulation of financial enterprises that play with other people's money.

The year I joined Lloyd's my older son was not yet in law school. When I began to get cash calls in 1990 he was a practicing lawyer on Wall Street. He asked to read the papers I'd signed to become a Name. When he finished he shook his head and said, "If I'd been a lawyer at the time, I'd have broken your arm before I let you sign these papers." Now, by consent agreement, I sign my Christmas cards myself. Everything else gets John's approval first.

Although I resigned in 1987, Sedgwick still sends me annual statements of increasing losses. The resignation won't be effective until all the losses on policies written in my name by Merrett Underwriting Agency are finalized. Auditors Ernst and Young have been unable to set a figure for the total amount of deterioration in the future—a very unpleasant reading.

Attempting to understand my plight has led me to live in London for most of the past three years. When I look over the notes I took three years ago, I feel I don't know the woman who wrote them. I've read sky-high stacks of legal and business reports, and I've interviewed more than two hundred people. Some became good friends. Each one had a different perspective, making even the court cases fascinating. Aside from bearing four children, this has been the most challenging period of my life.

CHAPTER 2

"A Unique Institution"

"The Society of Lloyd's," its future chairman David Rowland wrote in a 1992 internal report, "is a unique institution, unlike any other in the world."[1] For good or ill, there is a lot of truth to that statement. Insurance has become one of the world's biggest businesses, generating more than $300 billion of premiums a year, and nowhere else in this vast service industry is there anything like the Lloyd's system for generating insurance policies. The world has many trading floors now, markets for paper having become the center of a triumphant capitalist age, but Lloyd's is of necessity the largest, because it is the only one where the participants are sitting down, and people sitting down take more space than people standing up. The Lloyd's "box," on which the insurance underwriters sit, is an idiosyncratic piece of furniture, quite literally a box, closed on all sides with a hinged top on which the underwriter sits and a straight wooden back against which he can rest his shoulders. On a more romantic level, the history of Lloyd's is uniquely adventurous, a combination of derring-do and commerce that survived, generating security for its customers and rich rewards for its traders, for more than three hundred years.

Looked at purely as a modern-day commercial *institution*, however, Lloyd's today seems less than unique; indeed, it resembles much less august organizations that have proliferated in the United States in the past dozen years. For all its romance, drama, and history, the Society of Lloyd's is at bottom a franchise business, like McDonald's or Holiday Inn.

Like the owners of franchised properties, the insurance brokers and insurance underwriters who work in the building and identify themselves as part of Lloyd's pay an annual fee for the privilege and agree to abide by the rules and regulations established by the board that controls the use of the name, in this case called a council. The first of these rules is that a Lloyd's underwriter transacts his business only on the floor at Lloyd's, accepts business only from a Lloyd's broker, and sees to it that every policy he writes goes through the Lloyd's clerical process and comes out carrying the Lloyd's rubber stamp. His premiums are paid to him through the Lloyd's clearinghouse. Unless he is the lead underwriter on a policy, a Lloyd's claims office is normally his source of information about the losses he must pay for under the policy, and he (or, rather, the Names that back his policies) will pay those claims through the same Lloyd's clearinghouse. (The other modern commercial institution with resemblances to Lloyd's, as Names have learned to their distress, is the collection agency that acts on behalf of a number of creditors to force debtors to pay up.) The council presumably sets policy for everybody and by assumption—for the Lloyd's Act of 1982 identifies it as the regulator of its insurance market—controls standards of performance. It is distinguished from the board of directors of McDonald's only in that the franchisees themselves dominate the electorate that votes on the council members and therefore have a lot more clout than more modern franchise operators permit.

Particularly now, with the number of underwriting syndicates active at Lloyd's down from 401 in 1990 to 170 in 1995, it may be easier to get franchised by Lloyd's than to start a McDonald's. The Lloyd's annual fee isn't very large, and the initial investment for entry is tiny—a managing agency that operates insurance syndi-cates that will take risks totaling in the hundreds of millions of dollars can win a place on the Lloyd's floor with a deposit of less than $20,000. It doesn't take much capital to start an insurance company, because insurance is one of the few products people pay for even before it is manufactured: The house is always playing with other people's money.

But the managing agencies are not at risk, anyway. They are merely the franchisees: The syndicates that accept premiums to write insurance policies are simply a club of the individuals who have agreed to back the policies. When American Names wanted to sue syndicates for defrauding them, Judge Morris Lasker of fed-eral district court in New York ruled that they couldn't, because the syndicate had no legal existence other than themselves.[2] Suing the managing agent that operates the syndicate wasn't especially promising either, because since World War II some managing agencies have transformed themselves into corporations with lim-ited liability. . . . The Names, in short, are at risk for all they've got, but the people who decide what risks they should bear can't be called to account except to the extent that their companies have malpractice insurance. Not so in England: Managing agents suc-cessfully sued by Gooda Walker, Feltrim action groups, and Mer-rett 418 Names are in court claiming damages from Merrett Underwriting Agency.

"Working members" of Lloyd's must also buy from Lloyd's the insurance industry equivalent of the French fries and the meat. Before a Lloyd's policy can come into force, it must receive a final rubber stamp (a trademarked anchor) from the Lloyd's Policy Signing Office (LPSO). This was not in the past an especially ar-duous requirement. Though prepared boilerplate clauses for in-sertion into insurance contracts were widely used in the market, Lloyd's underwriters were entitled to write their own policies in their own language, and could use just about any form they liked. The first time someone got insurance at Lloyd's, his policy was likely to be written on what was called a "J" form, which was a plain piece of paper with two required clauses, one disclaiming payment on claims growing out of a policyholder's own fraud, the other holding the insurer harmless if the policyholder's claim grew out of an act of war, unless separate war risk insurance had been purchased.

In real life, because the brokers were part of large international agencies while the underwriters were locals, a Lloyd's policy was most likely to have been written by the broker who brought it to the underwriter. The brokers had much better filing systems. They kept the policies; the underwriters themselves kept—at most—what they called "skeleton cards." The result was that policies moved slowly, slowly through the Lloyd's Policy Signing Office. To take one of the relatively few contracts on which we have information, the reinsurance of asbestos risks from the Sturge syndicate at Lloyd's to Fireman's Fund in San Francisco—making Fireman's Fund responsible for all claims over the first $20 million submitted by companies that had insured the safety of their workplaces and products before 1969—was agreed on October 7, 1974, but not actually signed until March 25, 1975. And the policy by which Fireman's Fund unloaded these risks back onto Lloyd's was negotiated on November 11, 1981, but not actually signed until January 26, 1982.

These delays haven't mattered much to policyholders, who are covered from the date the underwriter signed up with the broker, and who put in their claims through their brokers. (And in the Lloyd's market the brokers themselves usually pay the smaller claims, collecting later from the Lloyd's syndicates that were paid to accept these risks, assuming that nobody is going to fight what the broker considers a legitimate smaller claim.) But the shift of premium income from one year to another did matter a lot to the underwriters and their Names, because they were credited with the money in the year when the LPSO put the Lloyd's stamp on the documents, not the year when it actually came into effect. Since January 1, 1994, as part of the drive to rationalize this famously disorganized place and help the computers keep the accounts, the LPSO has made available to brokers and underwriters standard-form policies that can be processed more quickly than the custom-designed policies somebody at the LPSO offices previously had to check through for form and style.

All Lloyd's policies were and are written for one year at a time, though they can be "reinstated" within the year (until recently at the same rate) to maintain coverage if the disaster insured against occurs. The profitability of the participants in the market is measured in the "year of account," which is the year the policies were signed. The profitability of an insurance policy is determined only in part by the relationship between the premium charged and the losses claimed under the policy, because a policy can be profitable even if the claims exceed the premiums, if the insurance company earns enough on its investment of the premiums during the time before the claims must be paid. Indeed, most of the profits of the casualty insurance business in the first half of the 1980s derived from the high interest rates the companies received on their premium trust funds—which is not the least of the reasons why the market got in such trouble in later years, when interest rates fell. In the eighteenth century, ships might be at sea for more than a year, and the Lloyd's rule became that the "year of account" should "close" only after two additional years had passed. Thus the 1991 year of account closed on December 31, 1993, and Lloyd's reported the results of insurance underwriting for that year (another $3 billion of losses) in May 1994.

Again, the Society of Lloyd's is a "market" and not itself an issuer of insurance policies. Its franchisees, "members" and "subscribers," settle their transactions with one another (deliver the policies the underwriters sign, collect the premiums the brokers have agreed to pay, and pay the claims the brokers have asserted on behalf of their clients) as though they were buying and selling futures contracts at a commodities market. Until quite recently, what the LPSO sent to the members to help them process this settlement was a biweekly stack of old-fashioned stiff IBM cards they could run through their own old-fashioned IBM processors. Today the trading floor at Lloyd's is full of notebook computers hooked into the Lloyd's Policy Signing Office computer, which acts as a clearinghouse for the market. The brokers pay their clients' premiums to Lloyd's and collect their clients' claims from Lloyd's; the underwriters get their premium income from the same office at Lloyd's and pay their losses to Lloyd's.

And, of course, the franchisee will have to subject himself—or herself, for since 1970 Lloyd's has accepted women brokers and underwriters, and there are plenty of ladies' rooms in the new building—to whatever rules the council may make. These rules are usually not very restrictive, but some of them are indeed rough. For example, an underwriter at Lloyd's does not discharge his obligation by paying a claim to a Lloyd's broker acting as agent for the policyholder. If the broker goes bust before paying his client—and in the atmosphere of Lloyd's in the 1990s, nobody pays outsiders very fast—the underwriter will have to pay again. The underwriter can lose on the other side, too: The minute the insurance policy is signed by the underwriter's agent, it goes into effect (in the language of the trade, there is a "binder"), and for some time thereafter, claims can be made under its terms even if the premium has not been paid.

In return, the Lloyd's brokers, agents, and underwriters get the use of what was until recently one of the great brand names of the world. "Individually, we are underwriters" was the cant line. "Collectively, we are Lloyd's." It was a brand name that combined solidity with imagination, an absolute assurance that a valid claim under the terms of an insurance policy with the Lloyd's label would be paid and a likelihood that even if nobody else in the world would insure a risk, somebody at Lloyd's would find a way. Betty Grable's legs. Bob Feller's fastball. Snow on the ski slopes. A space shuttle sent up to repair a satellite.

But in one major respect the Lloyd's franchisees were different from the proprietors of a well-regarded hotel or restaurant franchise. They worked geographically in the same place, which meant that they saw a great deal of one another and very little of their customers. An American Name visiting Lloyd's a few years ago asked the underwriter for an aviation syndicate he backed how often he visited Boeing, his largest insured—and was astonished to hear the man reply that he had never been in the United States in his life. Since they were mostly in good repute with one another, and had learned to avoid but tolerate those of their fellows who were not of good repute inside the building, they did not entirely understand that everyone had responsibility for the brand name.

Anyway, they were in competition with one another, unlike the franchisee who receives exclusive use of the trademark in his location.

To commemorate the 1857 salvage of much of the treasure from the 1799 shipwreck of the HMS *Lutine,* the ship's eighty-pound bell was installed above the podium at the front of what was then Lloyd's trading floor in the Royal Exchange. Each time Lloyd's moved, the *Lutine* bell moved with it, and it is now in a kind of pulpit in the middle of the trading floor in the snappy new building. For four generations, this bell has been rung to announce the arrival of news of an insured disaster.

This does not mean that the sound of the bell makes everybody unhappy. The American politician Sam Rayburn once said that on most issues you could predict where a man would stand by looking at where he sat. The reaction to a disaster among the underwriters was inevitably a function of whether they themselves were or were not among the insurers of this particular risk. People who operated in the same market but had not insured this ship that sank or this factory that blew up might even be pleased to hear the news, because it meant the crippling of a rival for business—and an increase in the rates everybody's customers would pay for such insurance.

In 1970, Arab guerrillas blew up four hijacked passenger jets at Dawson Field in Jordan. The bell tolled. Ian Posgate was one of the most adventurous underwriters at Lloyd's. He was called "Goldfinger," because he collected large premiums for accepting large risks and rarely had to pay out on claims, or so it seemed. (Those who hero-worshiped him were not aware that he reinsured his positions with little companies he and some friends owned in tax havens around Europe and was alleged to siphon off profits for himself. However, when sued on the allegations, Posgate won.) On this occasion, as a young man, he lost his nerve. He went to the veteran Roy Merrett to tell him he expected to pull out, the aviation market had become too dangerous. "Nonsense," Merrett said. "We'll put up the rates and do it on an hour by hour basis."[3] In 1992, after Hurricane Andrew had done more damage to Florida than any storm in fifty years, Maurice ("Hank") Greenberg of American International Group got in trouble with the media in the United States when someone leaked a memo his son had written to senior staff that the storm was a God-given opportunity to boost premiums.

In such an atmosphere, underwriters who worked on the same open trading floor might be content to see their rivals goof. Bertie Hiscox recalls that when he was working on the floor every day, "you'd see a risk that was dynamite, and you'd say to the broker, 'I won't, but *he* might'—and then you'd watch with a kind of delight while *he* wrote it. After all, we were competing. Years later, I realized that this was going to be bad for Lloyd's."

Presumably, the reputation of the brand is the special responsibility of the elected leadership, but until very recently that leadership took the position that their task was "to keep the coffeehouse." Until 1993, the post of chairman of Lloyd's was unpaid, and the people who held it continued to work on the floor. When David Coleridge was chairman, in 1992, he said that the Lloyd's corporation was responsible for getting the floors swept. Lloyd's was the place where people did unconventional things, even the most established of them. "I've never understood why people regard insurance as a conservative business," says Robert Hiscox. "Really, it's bookmaking." Like every financial market, the Lloyd's floor has a bulletin board where news from the rest of the world is posted and regularly replaced. What makes the Lloyd's board different from others is that it includes virtually all the horse race news that moves on the wires in Britain.

●

Edward Lloyd, whose name is perpetuated, was not an insurance man but the proprietor of a coffeehouse opened in 1687, where workers in the City of London gathered to drink what was then the newest addictive beverage. Early in the eighteenth century, Lloyd's coffeehouse became the site of auctions where wine and brandy—and the ships that carried them—could be bought and sold. Shipowners frequented the auctions, as did rich men who supplemented their income by splitting risks of disaster with the owners of ships that might sink.

The principles of insurance were thoroughly understood in the eighteenth century (indeed, there is evidence from ancient Greece and Phoenicia that they were understood before the birth of Christ). Almost a century before Lloyd opened his coffee-house, Queen Elizabeth I had signed into law an act of Parliament proclaiming that "it has been tyme out of mynde an usage amongste merchantes, both of this realme and of forraine na-cyons, when they make any great adventure (speciallie into re-mote parts) to give some consideracion of money to othwer persons (which commonlie are in noe small number) to have from them assurance made of their goodes, merchandizes, ships and other things adventured." Through such a "policie of assur-ance," the act continued, "it comethe to passe that upon the losse or perishinge of any shippe there followeth not the undoinge of any man, but the losse lighteth rather easilie upon many, than heavilie upon few."[4]

Government regulation of a sort came to the British financial world in the aftermath of the South Sea Bubble, in 1720. Tens of thousands of Englishmen traded their government bonds for shares in a company that had a monopoly on trade between Britain and South America (and the Pacific Islands), and soon lost all they had. Jonathan Swift wrote a poem:

Subscribers here by thousands float,
And jostle one another down,
Each paddling in his leaky boat,
And here they fish for gold and drown. . . .

Meantime, secure on Garraway cliffs,
A savage race, by shipwrecks fed,
Lie waiting for the foundered skiffs,
And strip the bodies of the dead.

Parliament wrote a law, restricting participation in various kinds of financial enterprise. The insurance rules were to be among the most restrictive. King George I had received gifts of stock in two companies being organized to write insurance. Only those companies, he urged, should be chartered to do such business. But the individual underwriters of Lloyd's were already too well placed to be shoved aside in that way, and the Bubble Act, as it was called, in the end provided that no *companies* other than the Royal Exchange and the London Assurance could offer insurance—but any *individual* who wished to enter the business could do so on his own.

All this seems (and was) corrupt. The men who made the modern economic world had all the bad habits we now associate with Third World operators. It also seems foolish, because the principle of risk-spreading inherent in the insurance *company* that wrote a lot of policies was lost when an individual bore all risks. But the "sole trader" as an insurance underwriter was not foolish at the time. In the smaller world of the mid–eighteenth century, individuals owned and operated most of the world's businesses. "Incorporation" would give an enterprise a legal entity separate from its proprietor and thus a better chance to survive after a proprietor's death, insulating its stockholders from losses beyond their actual investment. But it was relatively rare, requiring until the nineteenth century an act of the legislature or an extraordinary specific approval by an official whose powers to grant such favors were hedged about with cautionary restrictions.

In the marine insurance nexus, incorporation was not necessarily desirable. The policy the insurance underwriter sold the insured was limited in time, usually covering a single voyage of a single ship. The immortality of the corporation might have a value if the corporation built up reserves every year instead of distributing its profits—indeed, Lloyd's is in even deeper trouble than it would otherwise have been because for so many years the profits of the fat years were distributed to the Names rather than salted away in reserves to meet possible demands in lean years. (And the syndicates that remained profitable through the debacle were mostly those that had managed to salt away for the benefit of their future Names large reserves that earned enough investment income to overcome the underwriting losses.) As an assurance of payment on claims, however, corporate status was worth less than nothing to those who did business with a company that could go bankrupt—especially as the estate of a sole trader who died was (and is) obligated to pay off on an insurance policy he had backed, while a dead corporation gets buried in bankruptcy.

Incorporation limited the recoveries the insured could make on their policies to the resources of the company that wrote the policy, and because entry into the insurance business required so little capital investment, these resources could be trivial next to the demand upon them in a world where ships could sink with a total loss. No matter what the circumstances, the stockholders of a corporation had "limited liability." With few exceptions, they were not at risk for more than they had invested. In fact, what Americans call a corporation was until recently known in England starkly as "a limited-liability company."

Under these conditions, a sole trader with unlimited liability and great personal wealth might well offer a more certain guarantee than any corporation that the policies he backed would be paid off. John Julius Angerstein, the leading figure at Lloyd's in the time of the Napoleonic Wars, once wrote a policy on a "treasure ship" that could have paid more than £665,000—the equivalent of about $50 million in modern money. If the ship had sunk, he probably would have been good for it, a boast that no limited-liability company in England, except perhaps the Bank of England, could then have made.

A major advantage of a place like Lloyd's coffeehouse was that news got there early, and was shared. Ships at sea had no means of communicating to land beyond sight lines, and until Morse invented the telegraph in the mid–nineteenth century, messengers on horseback were the fast way to communicate information on land. Much of the insurance written at Lloyd's was on ships that were overdue (a matter the shipowner was not required to mention when he made the rounds seeking insurance). If someone had early news that in fact the ship had already made land, he could pocket a sure profit by taking some of the risk from its worried owner; the great diarist Samuel Pepys wrote insurance on British merchant ships—while he was Secretary of the Navy!—and denounced himself as an "asse" for running to friends with his news that an overdue ship had docked safely in Newcastle, missing "an opportunity . . . to have concealed this and seemed to have made an insurance and got £100 with the least trouble and danger in the whole world."[5] If an owner had exclusive news that his ship had already sunk, he could still cover his losses by purchasing policies from the ignorant. The *Titanic* was insured after it had sunk, by a London broker who had received a frantic telegraphed order to do so from a colleague in New York, where the news of the disaster was closely held but known to insiders.

As a shipping insurer, Lloyd's supplemented its financial operations with salvage expertise. Having paid the owners of the ship and its cargo, the insurers in fact owned the wreck, and commissioned divers to get to the site if possible before Swift's "savage race" on the Garraway shores could pillage the remains. It was Lloyd's underwriters who took the lead in forming The Salvage Association, which obtained a royal charter as a nonprofit organization in 1867 and has ever since served as a nonpartisan source of information on damage and the danger of damage for insurers, governments, shipowners, banks, and lawyers. Its slogan is

"*Quaerite Vera,*" which means "Seek the Truth," and its hundred-plus "surveyors" work out of offices in thirty cities on four continents. (South America, oddly, is covered from the New York office, and Australia from Singapore.) The surveyors also do what are called "Warranty and Condition Surveys," most frequently at the insistence of Lloyd's syndicates being asked to insure a ship. Through The Salvage Association, Lloyd's performs the highest (though often forgotten) function of an insurance company: requiring the insured to pay attention to safety in performing insured functions.

Their work is not always welcome. Bryan M. Roddick, a former Lloyd's underwriter who became chairman of the "SA," wrote in his 1993–94 report that "it is not unknown for an owner, having paid in advance for a survey, to demand the certificate before the surveyor has been on board, on the premise that the certificate is bought and not earned!"[6] General Manager Michael Ellis reports on the difficulties of evaluating claims in places where the lead underwriter is a local who may have kept only 1 percent of the risk, and is under enormous pressure to pay what has been asked. "Those pressures can be transmitted to our surveyors. The association was founded to resist those pressures and to form objective assessments. Sometimes, though not often, we are instructed by underwriters who would like us to find reasons why the claim should not be paid. We were not founded for that purpose—we are there to be fair."[7]

Salvage led to proficiency at recovering lost or stolen valuables, and the creation of a Lloyd's silver medal "for extraordinary and meritorious effort in the rescuing and preserving of property." In 1984, in a ceremony at the White House, this medal was awarded to five astronauts of the space shuttle *Discovery,* who had brought back to earth an errant communications satellite owned by the government of Indonesia and insured by Lloyd's, which had paid NASA for this mission. If the satellite hadn't been recovered, Lloyd's as insurer would have been responsible for paying someone to build Indonesia a new one. In thanks to President

Ronald Reagan for participating in the presentation, Lloyd's gave him a gold coin salvaged many years before from a sunken ocean liner.

In 1734, Thomas Jemson, who had bought the coffeehouse from the original Lloyd's son-in-law, began publishing what he called *Lloyd's List*, a daily compendium of shipping news that had come into his place. (Still published every day, *Lloyd's List* is the oldest continuing newspaper in the world.) Obviously, his customers saw it first, which gave them an edge. On the other hand, the great advantage that being part of the house gave the denizens of Lloyd's drew some most unsavory people into the business of writing insurance. There was always a disreputable gambling element hanging around at a coffeehouse, an element that included most of the insured, virtually all of them sole traders themselves, shipowners whose ships could any day carry their fortunes to the bottom of the sea.

The mid–eighteenth century saw a succession of scandals involving Lloyd's, which was virtually taken over by touts and tipsters who solicited bets on such things as whether the defendants in notorious criminal trials would be convicted, or members of the royal family reported to be ill would recover or die. In 1769, the more conservative denizens of Lloyd's backed the headwaiter of the establishment when he started his own coffeehouse with the same name, a few blocks away.

This new Lloyd's was made permanent four years later when 71 of its underwriters under the leadership of Angerstein, a German-speaking Russian émigré, rented the second floor of the Royal Exchange, opposite the Bank of England, for the exclusive use of Lloyd's—which still served coffee in the new surroundings—as an insurance market. The market would remain at the Royal Exchange for 155 years, with occasional time elsewhere for the repair of the facilities after fires. In this permanent home owned by the insurers themselves, more professional attitudes dominated the gambling instinct. In the nineteenth century, the roster of "subscribers" was reduced from about 2,250 to about 700 by a requirement that men be approved by a governing committee and pay a "subscription" to defray the expenses of the rooms before they would be permitted to do an insurance business at Lloyd's. But until late in the century, even members did not have to put up any capital to convince the Lloyd's committee that they could back the policies they wrote in the coffeehouse.

As international trade increased toward the end of the century, shipowners incorporated and expanded, and the demand for maritime insurance ballooned. There was a limit to how much an individual underwriter could do for a ship-owning company, and Lloyd's began to lose business to the joint stock insurers. The solution to this problem was the formation of syndicates at Lloyd's to share risks among several individuals, who remained sole traders, each liable for the fraction of the loss that matched the fraction of the premium he received. Still, the risks remained under control. As late as 1891, Michael Ellis of The Salvage Association reports, a tramp steamer insured at Lloyd's might claim a value of $15,000, and might be insured by half a dozen Lloyd's Names and non-Lloyd's insurance companies, each taking a $1,500–$3,000 share of the risk.

When the market was new and for many years thereafter, all the Names inscribed on the back of a Lloyd's policy would be those of men who actually worked at Lloyd's. But just as the dimensions of the risks being undertaken in the eighteenth century forced a change from strictly individual liability to syndication, the growth of the insurance business in the nineteenth century compelled the recruitment of backing for the policies from men who did not work in the insurance market but were prepared to support the judgment of friends who did. Soon several thousand men were somehow involved with the insurance policies written at Lloyd's. When Dickens created a thickheaded rich Victorian who lived for nothing but money and what he considered propriety—Mr. Podsnap, whose dining room featured a silver service that called, "Wouldn't you like to melt me down?"—he noted that Mr. Podsnap "did something in marine insurance."

The essence of the arrangement was that those who were promising to pay the policies Lloyd's wrote signed on the back of the document. Hence the term "Names," for the people who bore these names were what guaranteed the insured. Where an "underwriter" working for a number of Names signed on their behalf, he supplemented his signature with a "stamp," a standard rubber stamp bearing his syndicate's logo. Hence the word "stamp," which is now also used by extension ("stamp capacity") to indicate the limit on the amount of insurance that Lloyd's will permit a particular syndicate to write in a single year. If an underwriter can't find Names to back his policies, he is out of business; this is what happened to Stephen Merrett in 1994. Conversely, if the better underwriters have all the capacity they want for the business they plan to do, new Names can't win places on that syndicate. From the early days, Names became "members" of Lloyd's. They could and sometimes would drop in to the coffeehouse to see what use was being made of their risk-taking. Each Name's promise to pay was backed by all his personal wealth, and the harsh English laws that jailed debtors who didn't pay their debts assured that he would be sincere about it.

At Lloyd's in the late twentieth century, the risks were spread even wider, as syndicates that included thousands of Names split risks with other syndicates, large and small. The policy became a loose-leaf book with the risks to be insured described in the first pages, followed by a number of "slips," bound into the loose-leaf at a rate of three or four slips per page, which different underwriters stamped and signed to signify their acceptance of a specified fraction of the whole. The individual Name now signed not an insurance policy but a contract with a Name's agent, who in turn contracted for his Names with an underwriter, authorizing the underwriter to accept premiums on the Names' behalf—and to draw upon the Names' financial resources to pay claims under the policies for which he had become an underwriter.

●

Lloyd's emergence from concentration on shipping was largely the work of one man, Cuthbert Eden Heath, son of a Navy family who was barred from service because he was hard of hearing. Lloyd's had long had a minor role in fire insurance; Heath expanded it to include burglary insurance and insurance to businesses for loss of profit associated with a fire. Heath also wrote insurance to cover damages from an earthquake. When the Big One struck San Francisco in 1906, other insurers tried to distinguish between fire risks they covered and earthquake risks they didn't cover. Heath made the reputation of Lloyd's in the United States by sending his agent a cable: "Pay all our policy-holders in full irrespective of the terms of their policies."

Cuthbert Heath was father or godfather to the huge expansion of insurable risks that was a prominent feature of capitalist societies in the early years of the twentieth century. In 1885, he started the first specifically "nonmarine" syndicate at Lloyd's; it continued in business until 1992, when it collapsed with losses to the Names estimated as high as half a billion dollars. Cuthbert Heath invented the "blanket bond" by which bankers could be protected against awards to irate stockholders at a time when bank charters did not give stockholders completely limited liability: If a bank went broke, a stockholder might be called on to contribute above and beyond the money he spent to buy his shares.

And it was Cuthbert Heath who as long ago as 1887 began the practice of insuring the diamond market, which in practice gave Lloyd's profitable connections with the De Beers diamond cartel and with various shadowy communities in the world that can find out what criminals are doing. Lloyd's rarely has to pay off on lost or stolen diamonds, even today, because somebody usually "finds" them and turns them in. The diamond market gets protection as well as compensation from its Lloyd's policies. From the underworld connections required by insurance in the diamond market grew Lloyd's most remarkable specialty—"K&R," for kidnap and ransom insurance, a staple product now for corporations that do business in "developing" countries.

Largely because Cuthbert Heath was always reaching for new ways to use insurance, Lloyd's became the place where a movie company would go to insure itself against losses if its leading man got caught snorting coke, where inventors of medications insured themselves against baleful side effects. As the risks grew bigger, Lloyd's became even more dependent on the creation of syndicates with many Names, and on winning a multiplicity of syndicates for each risk.

Intellectually, Heath's great contribution was the idea of vertical reinsurance. The principles of insurance noted by Parliament in the reign of Queen Elizabeth were *horizontal* insurance: A risk was too great for any one insurer to bear, so it was split up among a group of them—8 percent to me, 5 percent to you, 17 percent to him, and so forth. This may be done before the policy is written, in which case the broker representing the insured signs up a number of insurers, or it may be done after the policy has been agreed upon through some form of "quota share" reinsurance arranged by the original insurer. This procedure is especially suitable to situations where the total risk is known—the ship and its contents are worth, say, a million dollars, no more and no less; the insurer's liability for an 8 percent share is at most $80,000. Such horizontal risk-sharing is especially economical for an insurance syndicate that runs out of a trading floor at Lloyd's, because the man who runs it believes he can trust the "lead underwriter" on the risk to know enough about what he is insuring to protect those who follow his lead, both in setting the premium and later in deciding whether or not a claim is valid.

But this arrangement may not meet the needs of the underwriters stamping the original policy. When the maximum risk is whatever you can write as a worst-case scenario (two fully loaded jumbo jets crashing in the United States, where a jury can assess punitive damages and a judge can award *ad lib*), the insurance company dealing with the insureds may not wish to play Russian roulette. What Cuthbert Heath and later others at Lloyd's saw was that an insurance policy could itself be seen as an insurable risk, with a deductible to be paid by the insured. A company writing earthquake risk insurance in San Francisco might be willing to take, say, the first $50 million of losses but didn't wish to bet the business. Cuthbert Heath stepped into the breach with an "excess of loss" policy that began to pay only after losses on the original policy went over that $50 million limit. That excess of loss policy itself could be reinsured either horizontally, by putting a number of different syndicates into it from the start, or vertically, through placing a ceiling on the losses covered by this reinsurance—say, another $50 million—and reinsuring everything above $100 million with yet other syndicates. The terms of art in the business are "retrocession" for the reinsuring of a reinsurer, and "layering" for a multiplicity of vertical insurances. Some reinsurance applies only to specific risks in individual policies or classes of policies; some protects the originating syndicate from all its mistakes, through reinsuring the "whole account," limiting the maximum the originating syndicate can lose on all its policies.

When the division of risk is horizontal, the different insurers simply take a share of the premium paid for the policy. But at each step of a vertical reinsurance procedure someone has to calculate a suitable premium, measuring the unlikelihood that the policy will be invoked against the magnitude of the loss if it is. We put in our pocket for later examination the fact that this kind of reinsurance generates new profits for brokers, who take a commission from each reinsurance premium, every step of the way.

Reinsurance also became necessary within the Lloyd's market itself when the insurance of ships was no longer the dominant element in the business, and when syndicates began to rest on a number of Names, many of them with no other connection to the insurance market. "Marine" insurance was written for a single voyage; when the ship came home safe (or sank), the insurer pocketed the premium as profit (or paid out the losses). Fire and theft and accident and other bad luck insurance were written by the year, and some claims in these situations, even when a Lloyd's syndicate was the direct insurer, might not be lodged for some time. When Lloyd's was involved as reinsurer of the company that had written the original policy, the time lag might be considerably greater, as claims that had been paid gradually worked their way up the ladder of vertical reinsurers. Meanwhile, of course, each syndicate on the ladder could invest the premiums for its rungs.

For some, the art of making money consistently at Lloyd's became one of arbitraging between the premiums clients paid their underwriter for their insurance and the premiums the underwriter paid other underwriters for the reinsurance that protected him. Ideally, one shifted as much of the risk as possible to other shoulders, leaving as much of the premium as possible in one's own hands. To the extent that an underwriter could play this game, he became exposed to a "moral hazard"—that is, he could write policies without much concern about whether they made sense for the insurer, so long as his own operation was sufficiently protected by reinsurance "treaties." Especially as the market expanded in the 1980s, and new Names arrived with agents looking for ways to commit the new capacity, reinsurance became a larger part of Lloyd's total business—and a greater danger.

In the early years of the twentieth century, after some embarrassing episodes that had seen Lloyd's underwriters live high on the hog out of premium income that should have been reserved to pay claims, the market's governing committee promulgated a rule that all premium receipts had to go to a trust fund that could not be paid out to the backers of the syndicate until the results of the underwriting year were known. Because the ship contracts had contemplated voyages as long as two years, the rule placed the premiums collected in any one year in trust until two further years had passed. Even then, of course, it was possible that further claims against these policies might appear, especially in the case of what came to be called "long-tail" insurance—workmen's compensation, for example (another Cuthbert Heath invention), where the harm done to hatters by ingestion of mercury on the job could take some years to reveal itself.

To make certain that the insured would continue to be covered after the original syndicate had taken its profits and dissolved, Lloyd's insisted that the underwriter estimate not only the value of already known claims but also future claims "incurred but not reported" (IBNR). The syndicate would then offer a premium for a policy of "reinsurance to close" (RITC), which would transfer the risk from the policies written three years before to a current syndicate, which would usually be the next year of the same syndicate (same managing agent, same underwriter, same Names, same identifying number at Lloyd's) as the syndicate being closed. As a normal matter, the older of the underwriter's continuing syndicates would write the reinsurance to close. Policies written in the 1922 year (including the reinsurance of the 1921 year) would be in effect rolled over to the 1923 year when 1922 was "closed" on December 31, 1924. For many syndicates, the largest single contributor to premium income was the RITC from the most recent closed year. But in some "long-tail" situations, where venturesome syndicates might like the idea of years of income from investing premiums to cover claims that might never come, outside, entirely separate syndicates might give an underwriter his reinsurance to close. Richard Outhwaite told me that if there had been no claim under a policy for five years, he would reinsure it without further investigation. This relatively common approach to the analysis of reinsurance risk proved very costly.

Business came to London to use Cuthbert Heath's commercial aggressiveness (never personal aggressiveness—he was the model of an admiral's son, with none of the appearance or flash of a gambler; he was the source of Lloyd's flattering twentieth-century self-image). Lloyd's wrote its first insurance on motorcars in 1904, its first insurance on an airplane in 1911. Eventually, these fields would grow to become recognized specialties at Lloyd's. In 1962, the aviation section would be expanded by coverage of communications satellites, in policies that commanded premiums as great as 15 percent of the value of the satellite.

By mid-century, Lloyd's housed four more or less separate markets—marine insurance, nonmarine insurance (fire, pestilence, natural disaster, all the oddities), aviation, and motor. Names were considered diversified if they backed one syndicate in each of the markets. With the growth of the market and the "stamp capacity" of all the syndicates, however, underwriters became much more opportunistic. The motor people remained specialized in the reinsurance of automobile and truck policies, but others branched out. Merrett 418 was a "marine" syndicate, but its future was dominated by reinsurance of American product liability, toxic waste, and malpractice risks—plus some insurance of "errors and omissions" (the British term for malpractice) in the Lloyd's market itself. . . .

Indeed, the Council of Lloyd's permitted marine syndicates to have 70 percent of their business in nonmarine risks when the rates on marine insurance were considered too low to sustain the profitability of the enterprise. Christopher Moran remembers being called before a Lloyd's disciplinary committee because more than 70 percent of the risks his marine syndicate had insured were nonmarine. The chairman of the committee was Stephen Merrett. Moran had done some homework, and noted that more than 90 percent of the risks in Merrett 418 were nonmarine. "When I do it," Merrett said grandly, "it's proper."

●

The underwriter's "box" is part of a bench long enough to seat three. A cushion intervenes between the box itself and the underwriter, but the lid of the box can be raised and papers stowed in it, which was within the memory of man the initial filing system for most Lloyd's underwriters—and still is, surreptitiously, for some. Pictures from the years at the Royal Exchange show dark boxes very nearly as simple as today's, standing in serried rows, like schoolchildren's desks, facing a podium (and the *Lutine* bell) at the front of the room. Then as now, a solid wood back, also cushioned, rose behind the box, partitioning each syndicate off from its neighbors. Until the new building opened in 1986 with uniform furniture for everybody designed by the same architect, underwriters could design their own variations on the box. The

Merrett box in the old building, for example, had a small two-row amphitheater of benches behind it, so that juniors could watch the action and make the indicated telephone calls while the underwriter talked with the brokers.

There are six places at a box, three on each side of a table. In the new Lloyd's building, where the trading floor covers all of a fairly large city block, six-place boxes in teak veneer butt lengthwise against one another in pairs. An elevated book rack runs the length of the box, leaving eye level clear for the underwriter and his staff to look at one another. Various reference books and loose-leaf binders are on the bookshelf, where everyone has access to them. Today, as one of the many modernizations the 1990s have brought to Lloyd's, each place at the box has a notebook computer, which is wired into data sources of various kinds and provides the point of entry into the syndicate's own records plus a facility by which Lloyd's itself can track its underwriters' commitments to insure a risk.

All six of the seats at the box are occupied by the "active underwriter" of the syndicate, his deputy or deputies, and apprentices who can look up information or make phone calls while the underwriter schmoozes with the broker. A pull-down seat beside the underwriter may have a series of occupants, as the brokers arrive to present their risks. The underwriter is usually an older man wise in the ways of risk, though Lloyd's in every generation has shooting stars that may or may not become fixed in its firmament. Recently, as syndicates broadened but risks grew more specific to the business seeking insurance, underwriters have hired as deputies men or women who are specialized in electronics or space science or biotechnology and can advise on risks once unknown. In theory the underwriter operates according to a business plan adopted by the managing agent's firm of which the syndicate is a subsidiary, and reports to the head of that firm (which may be himself) and its directors. Most managing agents now operate several syndicates, each of which usually has its own underwriter. Merrett Holdings PLC before its collapse managed no fewer than seventeen syndicates.

But the underwriter at the box is the captain of the ship. In the lingo of the "Room," he "holds the pen." Though deputies may be empowered to write renewals of relatively standard policies—and some policies are in effect signed by agents abroad who have "binding authorities" from the managing agent—in general no risk can be accepted without the approval of the underwriter. In some syndicates, a photocopy of each slip is kept and signed by all the people working at the box to indicate that the underwriter has had his people check through the details of the policy.

Brokers, mostly young men and women conservatively dressed—the men in pinstripes, the women in tailored worsted suits—come down the aisles between the boxes, leather folders under their arms containing the papers that briefly describe the risk to be insured. They wait patiently in line, sometimes sitting on seats made available to them for the purpose, while one of their number sits beside the underwriter explaining the risk his client wishes to insure. It is a convivial world: The brokers in line talk with one another, and sometimes over the underwriter's head with the juniors who sit on the inside of the box. Most of the visits by the brokers are quite short: Once the first three or four leading underwriters have signed off on their willingness to take this risk at this premium (especially in the most common case, where the policy on offer is essentially another year's worth of something this underwriter has backed before), the other dozen or so who will complete the acceptance of the policy need no more than a few words describing the risk and the sight of the slips others have already signed. One should note that not everyone in the London insurance market considers this an ideal way to do business: Matthew Harding, whose Benfield Group of brokers has made him one of the five hundred richest Englishmen (and has given him the resources to buy a large share in the Chelsea Football Club), has said scornfully that in the age of the telephone "Benfield brokers do not go out with their binders and tramp through the streets on a wet Wednesday afternoon."[8]

Even when it's a new policy and an unconventional risk that's hard to price, the underwriters consider it bad form to take more than fifteen or twenty minutes to consider it. In really complicated matters, a broker may get the paperwork to the managing agent the day before, to allow consideration by the underwriter before he comes to the floor. But the broker arriving at the box doesn't know his fate, and often enough the conversation ends with a head shake rather than a handshake, sending the broker off to try his luck with another underwriter at another box.

Moreover, this is a *market*. What makes Lloyd's different from the upstairs world of insurance companies in offices is that a broker can shop a number of underwriters for a price before accepting one underwriter's bid to "lead" the policy. "Leading" the policy— establishing the size of the premium and the description of the risk, the deductible, the conditions under which loss may be claimed—is central to Lloyd's self-image. The 1992 annual report takes a whole page for a double boast in large print: "Two-thirds of all business in the London market is led by Lloyd's underwriters, who provide their policyholders with unparalleled security."

Lloyd's established rules for admittance to its floor as long ago as 1843. The world was divided into four different categories of humanity: "members," who could underwrite (this category includes all Names); "annual subscribers," who could not underwrite but could do other business on the floor (mostly brokers); "Merchants Room subscribers," who could come onto the floor for professional purposes (usually accountants and lawyers); and "Captain's Room subscribers," who could not do business at Lloyd's but had the use of the restaurant. Uniformed Waiters, wearing tailcoats (but not the black tailcoats of the restaurant waiters), guarded the doors and served the coffee at the Royal Exchange in the nineteenth century. Similarly garmented, but no longer delivering coffee (indeed, it is forbidden to eat or drink at a box, as on the floor of a stock exchange), today's Waiters still serve the insurance market as guardians of the gates and sources of information.

When the first Lloyd's building opened in 1928 (on the site of

today's building), it housed virtually all the London maritime insurance market. Lloyd's had the ground floor for its trading room,
and the insurance companies that did marine risks occupied the
second floor, enabling brokers to do all their business without
leaving the building. Thirty years later, the market had outgrown
that home, and a new semicircular marble-faced classical structure
in quiet 1950s style (even the heating ducts were sheathed in marble) was built across the street, connected to the older building
with a bridge over Lime Street. Its open (but pillared) high-
ceilinged main floor was the largest trading room in Europe. Elizabeth the Queen Mother (and her granddaughter Princess
Margaret) came to the ceremonies opening the building, which
concluded with what was probably the most elegant state dinner
of that season—the cabinet, leaders of the armed services, judges,
and ambassadors of the larger foreign countries all present and accounted for. The 1958 Lloyd's building still survives, housing
Lloyd's claims office and their related offices and meeting rooms.

The market's space-age current home, twelve stories high with
elevators and fat tubes for utilities climbing the outside walls, features a long and narrow center atrium that goes the full height of
the structure. It was designed by the British architect Richard
Rogers, with the utilities and the elevator towers outside the structure. Everything is a gleaming gunmetal gray. Because the block is
long and narrow, the building is long and narrow. The outside pip-
ing has given rise to bad jokes, especially since the market began
losing money. (The best, or the worst, is that the Lloyd's building is
the only creation that has its intestines on the outside and its ass-
holes on the inside.) This new Lloyd's is at its most beautiful at
night, when ghostly blue floodlights illuminate its entire height.
Day or night, one rides up the elevators in their glass tubes at the
ends of the building and looks out on an urban fairyland.

The fluorescent-lit trading room, up a short flight of steps from
street level, covers the entire footing of the building. The Captain's Room and lesser restaurants are on a subfloor a few steps
down from street level. Office space, with windows on both the

atrium and the outside, starts three stories up, served from inside by escalators built with glass walls to display the machinery below the steps. Hallways in the office areas are formed by modular wood panels, and look rather like the corridors in the great Cunard liners of a generation ago. The cost of the building in 1986 was about $270 million. In 1993, Lloyd's chief executive, Peter Middleton, told an American reporter that he thought the market might move back to its old, cheaper home before the turn of the century: "I just don't know whether, in four to five years time, underwriters will want to continue sitting in such high-cost premises." The atrium, he thought, would make a fine art gallery, with a shopping center around it—after all, the City of London lacks a shopping mall.[9]

The top two stories of the new Lloyd's, marble-floored with glorious views over the City and the church spires and the Thames, are reserved for Lloyd's executive offices and entertaining. The thought was that nonmember insurance companies would rent much of the office space, restoring the convenience the 1928 building had offered the market when it was new. As "subscribers," for a modest fee, they could also gain routine access to the trading floor itself. But the rents were too high and the insurance business too unprofitable. Much of the space in the new building remains vacant, both on the floor and upstairs.

Even so, the trading room is crowded, with something like two thousand people in the room at a busy time of day. (Three thousand is capacity.) Guards check passes for entry at each of the four doors to the great room. There are three categories of people who can go unescorted to the floor: members and the staffs of the underwriters who work at the boxes; annual subscribers, including the lawyers and accountants as well as the brokers; and substitutes for members, who are admitted when their principals are occupied elsewhere. About $10 million of the cost of running Lloyd's comes from fees charged for giving substitutes access to the floor. All Names, of course, are automatically members, even those of us who are no longer underwriting and wish we were no longer

Names. (Among them, members pay total fees of more than $100 million toward the cost of operating Lloyd's; this money is deducted from your "funds at Lloyd's" for as long as any of your syndicates has not closed; if you no longer have any "funds at Lloyd's," it becomes part of what they sue you for.) Names' cards are gold, and have photos, like drivers' licenses. Names' agents come onto the floor as Names themselves: They have no function in the actual market.

At the end of this process, a broker leaves the Lloyd's trading room with a loose-leaf notebook, in which the front pages contain a description of the risk being insured and the premium being paid (normally expressed as a percentage of the total at risk, where that total is known), and the back pages contain a series of "slips" insurance underwriters have stamped and initialed with a percentage of the total risk they are prepared to assume for the same percentage of the total premium. This notebook is the property of the broker; the underwriter may or may not retain his own copy of the descriptions. He knows which of his fellows has underwritten what percentage of the risk before the broker came to his box for his stamp, but often he does not know who is on the policy subsequent to his acceptance of it.

When a claim is made under the policy, the broker must submit the claim to the lead underwriter on the slip, meanwhile notifying the Lloyd's claims office, which also eventually tells the lesser underwriters that their syndicates must cough up some quantity of pounds or dollars. And everybody tells his Names that they have a check coming plus an addition to their "funds at Lloyd's" as a reserve, or that the premium income credited to their account in the first year of the syndicate will not cover the losses on the policies, and they must now put up some cash, by July 31, please, or interest will accrue. The Names won't find out how their syndicate made them money, or, except in the most general of terms, how it lost them money—or why they should get ready for more cash calls in the months or years to come.

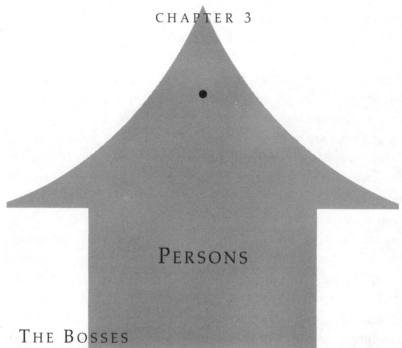

CHAPTER 3

PERSONS

THE BOSSES

Peter Middleton, who became chief executive officer and deputy chairman of Lloyd's at the beginning of 1993 when still in his forties, is a conciliator at heart. He has black hair and regular, strong features in a long head, his clothes always look relaxed and even a bit rumpled, his ties tend toward the bright red, and he has a country manner, courteous and slow. Lloyd's is his first significant contact with the insurance industry: He came from a career as a foreign service officer, serving as second secretary in Djakarta and in Dar es Salaam before ending as counselor in Britain's Paris embassy, whence he was recruited to Midland Bank International. From 1987 to 1992, he was chief of the bank's Thomas Cook subsidiary, revitalized it, and sold it to a German bank. He's from the north country, and his accent in English is the kind Americans find easy to understand.

At the ages when other Englishmen of similar prominence were going to "public school" (which means a private boarding school) and to university (which means Oxford or Cambridge), Peter Middleton was going to grammar school and to a monastery to prepare to become a monk. Until a couple of accidents smashed him up a bit, he rode to work at Lloyd's not in a chauffeur-driven limousine but on his motorbike, which he left parked at the front door. When he shambles to the podium at a meeting, he always pauses awhile before he speaks. He listens, apparently with great care and concentration, as though he were in a confessional, to what people say to him. His favorite line is "Give peace a chance." Names feel Middleton really understands them, he will intercede for them, he will take care of them. Really, he's Barney the Dinosaur.

His function has been to be liked, even loved. A letter to Lloyd's house magazine *One Lime Street* in February 1993 told readers that he "gave up some of his very limited free time to come down to an Oxfordshire village hall on Sunday 10 January to meet a group of impoverished Names who had suffered the double misfortune of having Gooda Walker as their members' agent as well as being on a range of disastrously loss-making Gooda Walker syndicates. . . . The meeting was very successful. The fact that Mr. Middleton was there at all speaks volumes. . . . He talked, but above all he listened. He comes to Lloyd's with clean hands, and the impression he gave was one of empathy and great integrity. Names left the meeting saying they felt fortified in hope and spirit."[1]

When Middleton failed to deliver to the Names a plan that would limit their losses, Chris Stockwell, the head of the Lloyd's Names Associations' Working Party, was like a betrayed lover who'd found his girl in bed with another man. If the truth is that Lloyd's is really stalling for time in using this year's premiums to pay off last year's losses, Middleton probably does not know it. Still, the facts on the ground prevent Middleton from delivering anything of substance to help the afflicted. There is nobody but the Names to pay the claims against the policies Lloyd's syndicates wrote, and if Lloyd's doesn't pay claims, it will quickly go out of business.

The pressure on Middleton has clearly been all but unbearable. He aged in 1993, his marriage went bad, and he began to lose control, not only of his motorcycle. He's not so patient and benign as he used to be. He was seen in London nightclubs with ever-younger ladies, one of them an employee of Lloyd's. One of them, returning with him from a trip to Singapore, let it be known by the press that she and Middleton were engaged, which drew from his wife the irritated comment that she didn't know bigamy was legal in England. He became something of a figure of fun. The Prufrock column in *The Sunday Times* took note of a robbery at his house, where "the desk drawer where he keeps business papers relating to Lloyd's had been emptied . . . documents had been taken out and examined, possibly photographed, copied, used to make darts—who knows what mischief went on in Middleton's drawers. . . . At least they left him his cufflinks."[2]

I was at a Society of Names meeting at the old Lloyd's building in late November 1993 when Middleton delivered himself of a tirade: "The American Names," he said in a voice that neared a shout, "may make the legal costs of collecting from them greater than the recovery of their debts to Lloyd's. And for the Americans who declare bankruptcy and move to Florida, well, that's the end of it. The Americans are giving Yeltsin only one year to turn around the entire Russian economy. We should be given five years to make Lloyd's profitable. And the Americans should remember it took them ten years to write their Constitution. And the Americans after that, one hundred years later, they had a CIVIL WAR."

He then left the speakers' platform and walked down the center aisle and out the door, without so much as a parting gesture. Outside the door, he realized he had forgotten his papers on the lectern, and walked back up the center aisle to the platform, took his papers, and again departed. Both exits were accompanied by absolute silence from both the audience and the other speakers on the platform.

In a private interview, moreover, Middleton was detached rather than sympathetic. He didn't look me in the eye for the first twenty-five minutes of our conversation. Instead, his gaze was always off somewhere to his right, in the middle distance. It was like asking questions of the Red Queen. But he was much more chipper a few weeks later at the 1994 Annual General Meeting of the membership, when others were dealing with policy questions and he had the chance to talk about *organization*. He sprang to life and spoke forcefully and happily about the technical innovations, especially computerized record-keeping, that had come to the Lloyd's trading room under his direction. Obviously, that's what makes him feel comfortable: organization. Other losing Names were appalled when they learned that Lloyd's had given him a couple of hundred thousand dollars in bonuses in 1993, because he'd reorganized so effectively to cut expenses. I thought he'd earned it.

If Middleton is the good cop, chairman David Rowland is the bad cop, a precise figure, thin hair slicked over a high forehead, very disciplined, rather like a Rolex watch, precise and expensive, with the consonant-swallowing speech of the British upper class. He's perfect. His soft gray suits *always* fit, very beautifully, and his ties never call attention to themselves. A Lloyd's veteran (Rupert Brett says he "has Lloyd's in his blood"), he comes from Sedgwick on the brokerage side of the insurance business, where he sold risks to underwriters rather than assessing them for Names, and he served on the council that ran the place in the 1980s.

In those days of "the old regime," he remembers, "social duties took a lot of time. Everyone of any prominence in the City was invited for old-style long lunches, with lots of ceremony. When the chairman of Lloyd's entered, everyone stood up. It was like royalty." Asked what he now wishes he had done differently on the council, he says, "I wish I had worked harder to remove more council members from office. The level of education at Lloyd's is lousy." He is a business school's ideal of a professional: smart, always controlled, directed toward his strategic objectives.

As long ago as 1989, Patrick Cockburn of *The Independent* remembers, Rowland was telling people that he wanted to be chairman of Lloyd's, which was a remarkable ambition: All but two of the previous chairmen had come from the underwriting end of the Society. (Of course, as a Name—accepting probably $800,000 of premium a year—he was an underwriter in reality if not in daily working life.) He had become chairman of Sedgwick, the company that owned my Name's agent as well as the largest British-owned insurance broker. The underwriter Murray Lawrence, an athletic, confident man, was then the chairman of Lloyd's, still publicly denying the danger to insurance companies from lawsuits asserting employers', and thus insurance companies', liability for health damage from the inhalation of asbestos on the job. Lawrence had reinsured his own syndicate out of asbestos risks as early as 1982, when he was serving as chairman of Lloyd's audit committee. After disposing of his own risks he wrote a memo warning other managers of underwriting syndicates—but not Names—to make sure they were adequately reserved against claims for asbestos poisoning.

Rowland was on the council while Lawrence was chairman, and he was forever complaining at council meetings about how badly the place was run. In 1990, Lawrence's deputy chairman and soon-to-be successor, David Coleridge, suggested that there were storms ahead and something really should be done if only to deflect the lightning. As David Rowland had made so much noise predicting trouble, he rather than an outsider or one of the underwriters should be commissioned to chair a task force to prepare the report *Lloyd's: A Route Forward.*

Coleridge had been a partner in the Sturge underwriting management agency, which also owned a large London stockbroker. When Sturge became a public corporation, he received shares worth something like $10 million. A big man with a large, lined face, staring pop eyes, and a mane of white hair, he is blue blood Lloyd's and beyond Lloyd's. Among his remote ancestors was the poet and table-talker Samuel Taylor Coleridge, also a very large man, author of "The Rime of the Ancient Mariner." Today's Coleridge did not shoot the albatross, but has had to wear it around his neck anyway. Coleridge owned more than 7 million of the 50 million shares in Sturge, which paid him dividends of about $600,000 a year over and above his salary during the time he was unpaid chairman of Lloyd's. He retired and sold his shares, just in time. In early 1994, the major Sturge syndicates ceased underwriting, and by late 1994, the question was whether Sturge Holdings could be restructured to avoid liquidation. One of the Sturge syndicates had losses estimated at more than $1.5 *billion.*

The disasters at Lloyd's that Coleridge had to report during his two-year tenure as chairman rolled off his huge back like so much water. In 1991, he predicted first that losses from earlier years wouldn't be bad and then that the market had already turned around and was profitable. Shortly before the annual meeting of Names that year, he told *The Times,* "We have the misfortune to blush very publicly. We had 30,000 members. Many of them will have lost money and they make a lot of fuss. . . . Most of the people who are bitching and whingeing are doing it because they don't like losing." In 1994, he still had little sympathy for the losing Names: "They went into a risk business," he told me scornfully. "Insurance isn't selling baked beans."

Coleridge chaired the first Lloyd's meeting for American Names which I attended, at the Waldorf-Astoria in New York, where I heard him answer a question from a distraught American with the statement that, yes, he would be expected to pay losses for the rest of his life if the syndicate he backed could not be closed. He was polite, but he was hateful. Later, I met him, and of course I found him a genial and likable personality, and extremely intelligent. If you had to spend a week with someone, it would be pleasant to spend it with Coleridge. He is a relaxed man who inherited a lot of money and a lot of education (he'd become chairman, he once told an interviewer, because he'd had more education than the other members of the council), and he doesn't feel pressured by anything in the world. He isn't awed by either his predecessor or his successor.

"Murray Lawrence," Coleridge said expansively, "is obviously not an Einstein. It was of course a good thing to form a group to study Lloyd's capital needs [Rowland's task force]. Rowland had left the council, his term had ended, and he was a vociferous critic of everything we were doing. He'd been a broker originally at Stewart Wrightson, which was sold to Willis Faber, and the result was an awful kerfluffle because Stewart Wrightson wasn't in good shape. Alan Cole had been their biggest money-maker, but he left. Willis Faber felt cheated. Rowland was lucky the chairmanship at Sedgwick came loose, because he wasn't going anywhere at Faber's. At council meetings, he acted as though he were in church delivering a sermon. He kept calling for change, change, change. I waited until he was away to get the task force approved, then I called him in Hong Kong and said, 'If you really think there's something to be done, you do it.' "

Coleridge could be cavalier about Rowland because he did not in his heart believe that Lloyd's as an institution was in serious danger. When I saw him in January 1994, I don't think he thought Sturge, his own company, was really imperiled, though that was the one subject he ruled out of our conversation. But he did admire what Rowland's task force did: "I must say, they worked hard. They took their weekends in a country inn, went there Friday, stayed till Sunday, and they didn't get paid for their work. We hired McKinsey to work with them. I must say the material was well chosen and well proposed. We didn't agree with everything in it, but Rowland insisted that everything be approved, and it wasn't worth the fight. I nominated him to be Lloyd's first paid chairman—at a salary, at his insistence, of 450,000 pounds [$700,000] a year. It was much more than he was getting at Sedgwick and twice as much as Middleton is getting."

Rowland himself is very, very proud of the task force report: "It's a masterpiece," he says. "Freshfields [a firm of British lawyers] and Warburg's [a British merchant bank] and the committee had to create a whole new structure for Lloyd's, and we did, in just one year, and it has the Names' confidence." (In point of fact, Warburg backed out.) He admits fighting hard for his huge salary: The first thing he said to me when we sat down to talk was,

"I needed the money. I was going through a divorce and subsequent remarriage while I was negotiating the contract. My salary allows me to devote myself full-time to Lloyd's, and I have no other conflicting financial interest."

He works in a fabulous birdcage of an office on the twelfth floor of the Lloyd's building, which is skyscraper height in the City of London. He has had the marble floor covered with a carpet, to express the new, no-extravagances style at Lloyd's, and he has reduced the costs of his office. When he came, there were four limos and four chauffeurs attached to the office of the chairman, with a Rolls-Royce for the man himself. Rowland sold all the limos and dismissed all the chauffeurs, cut back from four to two Waiters and from half a dozen to three secretaries. The lavish entertainments in the Adams Room are history; indeed, the room can now be rented for non-Lloyd's occasions.

ANDREW

Andrew Wade is about forty years old, a handsome, sensitive north country man who used to be a stockbroker in London but has returned home to Nottingham, Robin Hood country, where his family has long had a furniture factory. It's one of England's more successful small cities, a hill town dominated by Nottingham Castle, full of dark granite buildings, living off a lace industry that flourished through the long recession. The town's most popular export in recent years was the ice-dancing team of Torvill and Dean, Nottingham natives. Andrew remembers skating with them.

By the late 1980s, Andrew was ready to relish his London success. He had a nest egg of well over a million dollars, he was tired of being a stockbroker, and he had some ideas for entertainment businesses he might start in Nottingham. He was in love with a charming young lady who had a child from a previous marriage and was awaiting her divorce. They took a cruise around the world. His accountant, a partner in Deloitte, Touche, suggested to him that one of the ways he could generate income from his self-made wealth was by becoming a Name at Lloyd's. A meticulous man, Andrew kept a diary of his Lloyd's contacts and arrangements, and generously made all his documents available to me.

In spring 1987, his accountant introduced him to London Wall Members Agency, where he was personally taken in hand by Guil, Lord Strathalmond, managing director of the firm. He put up a bank guarantee of $150,000, about one-tenth of his net worth, which would enable London Wall to accept premiums of about $375,000 on his behalf in the 1988 year of account. As early as July, Strathalmond had proposed six syndicates on which he could take about $230,000 of premiums—there just wasn't enough business in the market, Strathalmond confessed, to let him reach his premium limit. But they would try to fill in his program later.

Of the first six syndicates in which Lord Strathalmond placed Andrew, one would lose him about $75,000, another would lose him at least $150,000, and the third would lose him more than $200,000. During 1988, London Wall was able to arrange space for Andrew on four other syndicates, two of them disasters, including one which would prove to be among the half-dozen worst at Lloyd's, costing Andrew well over $200,000. ("I have managed," Strathalmond wrote gleefully, "to find a further Marine syndicate for you to join and enclose the accounts of Eversure Underwriting Syndicate No. 740. . . . ")

Andrew could get on these syndicates as a newcomer to the market because they were the fastest growing at Lloyd's, and they were the fastest growing because they were taking risks of retrocessional reinsurance, where they wouldn't have to pay unless there were really big disasters—but would pay forever and enormously if they had to pay at all. The only reason Andrew's losses can be given with some certainty is that Lloyd's has now agreed that Andrew is broke and can pay no more. He can stay in his house, but he's had to sell his business. He believes it would be unfair to expect his fiancée and her daughter to move to Nottingham and live on his small allowance from Lloyd's; and that, he says, not his fortune, is his real loss.

Having put Andrew on the path to Lloyd's, Lord Strathalmond turned him over to Peter Graham, a London Wall director, who in turn made him a client of his son Richard Graham, who after a lunch with the others shepherded him through his Rota interview, a visit to the floor, and meetings with five underwriters in the syndicates London Wall planned to have him back. "I hope you did not find the Rota day too much of an ordeal," Graham wrote, "and that you found it a useful exercise to meet your underwriters and hear what they had to say about the future prospects in their respective markets." In November, Andrew paid his Lloyd's entrance fee of about $5,000, and was a guest at a formal lunch at London Wall, where not only Lord Strathalmond was in attendance but also R. H. Warrender, the CEO of London Wall Holdings. It was all downhill from there.

Andrew was given no indication in 1988 or 1989 that anything might be going wrong, though inside the market, people were beginning to tremble. In early 1990, in a conversation with Lord Strathalmond, Andrew "expressed concern about the U.K. storms at the beginning of the year. Guil," says London Wall's internal report on Andrew's account, "was not able to comment specifically but suggested that 1989 and 1990 would not be good years, and that AW should budget for a maximum overall loss figure of $75,000." What to do? Bucked up by Lord Strathalmond and by Richard Graham's certainty that "the market is firming" and that profits were right around the corner, Andrew decided that the best way for him to recover from his losses was to increase the size of his deposit at Lloyd's, the premiums he could therefore receive, and the number of syndicates he could back. In 1990, he paid his losses in cash and deposited a $150,000 line of credit from Norwich Insurance to supplement the securities already there.

The results of the 1988 underwriting year would not be reported until spring 1991. In February, however, a bomb dropped: The *1989* year of Devonshire 216 needed money to pay claims, and was issuing a cash call. Andrew's share was about $20,000.

Richard wrote a covering letter, explaining that the market as a whole was having a tough time with 1989, and 216 as a syndicate that reinsured other syndicates "is therefore affected more. . . . In their last report and accounts, they said that there would be a loss on the 1989 account and also referred to the possibility of a cash call. . . . I am now enclosing a letter from the managing agents, together with an extract from their interim report, a statement from the syndicate auditors and a confirmation from the syndicate bankers concerning the current overdraft facilities. . . . Could I therefore ask you to let me have a cheque for [$20,000] payable to London Wall Members Agency Limited in respect of the balance due. . . . We have discussed the matter with the managing agents, and are satisfied with the reasons for the call which will reduce the sterling overdraft of the syndicate. Claims arising from Hurricane Hugo have compounded the problems of a difficult year. . . . Full details will be provided with the annual syndicate accounts, but, at this time, we believe that both the 1988 and 1990 Accounts should be profitable. Andrew, I am so sorry that this cash call has been necessary and that you have only been given a month to settle it. The syndicate managers have tried very hard to avoid this option but their cash flow is so poor in this year that the call is now necessary." Poor dears.

Another, more general letter came in March 1991: "In the past we have resisted giving estimates at this time of the year, but because of the market losses expected for 1989 we felt that a 'broad brush' indication might be helpful. We regard this as being an exceptional circumstance which we do not anticipate having to repeat. These estimates have been produced by our monitoring department, from a computerised database which is being continuously updated in the light of the reports received from syndicates."

The long and the short of it was that Andrew should anticipate a loss of about $7,500 net on his underwriting for 1988, and about $25,000 for 1989—and when the accounts were final, these numbers would be about one-third the losses actually recognized in those years. "It is too early to make a detailed forecast for the 1990 year of account, but generally we believe that it will be profitable, although at a very modest level [in fact, the 1990 year of account would see losses of more than $4 *billion* for the market as a whole, $150,000 for Andrew]. . . . The increases in premium rating brought about by these losses, give grounds for optimism about prospects in the immediate future.

"I am so sorry," the letter concludes, "to give you this bad news particularly as 1988 and 1989 are your first two years. Quite clearly, we should meet in the next few months to discuss methods of funding and your future underwriting strategy. No doubt you will want to speak to me about which syndicates have performed poorly. Please do so whenever you wish."

From that day on, there was never any good news. Hopes, yes; beliefs, yes; sales talk, yes—but not good news. In 1992, Andrew's losses to be paid were $130,000. If he drew down his deposit at Lloyd's to pay some of them, he would have to cut back on his underwritings the next year. He borrowed from his mother, and paid his cash calls.

In the 1990 year of account, nine of Andrew's ten syndicates lost money, and his total losses for the year as calculated on December 31, 1992 (with five of his 1990 syndicates and three holdover 1989 syndicates still open and bleeding money), was about $140,000. Of course, there was good news for somebody. Between them, the members' agents' and the managing agents' fees totaled a little more than $15,000. If his syndicates had actually made money, the insiders would have charged him a "profit commission," usually 20 percent, on what they made. This commission was calculated off the top, before the deduction of taxes, fees, and managing agents' "personal expenses." Until 1990, when a new agreement between Names and their agents was adopted, Names' agents charged "profit commission" on every profitable syndicate their Names were on, even when the losses on other syndicates overwhelmed the gains from the profitable ones.

Lord Strathalmond, in his "Guil" letter to Andrew announcing this change, patted London Wall on the back for not raising its fixed fees, "although our earnings could be reduced as a result of the deficit clause." Some other Names' agencies did increase their fixed fees (to six-tenths of 1 percent of their Names' "capacity"). The prohibition of profit commissions for Names' agents when the Names had lost money did not, of course, apply to the *managing* agents who ran the syndicates, and Andrew in this disastrous 1990 year did pay about $600 in profit commission to a syndicate that wound up with a profit to him of about $2,800. That was Barber 512—owned and operated by London Wall itself. . . .

About a month before these results were finally announced, Andrew met with his accountant and Richard Graham, who advised him to join the "action group" suing Devonshire 216, arguably the very worst of his syndicates. "I am so terribly sorry that our meeting the other day was such a depressing affair," Richard wrote on May 11, 1993. "I cannot begin to appreciate the torment that you must be feeling but I will do whatever I can to help you through this appalling mess. Please let me know what date in July would suit you and Peter for our next meeting."

At that meeting, Richard was still proposing that Andrew could, in the favorite Lloyd's term, "trade through" his losses by continuing to underwrite. Andrew could defer payment of losses (of course, he'd have to pay interest, at 2 percent above the British equivalent of prime rate), take the 5 percent credit Lloyd's was giving all Names as an advance payment on the profitability assumed for the 1993 underwriting year, and shift over to a sort of mutual fund arrangement Lloyd's had constructed to allow Names to get around the rules on how much deposit was required to underwrite at each level. If all that was done, Richard could find a way that Andrew could pass his "solvency" test and continue to accept $600,000 in premium income and the risks associated with it for 1994.

But Andrew had now seen the light—or, more correctly, the darkness. With all those open syndicates, he was going to keep losing money at Lloyd's however well his new syndicates might do. He had to find a way out. Lloyd's had begun a "hardship" scheme, which would be closed down at the end of 1994 because management felt too many people were applying to Hardship, making it too expensive for the Society to support over six hundred Names in the program with more than 2,000 Names waiting to be processed. Under this Members' Hardship Scheme, people would cease underwriting but be able to keep the use of some of the money they had on deposit. It involved signing over to Lloyd's virtually all one's wealth, including one's home—in Andrew's case, a very substantial house on a charming street in Nottingham. In return, one could continue to live at home (though Andrew has had to divide the house into apartments for rent), and receive a small annual allowance for expenses from what survived in one's Lloyd's deposit. At Andrew's death, Lloyd's will own his home, and will sell it to meet his debts.

The hardship committee did not *excuse* anyone's debts; the failed Name had to acknowledge continuing legal responsibility for all losses already incurred and any further losses on his syndicates. If Andrew receives a legacy, he must hand it over. He had started a new business in Nottingham shortly before making his hardship arrangements, a wild mini–amusement park for young people, with laser guns and flashing lights and hard rock, where the winner was the one who got out "alive"—not my thing but very popular with nearby college students in the late afternoon and evenings. Attached to it was a pub with a high-tech dartboard, also very popular among the young. When this venture began to make some money, Lloyd's seized it, to Andrew's great distress. But the cash calls have stopped coming.

The living squirm and wriggle, even, as David Coleridge had it, bitch and whinge. Some of the horror stories are well publicized, in television shows, newspapers, books: Clive Francis, hero of the Battle of Britain, who became a property developer and made a fortune—then lost it all, and more, at Lloyd's; a retired secretary named Betty Atkins (a resonant name—the British equivalent of "GI" for soldier was "Tommy Atkins"), who was given a membership at Lloyd's as a retirement present by the insurance company that employed her, and found herself dunned for losses in the hundreds of thousands of dollars. I find myself drawn most to the people who are trying to fight back, protect themselves and their families, seek the truth behind what Names call "the Lloyd's speak" that so convincingly tells the Names nothing can be done.

FERNANDA

Fernanda Herford, now a lady of a certain age, an actress and a television "presenter," could be picked out in any room as a theatrical personage. She has a rich, wonderful, deep voice, and a lovely face. Her carriage alone gives her distinction. Very informal, she wears pants and oversized sweaters, but the result is really chic. Lloyd's has all her money now, but she still lives in a handsome Chelsea house, inherited from her mother, with her husband's fine collection of contemporary paintings in the reception room. Her husband is not a Name and he owns the paintings, and Lloyd's cannot touch "the matrimonial home." It duns her, however, for information about her husband's income and hints that everything he has should also be at risk for his foolishness in marrying a Name. Meanwhile, she tries to pay her current bills by using the top floor of her house as a bed-and-breakfast. Fernanda since 1992 has been devoting her time to fighting for the interests of a group of perhaps three hundred Names who had Anthony Gooda as their members' agent and were placed by the Gooda members' agency into underwriting syndicates operated by the same holding company, Gooda Walker. The Names were told these were conservative insurance operations: "We won't make you a fortune but we won't lose you one either."[3]

In fact, however, the Gooda Walker box wrote the most outrageously speculative policies written at Lloyd's, reinsurance that protected other insurance syndicates (including other Gooda Walker syndicates) against devastating hurricanes, shipwrecks, and the like. They would be very profitable if nothing went wrong in the world (though the Names didn't see much of the money, because the Gooda Walker people paid generous brokerage commissions, gave themselves big salaries, and took huge expense allowances for yachts and limousines). And they would be ruinous to the Names that backed them if a year produced a lot of big claims. At some point, because nobody stays lucky forever, there would be such a year. Probably more than one. Such years wouldn't necessarily ruin the people who worked for Gooda Walker, who would continue to receive their big salaries and perks, and even dividends from the profitable operation of the agency, but they would kill the Names. In the end, they killed Gooda Walker, too, because instead of diffusing risks, the underwriters in Gooda Walker concentrated them.

Gooda probably knew no better. He recruited most of his Names on the golf course, and after his world had collapsed, and he had loaded his sister, his friends, and his neighbors with a large piece of the billion dollars–plus lost in the Gooda Walker underwritings, he was dismayed that nobody wanted to play golf with him anymore. "He was very charming but clearly not very bright," Fernanda says. "He loved pouring the champagne. I think he still doesn't know what hit him." Nobody thinks Tony Gooda is hateful, though some people do sort of wonder if it is true he maintains the fleet of yachts for rent that was his side business and seems to keep him in luxury still. His brother-in-law Derek Walker, who was the underwriter, really is hated, because at best he didn't care what happened to the Names and at worst he was fudging the books for his own benefit, as indicated by a report from Kenneth Randall, a former head of Lloyd's Regulatory Services.[4]

Most of the Names in the Gooda Walker syndicates had been placed there by other agents, often enough because they'd had some good years and looked like money-makers. But Fernanda and her friends had been signed on to Gooda Walker syndicates by Gooda Walker Names' agents: They were "direct Names," victims of people who said they were acting in the Names' behalf but must have known in the last two years of the agency's life that they were leading the lambs to the slaughter. As of early 1994, the losses of the Gooda Walker direct Names averaged more than $1.5 million each. Jessie (Mrs. Alexander) Munn, another victim, author of the touching letter to the Lloyd's house organ about how nice it had been for Peter Middleton to come visit the Names in January 1993, wrote to Middleton himself in June, using information from Lloyd's own "loss report," that nearly all the underwriting capacity of the "GW Direct Names was placed on a narrow spread of high risk . . . GW syndicates *already* making losses rather than the profits stated." This time Middleton wasn't listening; her answer came from a functionary.

Fernanda has given me her correspondence with Lloyd's for 1993–94. Her good humor is as remarkable as her persistence. Gooda Walker Names Agency "went into liquidation" in September 1991. Among the questions Fernanda wanted answered was what the directors took out of the company. In 1989, they had given themselves a $2 million dividend, and up to the time of liquidation they continued to run the agency with their same generous expenses. Lloyd's refused to help: Brian Garraway, then the new director of market regulation (he died a few months later), admitted in March 1993 that "the loss review opinion contains clear and frank findings about the way in which the members' agency operated," but added that "Lloyd's has a duty to preserve confidentiality and privacy of individuals' financial circumstances."

There were thirty-two U.S. Names on the Gooda Walker direct list. Many of them, and some English Names who were taxed in America, claimed tax refunds for the taxes they had paid on false Gooda Walker profits. These tax refund checks were sent to the members' agents for forwarding to the Names, and virtually all the agents did forward. Gooda Walker direct Names, however, were now represented by a special Lloyd's-operated agency that had taken over their accounts after Gooda Walker disappeared. This agency seized the checks in partial payment of their losses, which required Lloyd's employees to open official U.K. mail and forge the signatures of the individuals to whom the checks had been made out.

Fernanda sent an astonished complaint on behalf of her friends. Garraway had an assistant reply that "external professional advice was sought as to the appropriate course of action. Once it was clear that the duty to policyholders to ensure the solvency of the association dictated a course of action the Board could not shrink from adopting this despite being aware that this would be very unwelcome to some Names."

Fernanda now decided she should be a little angry, and wrote to Garraway: "Even though it is now acknowledged that there is an element of fraud in the way these debts have been run up, Lloyd's is continuing to take as much money as it can, by whatever means at its disposal. . . . I think the time has come for the government to take a look at the way Lloyd's business has been, and is being conducted."

This sort of misbehavior has taken many forms. Richard Tropp, the American Name accepted despite his limited resources as an AID (Agency for International Development) official, received a cash call at the end of June 1992, for payment on July 31, and immediately instructed his Name's agent to honor it. The money was not actually drawn down by Lloyd's until late September 1992, after the pound had been devalued severely in the currency crisis of that month. The call had been in pounds, and Mr. Tropp's assets were in dollars, and on the day that they took the money from his reserves it took $6,000 less than it would have required in July to meet his obligation. Lloyd's nevertheless took his money at July's exchange rate, pocketing the profits from the devaluation of the pound. Mr. Tropp complained, and was told that the decision of the date on which to value the drawdown was exclusively at Lloyd's discretion. Then Lloyd's charged Mr. Tropp another $842 in interest (at the very high British interest rates) because his cash call hadn't been met by July 31!

Gooda Walker management was by Lloyd's rules covered by an "errors and omissions" policy, similar to malpractice insurance, that would pay victims of negligence by the underwriters. (The rules were changed in 1992 to permit managing agencies to operate from 1993 on without insurance, on the grounds that such in-surance was becoming awfully expensive: Somebody noted grimly that in the 1990s Lloyd's held itself out as a place where you could insure against any risk—except the incompetence of your agents at Lloyd's.) Some of this insurance was written inside the Lloyd's market, some outside. After looking at the Gooda Walker situation, both inside and outside insurers "avoided" (that is, canceled and denied any liability for) the agency's E&O policies, on the grounds that its actions were not just negligent but fraud-ulent.

Fernanda wrote to Middleton: "If the E&O insurers can claim that matters relevant to the insurers' decision as to whether to provide cover were suppressed, and so avoid the claim, could not the Gooda Walker Direct Names say the same as far as their losses are concerned? [The loss report] is clear that in 1988, if Gooda Walker as Members Agents had given their Names all the facts they knew with respect to certain Gooda Walker syndicates, many Names would not have underwritten on them in 1989. . . . I believe that if fraud is uncovered, and Names losses are not the result of bona fide underwriting, Lloyd's is in no position to demand pay-ment." At the Annual General Meeting of Lloyd's at the Royal Festival Hall in June 1993, one Name asked David Rowland how he could justify calling more than $225 million from Gooda Walker Names at a time when the Randall report had indicated fraudulent misstatements of results by the Gooda Walker manag-ing agency and the Serious Fraud Office was investigating the ac-tivities of the agency. "We have to see that claims are paid," Rowland said, "and that we handle the collection of monies within the Society's framework."[5]

On July 12, without alerting her that it was doing so, Lloyd's sold about $170,000 worth of securities from Fernanda's deposit, and took the money. There would be another million dollars or so to go. She sent Peter Middleton a fax: "Would you be kind enough to confirm in writing, that the sales of these shares from my de-posit are the result of legitimate Lloyd's underwriting business properly obtained for me by my Members' Agent." Middleton refused to give such an assurance. R. A. C. Hewes, who was a permanent corporation employee and head of regulation, informed Fernanda that Lloyd's was conducting its own inquiry, but its results would not be made available to her or the other Gooda Walker Names who were suing to recover their losses. She must pay her debts in any event. "You mention," Fernanda wrote in reply, "that you have been clearly advised that Names are liable for their debts, even with proof of dishonesty. No doubt the advice you have received on such an important matter is in writing. Please may I see a copy of the opinion."

Finally, in early 1994, Fernanda abandoned hope in Middleton. "We are the Can't Pay Names," she wrote, "so that however many writs and court orders are placed upon us, there will still be limited payment to Lloyd's." Between the Gooda Walker direct community and the Canadian Names who had been put on the Gooda Walker syndicates and had virtually no resources to begin with, Fernanda estimated, the shortfall on the Lloyd's cash calls would be about $900 million, so the game was not doing Lloyd's any good either. "I know you can hide behind the unknown, as our insolvency has not been tested that far, but taking the hypothesis that I have quoted, where will you pay the outstanding claims from? . . . I do appreciate that the problem is the size of the shortfall—or the fraud if you like. If the sum of money were less, I am sure you would have made us a particular case, and got us off your back. But this doesn't mean just because we have been hugely rather than slightly ripped off, that our case can be dismissed."

THE LEADERS OF THE OPPOSITION

Peter Nutting is a short, plump, genial fellow with a big smile, one of the few people in the governance of Lloyd's who never says anything terrible about anyone else. An old Etonian and a veteran of the Irish Guards, he wears a bright pink shirt that stretches tight over his stomach, and a flowered tie; he is contented with himself and with the world. I would be delighted to have him as my partner at a dinner party. An investment banker and a Name seriously punished by the losses of underwriter Richard Outhwaite, he was one of the early members of the Association of Lloyd's Members (ALM), an organization that does not forget its role as a complement to the corporation, officially the Society of Lloyd's. His partners in this early venture have gone on to head groups Lloyd's considers antagonistic to its interests—the bearded John Rew to Chatset, which prepares and publishes annual estimates on how much money the syndicates are *really* losing, and the fast-talking, darting Tom Benyon, who runs the Society of Names, which Rew describes as "a poor man's Association of Lloyd's Members."

Nutting's fifteen minutes of fame came when instead of going to a party at the Ascot race meeting, he attended a special meeting of Outhwaite Names trying to find out why their not very large insurance syndicate was asking them to pay losses of hundreds of millions of pounds, and found himself chairman of the Outhwaite Action Group. Outhwaite had specialized in reinsuring other syndicates at Lloyd's, and had been, to say the least, unfortunate in his choices.[6]

It was brave of Nutting, given his friends, his background, and his beliefs, to lead the first lawsuit against Lloyd's that actually came to trial—though not to verdict, for the Errors and Omissions insurer quit after much of the evidence had been entered, and arranged to have Outhwaite's malpractice insurers settle the case for about two-thirds of the losses the Names had already suffered before 1989. Unfortunately, that looks to be only about one-quarter of the losses the 1982 year of Outhwaite 317 will eventually impose on its Names. Nutting himself, not being a revolutionary or one of David Coleridge's "whingers" (though Coleridge had called him that in private conversation when the suit was first brought), returned to the fold at Lloyd's and became one of the Society's governing council. In early 1994, he boldly said he was sorry the Outhwaite Names had won. . . .

Another pioneer of action for the Names is Kenneth Lavery, a retired Canadian accountant, a straightforward, solid citizen who was a Name on, among others, Merrett 418 for 1985. Arriving a few days early for the Annual General Meeting of Names in spring 1991, and finding he got no satisfaction from his Name's agent or from Lloyd's when he inquired why this syndicate was still open and how bad it might get, he went to the Association of Lloyd's Members and asked for help in locating other members of this cursed syndicate. Val Powell, executive secretary of the ALM, told him he couldn't help because there hadn't been any other complaints about Merrett 418 (which was forgetful of him: I had already complained), and Lavery said that, well, he would then just have to print up a questionnaire and give it to all the Names as they entered the Annual Meeting. Powell said smugly that it was too late for that, because the meeting was the next day, and Lavery replied that Powell shouldn't worry, he knew a printer in London who would prepare a few thousand broadsheets overnight.

The next morning as he left the Army and Navy Club with his few thousand broadsheets in a satchel, Lavery received a call from Powell telling him that, on consideration, ALM would help him get a message to his fellow victims on Merrett 418, and from the response to that message grew the Merrett 418 Action Group, with more than two thousand contributors, which means $8 million, toward the legal fees. Of course, we will get all that back should we win the case.

John Rew, now a ruminative man of rural appearance, with a bushy gray beard and a barrel chest, was an investment analyst in the 1970s heyday of the expanding British stock. He has managed to keep some of that money, for he clearly enjoys himself in the world. When I come to London, we breakfast deliciously at Fortnum & Mason—unless, as happened once in 1995, he's off sailing in Venice. He decided to back some syndicates at Lloyd's as part of a retirement plan. "There I was," he says, "a hotshot gunslinger. I think, 'God, I was stupid.' One stumbled through this maze, kept stubbing one's toe on rocks of fact that were hard to uncover. I was looking around to decide which agents I wanted. One of them said, 'You're looking for so much information, I wonder if you're the kind of person we want at Lloyd's.' "

Rew was part of a periodic poker game that included Charles Sturge, scion of the Sturge family, the largest underwriters in the Lloyd's market. Charlie is still, indeed, protective of Lloyd's, though bitter about David Coleridge, who pushed his father out of the business that bears his name. Sturge had gone to work on the family box at Lloyd's, and as part of his self-organized apprenticeship had tried to explore how his own company's underwriters were doing. He was soon told in no uncertain terms that it was none of his business. The members of the poker game and three or four friends found that among them they were members of almost half the syndicates at Lloyd's, and in the course of events got at least summary information on what the syndicates they were backing had done. It is of the nature of reportorial ventures, moreover, that people who think they will come out of the story well are eager to talk, and people who fear they will come out of it badly can often be encouraged to tell their side to mitigate the damages. The poker players built a substantial dossier on the Lloyd's market.

By 1981, Rew and Sturge were publishing what they called "league tables" of how well different syndicates did (the reference is to the British soccer leagues, which run in separate divisions, the top two in each at the end of each season moving up, the bottom two moving down). They attempted to keep the proprieties by making the publication available only within the Association of Lloyd's Members—indeed, the first issues were given away as part of what a Name bought when he became a member of ALM.

These league tables would turn out to be much less of a help to consumers than Rew and Sturge originally thought, because syndicates that were running enormous risks well out in time looked great in their early years, when they had the premium income to invest and few claims to pay. Tony Gooda's work in recruiting people to the Gooda Walker syndicates was made infinitely easier because Rew and Sturge were ranking them at the top for return as a percentage of premium income. "We do have something to answer for," Rew says now; "we didn't understand how people would use the information. We always said we had no way of measuring risk against reward." Rew himself was put on several disastrous syndicates, and has lost his own country home.

Since 1992, when the market turned so heavily to losses, Rew and Sturge have published an annual *Chatset Guide to Syndicate Run-Offs*, predicting how bad the ultimate results will be on the syndicates that have not been able to buy reinsurance for themselves and continue to threaten their Names with unlimited losses. Every year Lloyd's denigrates the numbers, but most of the time reality turns out to be even worse than Rew's calculations.

"I'm writing an opera called *Tyrannosaurus Lloyd's,*" says Tom Benyon, a rather small man with thin brown hair and a sharp nose who talks very fast, and doesn't always care what he says. We always meet at the Royal Automobile Club, with its gold ceiling and showcase swimming pool. He is an operator, a former Labour Party member of Parliament, and a businessman whose businesses have not always flourished. "Two and a half years ago," he said in autumn 1993, "I called a meeting at the Lansbury Hotel, advertised it in *The Times, The Daily Telegraph,* and *The FT* [*Financial Times*]. John Rew and I had spotted that the spiral had blown [the reference—see Chapter 7—is to the out-of-control underwriting of reinsurance that was the cause of the devastation at Gooda Walker]. I knew there was a problem, I could smell it. Thousands of Names came, and I was like Dr. Stockman in *The Enemy of the People,* who sees that there's cholera in the water, and finds that he's regarded as the shit of the world. Nobody wants to hear the bad news.

"Whenever Lloyd's made an optimistic forecast, thousands of people poured money in. Nobody asked questions. You've got three hundred years of 'You're lucky to be here, lad; now, run off.' They had been conditioned, like Pavlov's dog. The end is ten thousand people running around the place with an identity crisis, because in this country your identity is in your possessions. Lloyd's has every theme but sex—it has royalty, mystery, theft."

Benyon makes what would appear to be a good living out of the Lloyd's debacle. He owns and operates an organization called the Society of Names (SoN), which prints (on shocking pink paper) an informative and sometimes scatological sixteen-page monthly journal called *The Son*. The headline on a recent issue was, "I Have No Gun, But I Can Spit." Each issue includes question-and-answer sections in which officers of Lloyd's respond to Names' concerns and Benyon's questions. SoN has an office in Piccadilly, but mostly Benyon runs it from his home in Buckinghamshire. He also organizes scores of meetings around the world, charging admission of $40 to $200, depending on the location of the meeting and the membership status of the ticket buyer, and the most senior Lloyd's executives come to them to make presentations and answer questions. These meetings are very well run, with an excellent choice of speakers, and the information in the literature passed out at the meetings is always accurate and helpful.

SoN will do hand-crafted analyses of their position for Names, charging as much as $400 for the service. Nevertheless, Benyon is critical of the action groups that are managing the class action lawsuits against the Lloyd's agents and syndicates, on the grounds that the committees running them are getting paid for what they should be doing as a charitable act. "The members of the Gooda Walker committee," he grumbles, "get a hundred thousand pounds [$150,000] each." This is denied, and very likely is not true. It is not only in the inner sanctums of Lloyd's that the people involved in this tragedy speak nasty of one another.

The man who chairs the Gooda Walker committee is Michael Eunon McLarnon Deeny, who is in fact a successful businessman, a deal maker, promoting entertainment events in athletic stadiums around the world, everything from Pavarotti to the Rolling Stones. He is a gray-haired man with a squint who wears gray shirts and gray suits, and walks vigorously back and forth behind his desk while he talks. He had a severe stutter, but being the chairman of the Gooda Walker Action Group improved his speaking abilities, and he doesn't hold up a meeting because he can't get the word out. After the meetings he chairs these days, people no longer say how brave he is to speak but rather how right he is in his opinions. Even when he does stutter, he is easy to understand, because the word he has trouble articulating is the truly important word. His action group has more than three thousand members, who paid out more than $10 million among them on the expenses of the case, and since early 1993, Deeny has been paid for his time, though a lot less than Benyon claims. And, of course, the Gooda Walker Names have won their case, though they haven't yet been paid.

Deeny has been perhaps the most formidable of the Lloyd's antagonists, because he is a businessman (originally, a chartered accountant). He believes that the essence of the problem at Lloyd's is that the underwriters were *not* businessmen, and he can cite chapter and verse, quite apart from the Gooda Walker mess. Eagerness to get the business—to get the premium income to invest—had driven prices below any reasonable calculation. "By the time the aviation underwriters were finished," Deeny says disgustedly, "British Airways were insuring their entire fleet for six one-hundredths of one percent of its value."

When Lloyd's offered a settlement to the Names suing to get out from under, the best offer as a proportion of their losses went to Deeny's group, and it was Deeny's analysis that, even for his people, there was more to be got from the court case that scuttled the settlement. At the same time, because he sees the chance to get some share of future profits for past losers, Deeny has publicly insisted that Lloyd's can make it, and that the ruined Names are not trying to destroy their destroyer. In private, he derides those who are "trading on" in hopes of making back what they lost: "A lot of them think that resigning now is like selling at the bottom of the market," he said in fall 1993. But he doesn't discourage them: Goodwill from the twelfth floor of Lloyd's remains an asset for him, part of his strategy to make a deal.

Christopher Stockwell, by contrast, has been proclaiming the doom of Lloyd's since 1992. He is the chairman of the Lloyd's Names Associations' Working Party (LNAWP), an umbrella organization of the chairmen of the thirty to forty groups suing their Lloyd's agents and syndicates for negligence or worse in placing their names and taking risks. ("It's called a working party," Deeny notes sourly, "to make sure everyone understands that its chairman can't negotiate for anybody.") A tall, slim man with light brown hair, quietly handsome with careful manners, Stockwell was a furniture manufacturer who built the business himself and lost it and everything else he owned, including his home, in Outhwaite 317. Benyon's description of him is that "he has the coolness of the north face of the Eiger and withering tongue of the head of the upper sixth."

Stockwell's newsletter, beautifully written, goes to all Lloyd's Names. His income as spokesman for the assembly of plaintiffs in suits against Lloyd's is all the income he has. Of all the people involved in the actions against Lloyd's, he had invested the most faith and hope in Middleton's ability to get a fair settlement of the Names' grievances. We had drinks together the evening of the day in November 1993 when Lloyd's presented to LNAWP the settlement offer it was prepared to make—and presented it, of course, on a take-it-or-leave-it basis. Stockwell was shattered, not only by the inadequacy of the offer but by Middleton's refusal to give him the analysis of the Lloyd's resources on which it was based. In effect, I was the first to know this first settlement offer would fail.

HISCOX AND KEELING

If Lloyd's has a future, it is in the hands of deputy chairman Robert (always "Bertie") Hiscox. Hiscox has become famous as the man who said of complaining Names that "if God hadn't meant them to be sheared, he wouldn't have made them sheep." When *The Economist* magazine quoted the line, he made himself even more famous by writing a letter to the editor arguing that just because he made such a statement doesn't mean he is unsympathetic to the Names. Hiscox was brought up in Lloyd's: His father, "an underwriter all his life," set up the Lloyd's American Trust Fund at Citibank in 1939. He is not, however, a blind loyalist. "When I first came to Lloyd's in the 1960s," he told me in autumn 1993, "I said I thought I'd come to a place for the mentally disabled. That's when the Lloyd's boys—the thick pin-striped boy made a member by his daddy—were washed out of the institution. Then in the 1980s we got a spiv [petty crook] element. We rightly are flagellated: We have underwritten *appallingly*. The average underwriter was an East End barrow boy [a wheelbarrow peddler from the immigrants' slum]. They were all traders; you could hear it in their voices."

All this in a rather small back room in the little building that houses Hiscox Underwriting Services, a Name's agent and manager of Lloyd's underwriters on one of the small blocks in the rabbit warren that is the City of London. Hiscox is a small, athletic man, as neat as Rowland, and he doesn't sit still as he talks. He plays with pencils and boxes on his desk, gets up and prowls around behind it. He is very intelligent as well as quick, and has been among Lloyd's most successful underwriters: Even in the disaster years most of his syndicates have made money. His responsibility in the new order has been to find corporate capital to back syndicates at Lloyd's on an entirely new, limited-liability basis.

In November 1993, he was enthusiastically certain that American companies would come roaring into Lloyd's. "They thought at the beginning of the year that nobody would come in. Then J. P. Morgan came, and Marsh and McLennan, and everyone else followed. The U.S. understands about venture capital. Americans do massive homework. The British rely on gut feeling, and it's only when they see the others there that you can bring them in."

Interestingly, despite Hiscox's ebullience, the Americans *didn't* come. Salomon Brothers and the brokerage house Morgan Stanley both tried to launch U.S. corporations to invest in Lloyd's syndicates in autumn 1993, and both failed. Morgan's deal had been with Stephen Merrett (indeed, Morgan and Marsh had already made a "quota share" arrangement with Merrett for a separately capitalized Bermuda reinsurance subsidiary to take one-quarter of his risks in the 1993 year and thereafter). Within a few weeks of Hiscox's comments, Merrett Holdings collapsed and Morgan disappeared from the Lloyd's scene, perhaps to return (when they did return, interestingly, it was to make an investment in Hiscox; we shall look at how and why this happened in Chapter 10). Lloyd's either does not have or does not regard as suitable for public consumption the kind of information required by American securities laws in "registration statements" for stock to be sold to the public. The corporate capital that did come to Lloyd's in early 1994 was almost entirely British, with a token $2 million company from Japan.

Hiscox's other mission for Lloyd's has been the development of a plan that would permit Names to sell their participation in syndicates—in sales that would presumably give the purchaser the right to continue to be a member of this syndicate in years to come. The advantage for Names would be their control of the time when they could cash in on the profitable risks taken in their names, which would enable them to pay with much less pain the losses on the bad risks. "Value" trading, however, would restrict the right of underwriters to choose the Names they accept on their syndicates, and it opens several cans of worms because the underwriters would have to fess up in detail about the risks they have written before the regulatory authorities in any country (even England) would permit the paper to trade. The plan was announced with much fanfare early in 1994, and a rather tentative version of it was actually launched that summer as part of Lloyd's frantic efforts to keep Names from jumping ship. The first auctions to sell places on famous syndicates were to be held in August 1995.

Lloyd's other deputy chairman in 1994 was Richard Keeling, balding but slightly younger than Hiscox, considerably more reserved yet at the same time more informal. His large office, high in the ultramodern Lloyd's building, is furnished in gracious

Georgian. He sits still with his legs crossed in a striped shirt, without a jacket. Like Hiscox, he is an underwriter, supervising the work of seventeen syndicates for the Murray Lawrence managing agency, which he chairs. His area of responsibility as deputy chairman of Lloyd's was the formation of the new company to work outside the Lloyd's framework and take over the claims on policies written before 1986. The new company was to be called NewCo; late in 1994, as a result of a competition Middleton launched with an announcement that he would personally give a bottle of champagne to the winner, it was renamed Equitas (the goddess of peace, Middleton says), but it still doesn't exist, and the sources we cite spoke about the plans for "NewCo." The year 1986 was chosen because it was then that the standard casualty insurance form, at Lloyd's and elsewhere, was changed to make insurance companies liable only for damages to individuals or property that result in claims during the life of the policy—"claims made" is the term of art. This clause virtually eliminates the danger of losses from certain "long-tail" claims, some of them forty years old but just emerging into the courtroom, that are devastating many of the syndicates.

"You couldn't set out to invent something more complex to do," Keeling says of NewCo. "It's the largest pricing problem ever—we're deciding the value of four hundred insurance companies. Their asset management, like everything else in this building, ranges from here to there. The most profitable Natwest branch [the reference is to Britain's largest bank] is the Lloyd's branch, because people at Lloyd's leave vast quantities of money on current [checking] account."

The theory is that NewCo will take some or all of the reserves of the syndicates that will be paying out for years for asbestos poisoning or water or soil pollution or other "long-tail" liabilities, call the Names to provide additional reserves for their syndicates as needed, and pay off the policies as the claims come in, from the income on the reserves and the reserves themselves. "The rules are," says Keeling, "one, that it must be fair to the Names, two, that it must be equitable as to the syndicates, three, that it must be sustainable as to the policyholders." The decision as to whether the third of these criteria has been met will be made by the Department of Trade and Industry in Britain, which will have to accept NewCo's claim of "solvency" before licensing it, and to some degree by the insurance authorities in the United States.

"If you want enough reserves to give a ninety-nine percent probability that this will work," Keeling says, "I will give you a number that will blow your socks off. Then we have to negotiate down. But I've sworn that I'm not going to move the mirrors: I ain't doing this on the basis that we leave a time bomb for the next generation." If NewCo works, which is a very large "if" that we shall examine in Chapter 9, the Lloyd's insiders and the surviving Names and the new Names to be recruited will be able to go about their business without worrying about the past—the claims under pre-1986 policies would be, in the emollient language of the Lloyd's business planners, "ring-fenced." In May 1995, in a last-ditch effort, Rowland extended the reach of "Equitas" to *all* Lloyd's policies written in 1992 or before: There wasn't enough money in what he began to call the "Old Lloyd's" to pay those losses either. The mirrors had been moved. But by then Keeling was no longer involved; he had declined to stand for reelection to the Council at the end of 1994.

As an underwriter, Keeling looks ahead to the ever-increasing risks of the insurance business everywhere. "Greenpeace came to me," he says, "and said, 'You are in the only business in the world that makes money if things stay the same.' We're funny bedfellows. But you have to remember that the lowest barometric low in history came in February '93. If Hurricane Andrew had hit fifty miles north of where it did, the losses would have been seventy billion pounds [$100 billion]. Global warming and holes in the ozone layer are a greater danger for us than for people in any other business. We're doing a lot of work with Greenpeace on ways to avoid changing the climate."

CHAPTER 4

APOCALYPSE NOW

You have to know the people to understand how *satisfactory* Lloyd's seemed to the thousands of Englishmen associated with it as Britain rebuilt after World War II. Like so much else that had made the British upper classes confident, the supremacy of Lloyd's in the world insurance market seemed part of the nature of things. It was a relic of empire, part of the tradition of the island people on whose dominions the sun never set. British banks financed world trade; Lloyd's insured the participants in world trade against loss by misadventure. Lloyd's installations could be found on all the world's shipping lanes, in the lighthouses that secured passage through the straits, which meant that Lloyd's had the resources in place to deliver the mostest information in the shortest time.

No doubt the pound was in trouble at $4.20 right after the war, all the newspapers said so, but that would be worked out with help from the American cousins. In fact, Lloyd's was already protected on that front: At the beginning of the war, National City Bank of New York (later to become Citibank and Citicorp) had worked out an arrangement whereby dollar premiums for insurance policies that could lead to claims in dollars were separately held in a trust fund in New York—a trust fund backed, if necessary (and, of course, it never would be necessary), by a line of credit from the bank.

As an institution and a socioeconomic system, Lloyd's met everyone's needs, with an almost mathematical neatness of fit. To the shipowners who were still by far the largest fraction of the policyholders, Lloyd's gave absolute assurance that losses deriving from misfortune at sea would be compensated. No Lloyd's policy had defaulted since the nineteenth century, and Lloyd's had a worldwide reputation for paying claims quickly and without much niggling about whether the money was really owed and how much was owed.

In the shipping area, a Lloyd's Underwriters Claims and Recoveries Office exists to serve underwriters whose global reach is less than that of the corporation, and a separate organization, the Lloyd's Underwriters Non-Marine Association, works with underwriters on claims that don't involve ships at sea. But Lloyd's itself does not usually investigate claims. Syndicates that wish to lead underwritings contract themselves with The Salvage Association or employ their own claims adjusters.

Since the 1930s, there has been an Advisery Department of the Corporation of Lloyd's checking up on how claims are treated, but its usual approach was to keep underwriters from contesting claims. After all, the Names in the syndicates, not Lloyd's or the underwriters who worked in the other syndicates, would bear the losses: each for his own part and not for any other. There was no rule or sanction, but a working party appointed by Lloyd's itself to look at the market in the late 1970s reported that "the practice" was that if a policyholder who had not been paid threatened to sue, an underwriter would consult with the department about "whether it would be in the best interest of Lloyd's for the action involving the Underwriter to proceed to trial. . . . The aim of this scrutiny is to protect the good name of Lloyd's and avoid the possibility of legal proceedings which would adversely affect (legally or politically) the interests of the Market as a whole."[1]

To the extent that Lloyd's underwriters were in competition for business with the rest of the world, this reputation for prompt and certain payment was a major advantage. Insurance brokers could offer business anywhere, but most of them, especially the brokers of shipping insurance, felt they had to be approved Lloyd's brokers certified to show requests for insurance at Lloyd's—and most policyholders were willing to pay a slightly higher premium for what was regarded as the better product of the Lloyd's policy.

For those who worked at Lloyd's, life was grand. Only a few score of the underwriters were "lead underwriters" who had to measure the dimensions of the risk and price the policies; the others could follow the leader and place their "stamp" on the brokers' slips without troubling too much about the perils of the deep. "You know," Richard Keeling says, "brokers need folk heroes, people of whom they can say, 'This guy is absolutely brilliant.' Then they take those names around the floor and fill the slip." Though a man who worked as an underwriter on the floor had to put his money where his stamp was, and share the risks and rewards of the policies with the Names who had agreed to back his syndicate, the insider's compensation was greatly enhanced and his risks reduced by commissions and expense budgets that came off the top of the premium income before it was allocated to the Names. For a managing agency that had more than one syndicate, as nearly all of them did, there was further protection in the profit commission Names had to pay on the winning syndicates while they swallowed all the losses (including of course the managing agents' expenses) from the losers.

There really were golden apples at the top of the tree. In 1992, two members of Lloyd's Council who considered themselves as representing the Names rather than the insiders—Peter Nutting and Lady Rona Delves Broughton—forced the Council to vote on whether the managing agents should be required to publish what they paid to their underwriters and other major officers. The Council grudgingly agreed to compel the publication of salaries, but not of bonuses and expense accounts. Even so, the news made a stir, because it turned out that many of the active underwriters were earning more than half a million dollars a year before perks and bonuses, even in bad years. Starting in the 1960s, Lloyd's permitted the incorporation of the underwriting syndicates, which meant (among other things) that the underwriters could pay themselves large dividends even though their Names were losing money, because the income of the syndicate as an operating entity related only distantly, as a source of bonuses, to the profitability of the policies it wrote. Several of the studies of itself that Lloyd's commissioned in the 1960s and 1970s laid it down as a good rule that agencies *should* be profitable from their return on the fees they charged, and should not be dependent on their profit commission on syndicate results (normally 20 percent—and the Names' agents also got a management fee assessed on the Names' entire stamp capacity, even if not all of it was committed).

The syndicate managers also benefited from the fact that people are invited to become Names in the "best" syndicates, the ones where the rewards are greater and the risks are less, because the managers of those syndicates know and like them or their Names' agents. The underwriters trust and feel a loyalty to the Names who have supported them for many years; these relationships are especially close at the small syndicates, as is to be expected. Placement on well-regarded syndicates is, says deputy chairman Bertie Hiscox, assuming royal prerogatives, "a matter of grace and favor." The first people who get placed on the best syndicates are the brokers who bring in the business and the managing agents who can put other managing agents into *their* best syndicates. A surprising fraction of the Lloyd's membership has never seen why this commonsense practice brings down criticism from outsiders and execration from Names who have lost money in the syndicates most of the insiders know enough to avoid. The conflicts of interest came out in the open only in 1994, when Hiscox as deputy chairman promoted his "Value at Lloyd's" plan that would establish a transferable right to be on a syndicate in perpetuity—and some managing agents insisted that any profits from the sale of such rights should be theirs, not the Names'.

Brokers had to talk in the morning with the clients who were buying the insurance before they could "broke" their risks on the Lloyd's floor. So the brokers did not begin to call on the underwriters at their boxes until eleven o'clock, which meant that the underwriters could be leisurely in their arrival. Most good underwriters reported to their offices at eight-thirty or nine in the morning, and discussed the previous day's business and this day's prospects with their colleagues before heading to the Room. People who share a box all working day tend to bond closely. It should also be noted that Lloyd's was an engine of social mobility in England, for all its aristocratic trappings and stern dress code (pinstripes for all, men and women). Young Cockneys could work hard at unskilled jobs, learn the business of insurance from the underwriter who employed them, and become wealthy gentlemen with gracious estates in Surrey.

Others were more casual. Lunch was latish, at one or so, and there was no reason why lunches could not be convivial. The fact that an underwriter might have been drunk when he stamped the policy slip was not grounds for invalidating an insurance policy, and there were risks that got taken to the floor only after lunch and shown only to selected underwriters because nobody who was entirely sober would stamp them. One senior man was known to the floor as "the nodding donkey," because he would hold his stamp under his chin and stamp policies with nods of the head that came naturally anyway after so liquid a lunch. The *Aragorn* case, one of the few lawsuits by angry Names that Lloyd's settled in 1993, involved an underwriter who had gone to lunch with a broker with an announced intention to take 2.7 percent of the risk the broker was offering, and after the lunch signed for 30.5 percent of it. And the claims on the policy turned out to be about eight times the premium the insured had paid for it.

Other lunches, held in Lloyd's own Adam Room, might be major occasions. Not infrequently, they were spectacular occasions.

Bolivia shipped a lot of tin. When the president of Bolivia came to London, he would meet with the prime minister of the United Kingdom and the foreign minister (at his suite in what is still called the Foreign and Colonial Office), have audience with the queen—and come to lunch at Lloyd's, where he would be greeted by uniformed Waiters and ushered to the Adam Room with crested china on the table with crystal and silver, where the Committee of Lloyd's would join him for champagne and caviar, crayfish from the Mediterranean, and good English beef to be washed down with Bordeaux from the best châteaus.

"People came to Lloyd's," says Bertie Hiscox reminiscently, thinking back to the days when he was an eager lad and his father was chairman, "the way they came to the Tower of London, it was part of England's great tradition." There was a real red carpet that was rolled out when royalty or foreign heads of state came calling. Sometimes the guests of honor were more plebeian, like the Dallas Cowboys, insured by Lloyd's, who came to call after winning the Super Bowl. They were entertained at a grand lunch (the British have become intrigued with American football), but they didn't get a red carpet.

The brokers had a life outside Lloyd's. Of the premiums paid for casualty insurance in London, only about a fifth went to Lloyd's. But Lloyd's was in many ways the best deal for the broker. The Lloyd's reputation rubbed off on all the underwriters, and a rubber stamp from a Lloyd's underwriter on a slip of paper representing part of a policy was a big help to a broker in persuading other underwriters, outside Lloyd's as well as inside Lloyd's, that they should want a piece of this action. The Lloyd's syndicates were physically small operations with a box on the trading floor and a small support staff elsewhere in the neighborhood. Lloyd's underwriters were exotic birds who could not fly from their perches. They had no sales staff, no agents in the field, and were dependent on brokers for their business. The brokers ranged the world; insurance brokerage companies were themselves bought and sold by other brokerage companies from other countries. In many cases, the voice was the voice of Lloyd's, but the hands were the hands of a giant American insurance brokerage firm—Alexander and Alexander, Frank B. Hall, Marsh and McLennan, Johnson and Higgins.

Many of the negotiations in the Room involved trade-offs, where brokers required a syndicate to take an unattractive risk or accept an unattractive premium on one piece of business to gain another, more lucrative piece of business. Or, if the power balance ran the other way, the underwriter might demand a bigger piece of a better risk he knew the broker was placing before he would put his stamp on the policy the broker had come to his box to create. And it was the lead underwriter on a policy who made the decision for all the insurers on whether to pay or fight a claim under the policy.

For the county families—the landholders of southern England—Lloyd's buttressed a way of life. When the original Lloyd's Act had been passed in 1871, nearly all the 675 "Underwriting Members of Lloyd's" worked in the City of London, but by the 1940s more than half the 2,500 Names were the family and friends of the brokers and underwriters who worked on the floor. Ian Posgate, hero underwriter of the 1970s and villain underwriter of the 1980s, says that was already too many: that the historic Lloyd's, where everyone was involved with shipping and trade, was a better insurance operation because the Names themselves had expertise. Once Britain no longer ruled the waves, and shipping was no longer the primary source of income for Lloyd's, a new and less careful attitude toward insurance came to dominate the trading room.

In the 1940s, the institution was still a club, and Names who came down from their country homes for a day or two might well use Lloyd's as they used a club, lunching in the Captain's Room or dropping by for a convivial drink. They were most likely members of only one syndicate, and they had a personal relationship with its managing agent or its underwriter. What characterized them most, from a foreigner's point of view, is that they seemed totally idle: Most of them did not work for a living, did not intend ever to work for a living, and did not see why anyone would expect them to work for a living. Their job was to tend their sumptuous estates, maintaining the land as they had received it for the use of later generations—a splendid burden, and one that does take time, skill, and effort to succeed at. They had inherited their wealth, and they turned that wealth into income by clipping coupons, renting land, and backing insurance policies at Lloyd's. Sport was a huge part of their lives—shooting parties for birds, hunts for foxes, fishing in the streams.

The Labour government of the postwar years was hard on the rich, but did not wish to discourage the operation of Lloyd's, which was a source of considerable dollar income for Britain. The most socialist member of the government, Chancellor of the Exchequer Sir Stafford Cripps, proposed and carried an amendment to the income tax laws that permitted Names to accumulate half their profits in personal reserves at Lloyd's, up to what was then $20,000 a year (perhaps $120,000 a year in 1994 dollars), without paying tax until withdrawal—and then much of what they withdrew would be taxed only at capital gains rates, which topped out at 30 percent even in years when British tax on "unearned income" went as high as 98 percent for the very rich.

The profits subject to tax accumulated naturally for almost four years under the Lloyd's accounting system, and the earnings on those profits, too, could be turned into capital gains by a process inelegantly known as "bond-washing." Lloyd's would buy a bond for the Name immediately after the payment of an interest coupon, when the price was down, and sell the bond immediately before the payment of the next coupon, when the price was up. Though interest paid on the bond would be income, the gain from buying just after and selling just before the coupon date was capital gains. This tax loophole endured until 1988.

The return on risk-taking at Lloyd's became on a posttax basis the most lucrative "investment" in England. Here again, by the way, insiders had an advantage, because passive income from investments was taxed in England at a higher rate than income earned from work. External Names had to pay taxes at the higher, passive-income rates on the profits of their syndicates; Names who worked at Lloyd's had their profits from underwriting as well as their fee/commission income taxed at the lower rates. Some at Lloyd's argued wistfully that one way to get more people to volunteer as Names would be to give all premium income a status as earned income, taxed at the lower rates, but Lord Cromer warned in 1969 that making such a proposal "might lead to a close scrutiny of the concessionary treatment of working members, which would be regarded in some quarters as too generous."[2]

(There were tax breaks for Americans, too, though none so lucrative. I used to get these voluminous, elaborate documents from Lloyd's, which I couldn't begin to understand; I'd turn them over to my accountant. In 1995, the U.S. Internal Revenue Service took back with a vengeance whatever tax advantages a Lloyd's Name had enjoyed, ruling that losses at Lloyd's could not be deducted from income for tax purposes until they were "final." The losses on syndicates that were still open were clearly not "final," and the IRS then twisted the knife by ruling that the losses on a syndicate that had closed into a subsequent year of the same syndicate were not "final." The IRS moved ahead one case at a time, and as of summer 1995, most American Names still did not know that this dragon was at their door, breathing fire.)

Finally, the entire arrangement was incestuous. At Lloyd's in the 1970s, as the drive to acquire new Names accelerated, managing agents owned brokers and brokers owned managing agents, and both of them owned Names' agents, a category that was expanding rapidly as the recruitment of new Names became a major goal of the Lloyd's leadership. At an informed guess, as much as a fifth of all the business done at Lloyd's in the early 1980s involved Names' agents placing the backing of their Names behind policies accepted by a syndicate operated by a managing agent who owned the Names' agency and was in turn owned by the broker who had written the policies the Names were now committed to back. And at every turn the insiders got expenses, a share of the premium, a salary, commissions, and a share of the profits when there were profits.

Lord Cromer in his 1969 report was especially troubled by the fact that brokers owned underwriters. "There is," he wrote, "a conflict of interest which cannot be ignored. . . . The broker is the agent of the insured and in any conflict with any underwriter should put first the interest of the insured. He should not even adopt the role of an arbiter in a conflict unless this can be seen to be to the advantage of the insured. If a conflict were to arise between an insured and an underwriter who happened to be an employee (even indirectly) of the broker to the insured the problem is most difficult. But, short of conflict of this kind, we find it difficult to accept that, in exercising judgment of what business to accept and what to refuse, an underwriter who is an employee of a broker-owned agency can at all times be wholly impartial. . . . In so far as any influence might be exercised it would be to encourage an underwriter to accept risks he would, if independent, refuse, so that the names of his syndicate could be carrying more than in the free judgment of the underwriter were desirable."[3]

In fact, as nobody realized, the ownership of syndicate managements by brokers protected the *Names*, who, once the brokers began dealing with the underwriters at arm's length, had no other protection. Brokers would not victimize underwriters whose managements they owned, if only because broking a bad risk into the syndicate would cost the managing agency the 20 percent profit commission that went right into the pocket of the broker-as-owner. Even the barest minimum of noblesse oblige would then keep the brokers from dealing with other underwriters in a predatory manner. As the underwriters were dependent on the brokers for their information about both risks and claims, such restraints on broker behavior were a first line of defense for the Names that backed the syndicates. Once the brokers were free to take an attitude of let-the-buyer-beware in their dealings with the underwriters, the Names would be the losers, both from the excess commissions the brokers would extract and from the bad risks they would induce the underwriters to accept.

Thinking along those lines was impossibly bad manners.

Even Cromer was reluctant to say anything mean. His paragraph after the one criticizing the apparent conflict of interest begins with the words "In saying this, we must not be thought to be critical of what has happened in the past." Still, the leaders of the Society of Lloyd's didn't like to hear criticism from anybody, and while the commissioning of the *Cromer Report* had been loudly trumpeted as a signal that Lloyd's was on its feet and dealing with its problems, the report itself was suppressed until October 1986 because it suggested that insiders had opportunities to profit at the expense of Names, and that some organizational arrangements were undesirable.

There was, after all, reason not to make much of a fuss. Cromer's study had been commissioned in part because some in the market feared that their capacity to write insurance was growing less rapidly than the capacity of the incorporated insurers outside the Lloyd's market. Nobody was seriously worried about Lloyd's policies themselves. That something so perfect and close-knit as all this could simply fall apart was beyond the imaginings of Lord Cromer or the members of Lloyd's at mid-century—and, indeed, for a generation beyond mid-century.

●

The central conflict at Lloyd's had always been, necessarily, between the interests of the policyholder and the interests of the Name being told to pay off on the policy. "Each for his own part and not for any other" looks good on paper, but it does not answer the practical question of who is going to pay the holder of what is a *Lloyd's* policy, registered at a *Lloyd's* Policy Signing Office since 1911, when an act of Parliament gave the Society exclusive use of the name "Lloyd's" for insurance purposes and prohibited anyone else from affixing the Lloyd's stamp on an insurance policy. A Name who has accepted $45,000 of premium on the policies written by Merrett syndicate 418 for the 1985 year of account, as I did, presumably stands at risk for about one-fortieth of 1 percent of the losses on those policies if the total premiums paid to the syndicate were $180 million. If I can't or won't pay my 0.025 percent share, a strict application of "each for his own part" leaves the policyholder one-fortieth of 1 percent short on a valid claim, and places in doubt not only the reputation of Merrett Underwriting, which actually accepted the risk on behalf of all its Names, but the reputation of "the market"—the entirety of the business written at Lloyd's.

For all the brief insistence on unlimited liability at the Rota interview, the possibility that a defaulting Name could multiply the losses of other Names in his syndicate was never mentioned. There had been two losing years for Names as a group after the splendidly named Hurricane Betsy in 1965 (the Cromer study was commissioned, indeed, because following those years the number of Names shrank and the capacity of the Lloyd's market to accept insurance risks was reduced), but even in those years more Names made than lost money.

Diversification was built into the system. Each syndicate as a whole wrote a lot of different risks. If it was a marine syndicate, it insured against losses not just in the North Atlantic, but on all the seven seas. The odds against massive losses on *all* the shipping routes were so high, nobody had to think about it. When the syndicates branched out of marine business to cover natural disasters, rain at the wedding, the extra expenses from having twins, hazards of the workplace and marketplace, the new insurance was added originally as part of the land risks in a marine package, retaining the odds against loss for the syndicate as a whole. Only later, as experience with these risks mounted, did syndicates begin to specialize in areas other than marine. By the 1960s, each of the four categories of Lloyd's underwriting—marine, nonmarine (disaster insurance in general), aviation, and automotive—had an almost actuarial base of information the underwriters could use to stabilize their risk profiles. Portfolio theory argued for diversifying risks, common sense argued for telling people to concentrate in underwriting the risks they knew about. Lloyd's offered those lucky enough to be Names the best of both philosophies.

As the market grew, most Names diversified their exposure to different kinds of risk. Names in the 1960s routinely accepted premiums from syndicates in all four sectors of the market. Taken together, the syndicates a Name backed were most unlikely to show a net loss for the year, especially when you considered that all the premiums paid to all the syndicates, held in trust and invested by the underwriters, would be earning money for the Names' benefit for three years. Losses on one policy written by a syndicate would often be covered by profits on other policies. When the group of policies written by the syndicate as a whole produced an underwriting loss on the "pure year" of risk-taking being measured, the earnings from investing the premiums would more than pay the loss. Even if one of his syndicates went into the tank, the Name had reason to expect that the profits on his other syndicates, including the earnings on their premium trust funds, would more than cover what was lost by the one bummer.

So the Names were safe. And so was the policyholder. The payment of his claims was backed

1. by the premium trust funds segregated in escrow by Names for just that purpose. In the United States, by state law, these funds could usually be invested only in the safest, short-term, government-guaranteed paper (Lloyd's was the biggest purchaser of paper issued by the Student Loan Marketing Association); then
2. by all the other Lloyd's income earned by each Name backing his policy (for Names were not permitted to take profits on any of their underwriting contracts so long as claims or potential claims on one of them remained unsatisfied, unless they had been reinsured in ways that protected the policyholder); then
3. by the reserves on past years' earnings that Lloyd's

quietly set aside for Names as a matter of course; then

4. by the Names' "deposit" at Lloyd's, in the case of English Names most commonly actual securities or bank guarantees secured from the bank's point of view by deeds to land, in the case of foreign Names after 1970 most commonly a letter of credit from a bank in the foreigner's home country, which kept custody of the assets (only stocks, bonds, and cash deposits from Americans) being pledged; then

5. by all the other worldly goods, the "net worth," of the Name, who had signed what is in hindsight the most binding contract in the world, giving incompetent as well as careful underwriters at Lloyd's unrestricted power to destroy everything he had worked a lifetime to achieve; then

6. though the Names who might become the victims of such an invasion of their assets didn't realize it, by the premium trust funds in the sterling accounts of all the other syndicates. Though the premium trust funds were in theory inviolate, the assets the sterling funds could hold were not tightly restricted. Among those assets could be loans to other syndicates (or to Lloyd's itself) that needed cash because Names couldn't or wouldn't pay; then

7. after 1927, by a "Central Fund" to which every Name paid an annual subscription of about one-half of 1 percent of the premium income allocated to his account. In 1992, the members of Lloyd's tithed 6.2 percent of that year's total premium income (almost a billion dollars at the then prevailing rate of exchange) to fill up this Central Fund, which was obviously about to be depleted by a combination of unexpectedly high claims and unexpectedly strong resistance by Names receiving cash calls.

In 1994, to enable Names to pass the solvency test, this fund earmarked from its roughly $1.1 billion of face value about $1.5 billion, partially for claims that should have been paid for by Names and partially for credit to Names' accounts so they could continue underwriting. About two-thirds of this money was later restored to the Central Fund. According to the by-laws, the Central Fund is not supposed to be tapped until the entire resources of a defaulting Name have been seized and sold, but in 1994 it had to be just a source of earmarkings to Names who had ignored cash calls from their agents at Lloyd's; and finally,

8. though nobody would ever say so, the payment of the policyholder's claims was guaranteed by the fact that the insiders at Lloyd's simply could not afford the awful publicity of a plausible claim on a Lloyd's policy that is not paid. There had been long delays on the payment of a handful of claims in the late nineteenth and early twentieth centuries, usually in the context of peculiar policies (guaranteeing the price of a security, or the selling price of a block of tickets for a coronation parade that was postponed when the new king got appendicitis—a guarantee that bankrupted Sir Brian Bartlett, a blue blood Name who had the wrong underwriter for a friend and had to sell 15,000 acres of land). Once the 1911 amendments to the Lloyd's Act put a Lloyd's stamp on all Lloyd's policies, the fact was that the proprietors of the brand name were going to move heaven and earth, and bankrupt all their external Names if they could, to prevent default on the policies. "The Names," says David Rowland, over and over and over again, "*will* pay."

The first time the market officially rallied round an underwriter who couldn't pay his debts was in 1923, when it paid the debts of

Stanley Harrison, a pioneer in insuring automobiles. Harrison had been victimized by a fraudster who lured him into underwriting insurance policies that backed the repayment of what turned out to be nonexistent borrowings by nonexistent purchasers of nonexistent cars and buses. Third parties had bought the paper generated by these fake sales because there was a Lloyd's policy behind them, and it was the unpleasantness of this experience that led to the creation of the Central Fund. Interestingly, it was a fraud with some of the same elements that began the Lloyd's market's descent into chaos and exposure in the 1970s. And it was the outrage of a number of high-status and high-prestige Names victimized by Lloyd's insistence on paying fraudulent losses that would blow open the first of the holes.

•

All the glorious things at Lloyd's could go wrong; and in the end, many of them *did* go wrong. The best way to understand what has happened is to look first at the principles that were violated, so we will have a map on which to place the horror stories as we come to them.

The first and easiest aspect of the organization to go wrong was the personal one. Lloyd's had a system built on trust. Brokers were honor bound to give accurate descriptions of the risks they brought to the box, and underwriters promised not to raise frivolous objections to the payment of claims. This system was vulnerable to abuse by the dishonest, the stupid, and the arrogant.

Dishonesty was invited in the outside world by the rather informal way the Lloyd's syndicates acquired their business. The underwriters sat on their boxes on the trading floor, and brokers brought them risks that the brokers' clients wished to insure against. The broker told the underwriter what premium was being paid for this business by other underwriters. A dishonest broker could quote a higher premium rate to one underwriter and a lower premium rate to another, charge the client for the higher rate, pay the lower rate to those who had accepted it, and pocket the difference.

If an underwriter had a lot of capacity—a lot of Names backing his syndicate—and the brokers weren't being friendly to him, he would have to find agents in the outside world who would bring him business. Though it was a rule of Lloyd's that only certified Lloyd's brokers could bring business to the floor, underwriters could give people in other countries a "binding authority" that in effect allowed them to write Lloyd's policies. If the agent who had been given such authority wanted to play footsie with the Mafia, the underwriter sitting on his box in a building in London would not know about it. If the Mafia, through its friend with the binder, insured a bunch of tenements and vacant storefronts for much more than they were worth and then burned them down, Lloyd's would be confronted with claims that would be hard to refuse.

Dishonesty was also possible on the inside. A premium trust fund had to be created after some underwriters in the nineteenth century lived high on the hog on premium receipts and had nothing left to pay the policyholders. More recently, the cheating of choice was on the reinsurance chassis. On the most rudimentary level, insiders could reinsure the "whole account" of a syndicate with an insurance company they had set up and controlled in a tax haven. The net effect would be to transfer the earnings on the investment of the premiums from the Names to the insiders. A chairman of Lloyd's was caught profiting from such a scam. The committee that investigated his speculations spent most of their time debating whether his conduct was "outrageous," or should be described with some other adjective.

Worse was not only possible, but relatively common. Looking at his book of business partway through the year, an underwriter could fairly easily distinguish the better risks and the worse risks. If he started his own reinsurance operation in Liechtenstein or Monaco or Guernsey, he could pay himself a premium to reinsure the better risks, and walk away with the money.

John Wallrock, a Royal Navy captain who had become head of the Minet agency, a company that combined brokerage and underwriting (and was partly owned by the St. Paul Insurance Co. of

St. Paul, Minnesota), was caught participating in reinsurance schemes that channeled interest earnings on premium income away from the Names in a syndicate to officers of the syndicate like himself. "I wish to emphasize," he said stiffly, criticizing a government decision to investigate this matter, "that this proposal had been approved by both lawyers and accountants possessing knowledge of Lloyd's practice."[4]

Or a reinsuring underwriter could form a "baby syndicate" at Lloyd's with insiders and a handful of favored outsiders as the Names, that would reinsure only the best risks from the syndicate backed by run-of-the-mill Names. This wasn't even against the rules until the mid-1980s. If the underwriter's judgment was as bad as his morals, the result of such reinsurance might well be a huge liability for the original, larger syndicate. A thoroughgoing crook planning an endgame at Lloyd's might even seek out bad business because the premiums would be higher, and thus the receipts he could milk from his private reinsurance fund would be greater. To pay the policies, Lloyd's might have to ask all its members to pay an assessment.

The temptation to play such dishonest games was greatly heightened in the 1970s and 1980s by the very high interest rates that could be earned on the premiums. Fools could make money from the availability of such rewards on virtually any investment of what was, after all, other people's money. Underwriters were supposed to limit their total premium receipts to the "stamp" provided by their Names, but in fact nobody was watching and a syndicate could bloat to three times its supposed limit without anybody at Lloyd's taking notice. High interest rates meant competition for premiums, which drove down insurance rates especially in the marine market, which was why so many marine syndicates wound up reinsuring asbestos risks and writing malpractice insurance for accountants. One accident every third or fourth year would put the aviation market as a whole in deficit on its underwriting for the period.

Stupidity would show up mostly as an inability to measure risk and reward. This was clearly a delicate question at Lloyd's, because the risks to Names with unlimited liability were so extraordinary. But in an economically rational society, taking more risk is the dedicated path (for some, some of the time) to higher rewards. In the insurance nexus, there was the additional temptation that the premiums came in today, while the payments that would have to be made on the greater risks would not come due for a long time. The underwriter who took "long-tail" risks or wrote vertical reinsurance (where the claims came only after a time lag) would appear to be the most profitable now.

The temptation dangled before the underwriter of "long-tail" risks was the annual "reinsurance to close" (RITC) that permitted the Names on one syndicate to take their profits for that year, laying off the surviving risks on their successors. Realistically, there was a large element of guesswork in estimating likely future losses on insurance contracts for the general liability of companies that manufactured or used asbestos and other potentially hazardous substances, or dumped toxic chemicals in the ground above an aquifer. And the guesser had a self-interest in setting his estimate low. The smaller the premium paid for the reinsurance to close, the greater the profits that could be taken out by the Names in the dying year, and the less well rewarded for their risks were the Names in the syndicate with another year to go, who assumed the risks. As the underwriters got profit commissions and bonuses when a syndicate closed, their own income was in part a function of their assessment of the proper premium for reinsurance.

The root problem here was the expectation that a syndicate would reinsure with the subsequent year of the same syndicate. Thus there was no *market* for reinsurance-to-close policies, and the underwriters were not required to tell anybody what was in their portfolios. Christopher Stockwell of the Lloyd's Names Associations' Working Party wrote late in 1994 in a submission to a Parliamentary committee investigating self-regulation of Lloyd's that "it would have been entirely reasonable for Lloyd's regulations to have required an underwriter to seek two or three quotations to

close an account, one of which could be from the successor syndicate he was going to be running. By this means market forces
would have been used to ensure a fair price was struck for both
groups of Names. This has never been the practice."[5] There were
two reasons it was not the practice: One, such a practice would require exposing the syndicate's portfolio to scrutiny by others in the
market; two, there was more money to be made by doing your
RITCs yourself.

Syndicates that showed these profits would be in high demand
by Names. "I went to a meeting of Names," Richard Keeling says
with remembered distaste, "and I came out of it thinking, These
people don't care if I stick up a bank; they just want me to write
it." Names would be booked into them by Names' agents who had
been recruited to Lloyd's for their contacts and good manners
rather than for intellectual acuity, and might not even realize what
was going on. Indeed, when one can find out who the Names were
in the very worst of the syndicates, the list invariably includes the
Names' agents themselves, in their personal capacity—though
Names' agents, unlike underwriters, are not required to participate in the syndicates they book for their Names.

On June 5, 1991, the Council of Lloyd's passed a bylaw ordering
that whenever a syndicate lost more than its total premium income
in a single year, an investigating committee of senior people in the
insurance market must be convened to find out how it happened.
The evidence gathered by these investigating committees demon-
strates pretty conclusively that incomprehension rather than knav-
ery was at the root of most of Lloyd's catastrophic failures.

Arrogance mimics stupidity. People who wanted to take risks
would get opinions from accountants and lawyers supporting
their desires, and then wave these apparent authorities in the face
of anyone who argued to the contrary. The consulting firm DYP,
serving the London insurance market (purchased in 1994 by
Lloyd's itself), wrote in 1990 that "a whole generation of entre-
preneurs aided by skilled lawyers and accountants saw the ex-
ploitation of gaps in the rules and traditions of the Society as a

major business opportunity. They replaced observance of the spirit of the regulation with a philosophy that saw all rules as a challenge, so that whilst sticking to literal observance of the regulations one could totally offend their spirit."

These "legal and accounting advisers . . . corrupted Lloyd's. The standing of some of the proponents overcame the ethical qualms of many Lloyd's underwriters and brokers whose morality would otherwise have been unquestioned. . . . The increasing complexity of the market helped to hide these changes and create other activities where unsuspecting but often avaricious newcomers wrote insurances and reinsurances that were almost certain to produce large losses."[6]

On Lloyd's trading floor, intelligent people saw that they were smarter than their rivals, and never had occasion to learn that in the outside world there were people who might be even smarter than they. In the 1980s, moreover, as the premiums booked at Lloyd's rose with the expansion of the insurance business and the Names roster, both brokers and underwriters found it possible to take higher and higher salaries and bonuses from the business. By the end of the 1980s, at a time when horrendous losses were piling up for the Names, half the leading brokers and underwriters at Lloyd's were taking home more than a million dollars a year. The fact that they were making more money than other people reinforced their sense that they were smarter than other people. Meanwhile, the old-line underwriters—the people who specialized in motor or marine, took risks only when the premium level justified them, and carefully overreserved to squirrel away resources for bad years—chugged along profitably with the old-line Names. Everyone was a sole trader; other people's problems were their own.

●

The second aspect to go wrong was the system itself. Whatever its virtues in the first quarter of a millennium of its operations, Lloyd's at some point in time might become an anachronism, an organizational structure unsuited to its modern role. And the reforms attempted by its leaders might make things worse.

Clearly, the main structural problem would be unlimited liability for insurers in a time when the losses on policies were openended. The insurer of a cargo ship could lose no more than the value of the ship and its contents. The families of dead sailors couldn't sue. It was not unreasonable for a Name or a small group of Names to stand liable for all the losses on the ship: They knew what their maximum loss could be. But in modern times the insurer of a tanker might find himself liable to the residents along the shores of the waterway polluted by the oil that leaked from the tanker when it sank. If the possible loss under the policy was unlimited, it no longer made sense for the guarantor of the policy to accept unlimited liability.

The problem was first of all American, because it was in America that courts had abandoned the doctrine of privity—the idea that individuals could claim damages only from firms with which they had direct business dealings—and had vastly extended the right of third parties to collect damages from people who were negligent in their actions and companies that produced dangerous products. The insurer of an airplane operated on domestic routes in the United States might have to pay whatever a jury thought suitable recompense and heartsease for the heirs and assigns of people killed in a plane crash. The insurer of the maker of a medication prescribed for pregnant women might have to pay for physical and psychic harm done to both mothers and daughters and even granddaughters in numbers to be determined at a later time. Names recruited to back such insurers had no sense whatever that they were running such risks, and after a certain number of shocks had dislodged them from their belief that their friends at Lloyd's had their best interests at heart, it might be extremely difficult to get them to pay.

These dangers grew as businesses demanded that their insurers undertake larger and larger risks, and to meet their demands Lloyd's found it necessary to enlarge the community from which the Names were drawn. Before the 1970s, there were no "Names' agents" at Lloyd's. "There were the occasional chaps who were well connected," says Alan Smallbone, an elegant older man with a finely tended mustache and a military bearing, who worked at Lloyd's in the 1960s. ("I had the misfortune to work under a man who was both incompetent and devious. I knew he was incompetent rather soon; it took longer to know he was devious.") Since the mid-1980s, he has been an ardent, well-informed gadfly. "Such chaps didn't do much except hold up the bar, but they introduced people to Lloyd's." Most syndicates had only a few score, at most a few hundred, Names. Only male British subjects were permitted to be members of the Society, and there was some substance to Lloyd's boast that men could become Names only on the introduction of a friend and an underwriter who would place them in his own syndicates. These people knew one another. It would have been *embarrassing* for a member of Lloyd's to solicit or accept a commission for introducing a new Name.

While Lloyd's was a close-knit club, insiders accepted fiduciary obligations that acted as a brake on cowboy behavior and moral hazard. Once the club was expanded to include masses of Names who really had no more contact with Lloyd's than they had with the corporations in which they owned stock, the sense of fiduciary obligation would be attenuated and would be dissolved.

The problem for the Names' agency was to find managing agents who would place these Names on their syndicates. By rule (though the rule was not always enforced), a syndicate was limited in the insurance it could write by the premium limits of the Names, which were specified multiples of the deposits and letters of credit they had pledged at Lloyd's. By the same token, the premiums a syndicate received had to be divided proportionately among the Names, according to the size they had agreed to underwrite in this syndicate. An expansion of the "stamp capacity" of the syndicate would have to be matched by an expansion of the business that syndicate undertook, or the managing agent would have to reduce the underwritings of his existing backers.

Names' agents, mostly owned by brokers and managing agents, received profit commissions only to the extent that their Names were on syndicates. An overwhelming pressure was felt throughout the market to find risks for new Names to underwrite. And there was an easy way to expand underwritings at Lloyd's: more reinsurance.

Reinsurance was riskier—especially "excess of loss" vertical reinsurance, where the reinsurer was on the hook for the original insurer's losses over a certain amount—and it was easier, because the business was already there on the floor, already vetted by a Lloyd's underwriter who presumably knew what he was doing. There were several different kinds of reinsurance to write: facultative, in which individual risks were reinsured; treaty, in which the reinsurer took the responsibility for a fraction of the reinsured's book; or excess of loss, where losses over a certain amount, incurred on a given risk or on another underwriter's portfolio of risks, would be carried by the syndicate for a premium reflecting the market's view of the likelihood that the losses might rise that high. Normally, a syndicate that reinsured another underwriter's portfolio would seek a "retrocession," a separate reinsurance that set a limit on the losses the original reinsurer would bear. One could also write "stop-loss" policies for individual Names, to protect them against losses over a certain amount. A collection of stop-loss policies could be reinsured in turn, and retrocession could be bought to protect the reinsurer. The sky was the limit.

The American financial writer Andrew Tobias saw the danger as early as 1981, when this sort of incestuous reinsuring was uncommon. "If everyone is insuring everyone else, might not the whole house of cards come shuffling down some terrible year?" But his fears were stilled: " 'I had the same question,' says a bright young member, 'and they assured me that the syndicates that take on such risks are *very* well-heeled.' "[7]

"Good Lloyd's syndicates," says former deputy chairman Richard Keeling, "never did vertical reinsurance." But the growth of capacity, the expansion of the number of Names who had to be serviced, would inevitably fertilize such ventures. The publication of "league tables," reporting on the profitability of the different syndicates, would create enormous demand. The proportion of Lloyd's premium income represented by reinsurance would rise, year after year, concentrating the dangers of a bad year rather than diversifying them—especially as most of the reinsurance was written inside Lloyd's itself. Indeed, Lloyd's, to its later discomfiture, directed reinsurance activity back into its own market by giving 100 percent credit as reserves for reinsurance policies written by Lloyd's underwriters, while insisting on reducing by 20 percent the credit that would be given for protection bought outside the Lloyd's market. This preference for inside reinsurance would later become one of the most compelling arguments in the lawsuit against Lloyd's for violating the antitrust rules of the European Union.

On their trip to the Scottish isles in the mid–eighteenth century, Samuel Johnson and James Boswell made fun of the women of the Hebrides, who made a living by taking in one another's washing. Lloyd's could pretend to operate on such principles—but only for a while. Ultimately, a different danger appeared. Because the profitability of the insurance written was in large part a function of the premium income that could be kept after reinsurance, pressures grew to buy reinsurance cheap—from, say, the [North] Korean Foreign Insurance Company based in Paris. Pressure to buy reinsurance away from London would also be fed by the desire of Third World countries to keep in their own communities some fraction of the premiums their business paid to buy insurance from Lloyd's. Even after the haircut—which could be balanced inside the syndicate by reduced premiums for the internal reinsurance to close—such doubtful reinsurance might be profitable. The insurers who loaded their reinsurance onto such entities would still have the risks they insured originally—plus the risk that the reinsurer couldn't or wouldn't pay on his contract. Among the grand fallacies of the people who are touting the revival of Lloyd's and the "ring-fencing" of old liabilities, Kenneth

Randall says, is the belief that the reinsurance carried on the books of the Lloyd's syndicates as a protection against future losses will actually pay off.

Overcapacity led to inadequate premiums for the risks being run not only in the original market, but also in the reinsurance and "retrocessional" market. For the original insurer, who might find he could lay off two-thirds of his risk for half his premium income, an aggressive reinsurance market virtually guaranteed the profitability of the underwriting year. Meanwhile, Names' agents and managing agents got fees and "profit shares" that would not have to be returned if the profits later proved illusory, and brokers got commissions. Largely because underwriters had relied on brokers to do their clerical work (often including the records of which underwriters had signed on the policy), the Lloyd's cost structure had been far below that of the insurance company world outside. In the 1980s, as the Lloyd's market became increasingly involved in reinsurance rather than direct insurance, the balance shifted: The insurance companies cut their costs, and Lloyd's went from a cost ratio of 12 percent of premium income to a cost ratio of more than 20 percent of premium income.

Inbreeding was often presented as a virtue. Names were likely to be pleased if their agents put them into syndicates controlled by the same company that owned the Names' agency; people with any trust at all in the insiders handling their affairs could scarcely imagine that *their* agents were placing them in home-team syndicates that other Names' agents considered too risky or incompetent to back.

Within the market, the danger was that an information structure well suited to deliver early information of the movements of ships might be inadequate to measure the risks involved in newly created toxic chemicals, or nuclear power plants, or offshore drilling rigs. Adventurers who wrote the policies more sober underwriters avoided could be victorious for a while, but in time the odds would run against them. Because the leaders of Lloyd's had never asked for or received power to limit the policies members might write, there was no way to police the gambling that might go on in an environment where risk was everywhere.

The fragmentation of a market that created what was presumably a common guarantee—the policy with the Lloyd's stamp on it—might encourage criminal elements to exploit weak sisters in the underwriting cadre. The officers of Lloyd's itself would urge underwriters to pay off claims that ought to have been contested, in the interests of preserving the "good name" of the Lloyd's policy, especially when the insured were in foreign countries where Lloyd's was trying to increase its market share. The costs of promoting payment on doubtful claims would be borne by only a small fraction of the community of Names, but the benefits would redound to all. The danger here was that when the afflicted Names learned why they had lost their money, they would seek revenge in what Godfrey Hodgson in his history of Lloyd's delightfully called the revolt of the first-class passengers.

●

The third aspect to go wrong was the very practice of commercial risk, always there. The original Lloyd's insurers were gamblers, and an authority as great as Bertie Hiscox, deputy chairman of Lloyd's, says that the sort of insurance in which Lloyd's specializes still is a gamble. Spreading the risk is supposed to make insurance actuarial, resting on predictions of probability that grow from the statistical analysis of past experience. Statistics, however, is the home of Murphy's Law. Though the odds have no memory—and yesterday's hundred-to-one shot remains a hundred-to-one shot today whether or not it happened yesterday—statistical analysis says that if you do it often enough, the likelihood is that the worst will happen. This is why governments require insurance companies to keep reserves over and above their premium trust funds. My Name's agent, Sedgwick, demands that Names build special reserves, over and above their deposits, and asks them to keep additional personal reserves in Sedgwick's care at Lloyd's. Even if the syndicate is properly reserved for any one or even two disasters, a succession of windstorms, earthquakes, oil rig explosions, or jumbo jet crashes can put any casualty insurance company in jeopardy. If the reserves have already been committed to "long-tail" liabilities and unexpected calls on the higher pieces of vertical reinsurance, a run of bad luck could be fatal.

The fact is that unlimited liability made diversification a danger rather than a hedge. In the stock market, the loss on any investment is limited by the size of the investment—you can't lose more than you put in—while the profit is potentially unlimited, because Haloid can become Xerox. At Lloyd's, under conditions of unlimited liability, the profits are limited by the premium income your deposit entitles you to receive—but the losses are boundless.

If the losses are beyond the ability of the individual Names to pay, but the claims must be paid anyway, Names cannot be sole traders responsible only for their own losses. "Mutualization" of the market becomes inescapable. Which makes Lloyd's not a collection of sole traders, but in effect a corporation—the one and only unlimited-liability corporation.

•

It may be that what made unlimited liability impossible was not the American courts and the lawyers who feed from them, and not the rush of catastrophes that generated gigantic claims in the years 1987–92, but the change in the politics of the market. Most of what has been written about Lloyd's, historically and in recent times, assumes that the underwriters are the lords of the manor. It is they who decide what risks can be insured, their talent for innovation that opens new fields for insurance, their expertise and judgment that controls. Bertie Hiscox insists that his most important talent during the quarter of a century he sat on the box was his ability to look a broker in the eyes and see if the man was telling him the truth. Brokers thrived because underwriters trusted them and gave them reasonable rates for the business they brought.

But with the passage of time, the dominant actor in the Lloyd's market became the broker. Underwriters thrived because brokers brought them business. It was Bill Brown of Walsham Brothers, broker to the Gooda Walker syndicates, who made the most money at Lloyd's in the 1980s—*$15 million* personal salary in 1989 alone. And in 1989, as the Deposit Defence Group brief to the European courts sourly reports, the Names backing the syndicates to which Brown had broked his policies were to lose more than $1.5 billion by accepting the premiums he brought. The London *Times* in its list of the richest men in Britain in 1994 valued Brown's holdings in Walsham Brothers just short of $200 million. No Lloyd's underwriter made the list at all. The Name's agent Robin Kingsley remembers going to lunch with an underwriter and Brown, who brought along with him a small man and a large man. "Who's the little guy?" Kingsley asked the underwriter. "He's Brown's jockey." "Who's the big guy?" Kingsley asked again. "He's Brown's land developer," the underwriter replied the second time.

From the founding of *Lloyd's List* in the coffeehouse days through the arrangements that gave Lloyd's news of ships passing important headlands, the underwriters on their boxes were the people who had the best information. They were themselves at risk on their policies. The Names who joined them in backing those policies received for very little cost the benefits of the information they used in deciding whether the premium offered was great enough to justify the risk assumed.

In the second half of the twentieth century, the international brokers, with clients all over the world, came to know more about the risks and the companies that wished to insure against them— and would do so, somewhere, whatever a Lloyd's underwriter on a box might think of it. They knew all the insurers, everywhere. They could bring their business to an insurance company in New York or in London away from Lloyd's or in Zurich or Munich or Paris. Worse yet, because they had always kept the files, they knew more than the underwriters could know about Lloyd's itself. Their fiduciary obligations were to their clients, not to Names. By promoting reinsurance that gave them additional commissions from additional premiums, they did not betray their clients, who were if anything more likely to be paid if the risk was spread around the entire market. They generated great profits for the managing agencies to which they gave their business. But they left the Names twisting in the wind.

CHAPTER 5

THE BEGINNINGS
OF THE CRISIS

The first serious cracks in the Lloyd's facade appeared in the late 1970s and were the work of the raffish fringe of the market, especially F. H. ("Tim") Sasse and the brothers Charles and Edward St. George, whose aristocratic name concealed a humble Maltese origin under another name. The link between Sasse and the St. Georges was horses: Both Sasse and Charles St. George were prominent owners at British racetracks, and in Britain in the 1970s the sure way of access to the royal family was through horseflesh. (Edward St. George had found another route, marrying—she was his third wife—the daughter of the Mistress of the Robes at Buckingham Palace.) When Sasse and the St. Georges' Oakeley Vaughan syndicates proved to be serious losers, a number of influential Names learned that their fortunes had been placed in the hands of irresponsible twits—and that the leadership of Lloyd's, when this irresponsibility was forced to their attention, decided to bury the information and press Names to pay rather than risk the bad publicity of fighting fraudulent claims.

The Sasse story is the simplest, and the earlier of the two to emerge. Sasse's office was outside Lloyd's, illustrated not very tastefully with racing prints and nude pinups, and he spent as little time as he could on his box. With a distinguished war record and a rich wife, he was skilled at getting publicity and at letting it be known that the 110 Names on his syndicate were on to a good thing, but he was not willing to take time to cultivate brokers. He took gambling risks like "tonners"—supposed insurance policies, really bets, that paid off if a certain number of tankers of a certain tonnage collided during the course of a given year, an ancestor of the "derivatives" that bedeviled a number of companies and securities houses in the 1990s. His also was one of the fifty-odd Lloyd's syndicates that signed on to a lunatic policy that insured banks against any loss of residual value in computers that had been leased to customers who could return them halfway through the lease if IBM or one of its rivals came up with a better machine. To use the "stamp capacity" of his syndicate, he made arrangements in America to give certain brokers there "binding authority" to write policies for the Sasse Turnbull agency, and specifically for syndicate Sasse 762.

One of the first rules of Lloyd's, enshrined in the Lloyd's Act of 1871, was that Lloyd's underwriters would do business only at Lloyd's, and that only those brokers who were recognized by Lloyd's could bring risks to the Lloyd's market. This rule had been stretched to permit the sale of Lloyd's insurance policies in foreign parts by brokers approved by a Lloyd's committee as "coverholders." The amount of premium income such coverholders can bring to Lloyd's is supposed to be tightly controlled by the Lloyd's underwriter who does business with them, to make sure that his syndicate does not exceed its stamp capacity. Stamp capacity had been intended as a "gross" number—the total premium income of the syndicate—but the rule could be twisted so that premiums paid for reinsurance were accounted for as a deduction from the syndicate's premium income.

As it turned out, Sasse 762 was handed a mountain of insurance policies written on abandoned properties in New York City's South Bronx, which were torched as soon as they were insured. The premium income (and thus the quantity of risk) accepted by the syndicate was ludicrously greater than its stamp capacity, a condition that was covered over by reinsurance purchased by the American brokers from the Instituto de Resseguros do Brasil, the state-owned Brazilian insurance underwriter. And in fact a lot of the premium income never came to Sasse or to the Brazilians, because it was skimmed through other reinsurance schemes arranged by the coverholders in the United States. When the claims came in from the companies whose buildings Sasse 762 had unwittingly insured, many suspected to be Mafia-connected, the Brazilians refused to pay.

Any number of Lloyd's rules had been broken here. The American broker (actually an expatriate Englishman) who had been allowed to write Lloyd's policies had not been approved by the committee appointed to authorize the issuance of binders. Income and losses had been shifted from one year to another by accounting trickery to make the earlier year look profitable when it had not been, keeping Names happy for another year. The reinsurance contracts provided that the premiums were paid directly to the Brazilians by the coverholders, leaving the Sasse syndicate with only one-quarter of the premium income it had expected.

Sasse signed up with his American broker in early spring 1975. Almost a year later the scheme was up and running. Almost immediately, Lloyd's New York lawyers—LeBoeuf, Lamb—began to hear rumors that insurance policies with the Lloyd's anchor on them were available cheap in the market and were being written in great quantity. The first LeBoeuf telex came to Lloyd's in March 1976. By July 31, Sasse himself had become terrified, and withdrew authority from Americans to write Lloyd's policies—kindly giving them a month's notice. They ignored his order. By the end of the year, Lloyd's believed that several of the Americans were crooks. Nevertheless, in January 1977, Lloyd's management ordered the Policy Signing Office to accept all policies written for Sasse 762 by coverholders through the calendar year 1976—and informed Sasse that however crooked the claims, he would have to pay them to preserve the good name of Lloyd's in the American market.

The 110 Names on the Sasse syndicate first learned that they were in trouble in 1979, when the cash calls began to arrive. Among them, it would soon become clear, they were going to have to cough up $40 million, which was quite a lot of money for a syndicate with only 110 Names. Further inquiry revealed gamy details of expensive binders in Canada, the computer leasing losses, the tonner contract, the acquisition of business far beyond the stamp capacity Lloyd's supposedly enforced upon the syndicates. Among the victims was the seventh earl Fortescue, whose forebears had borne shields for William the Conqueror. He was the first to say, in the House of Lords, that he was damned if he would pay: "I never agreed, nor do I now feel like agreeing, that I should accept unlimited liability if the underwriter or his agents act fraudulently or outside Lloyd's rules, or if in particular the loss is due to negligence or breach of duty on the part of the Lloyd's Committee [then the governing body]."[1]

Another on Sasse 762 was an international businessman named Paddy Davis, who in summer 1979 received a cash call (to be paid in three weeks) for more than $400,000. He went to Ian Findlay, chairman of Lloyd's, to suggest that the Lloyd's Central Fund should undertake to pay that part of Sasse's losses due to Lloyd's failure to hold the underwriter to its rules. Findlay said nothing could be done: "Bad luck, old boy. Wrong syndicate, bad luck." Davis went to a lawyer, and with help from several dozen of the Sasse Names began a suit against Lloyd's itself.

Lady Betty Middleton asked Findlay at the next Annual General Meeting of Lloyd's why nothing had been done to police the Sasse syndicate, and was patronizingly told that Lloyd's neither had nor wished the power to tell syndicates what to do. Then, she inquired, who could act in the interests of the Names? If she thought it important to have an organization that acted in the interests of Names, Findlay replied, she should start one herself. From this dialogue grew the Association of Lloyd's Members, which became active in organizing lawsuits and proselytizing among the Names it could find (for in those days the Names' agents would not distribute to Names the addresses of other Names).

The governing committee at Lloyd's was astonished that it could be sued, then frightened by legal opinion to the effect that the suit would probably be won. Godfrey Hodgson tells the story in fascinating detail in his book *Lloyd's of London: A Reputation at Risk.* The eventual settlement was not in fact reached until 1980, and in the end the Names agreed to bear about a third of the losses, an average of $120,000 each. But Lloyd's put up the remaining two-thirds, totaling about $25 million. To those who had participated in the negotiations, it seemed clear that Lloyd's was relieving the Names from most of their obligation because the committee couldn't afford to have the evidence of the syndicate's behavior presented in open court.

The Oakeley Vaughan story involves the leadership more directly, for the St. George brothers were on easy terms with Lloyd's chairmen and deputy chairmen. Sasse got in trouble originally because he didn't have enough business to keep his Names in premium income; Oakeley Vaughan got in trouble because from the start it booked a great deal more business than its stamp capacity justified. The company touched all the Lloyd's bases: It was an underwriter, a broker bringing itself business, and a Names' agency recruiting capacity for its own syndicates. A disgruntled former employee got the word to the Lloyd's committee that Oakeley Vaughan was "writing on the back of the Central Fund"—that is, issuing policies beyond the stated capacity of its Names to pay off if the claims were heavier than expected.

But it was worse than that. Edward St. George was deeply involved with the Pindling government of the Bahamas—he was cochairman of the Grand Bahama Port Authority—and the active underwriters who worked for his syndicates were writing policies carelessly for people who knew him or his brother Charles. The head of the underwriting operation, indeed, was Charles's son

James. Proselytizing by the St. Georges through their Oakeley Vaughan Names' agency had put some very distinguished people into the group's syndicates.

The Oakeley Vaughan syndicates were at their most active in the early 1980s, when many managing agents didn't care whether underwriting activities in themselves were profitable or not. Interest rates had risen so high that investing the premium receipts produced high incomes for all involved. Still, a syndicate that got a reputation for taking the risks others wouldn't take could wind up with so large a volume of bad business that the income from investing the premiums would be drained and then some.

Everything Oakeley Vaughan touched turned to junk, at a time when the rest of Lloyd's was (at least apparently) making money. The St. Georges controlled a range of syndicates, marine, nonmarine, and aviation, that could not be reinsured to close in the early 1980s and had to be put into run-off. This was an almost unheard-of catastrophe in those days. Names were not ready for the idea that they might be stuck for years to come with an uncertain total of losses from their underwriting.

The worst problem in this instance was that the results of Oakeley Vaughan's underwritings in the 1970s and early 1980s had been wrongly presented—recognition of claims had been delayed year after year, to enable syndicates to appear profitable (and to pay profits to their Names as they closed after their three-year run). Three times Lloyd's commissioned an investigation of affairs at Oakeley Vaughan, and three times the investigators appointed by the chairman were denied access to the agency's books without so much as a comment from Lloyd's leadership. But on the basis of interviews alone, the investigators came back with negative findings. In 1981, Edward St. George told Ken Randall, head of Lloyd's Regulatory Services, who had been asked to investigate Oakeley Vaughan, that "we plead guilty and throw ourselves on the Court's mercy." St. George sent Lloyd's chairman Peter Green a letter: "I will now be most interested to hear the outcome of your enquiry, and feel that in all probability your

Committee's conclusions will coincide with mine."[2] None of the reports was made available to the Names, who continued their support of failed syndicates.

The fact that Lloyd's had buried its own knowledge of Oakeley Vaughan's crimes and misdemeanors was the heart of the suit a group of forty Oakeley Vaughan Names brought against Lloyd's itself in 1988. Defending itself against this suit, Lloyd's was compelled to argue that the Society did not have a "duty of care" to its members—an argument upheld finally by the House of Lords in 1993. When the Names won a judicial order granting them access to Oakeley Vaughan documents that had been stored in a warehouse, the warehouse (a few hours after the judge's decision) burned to the ground following the explosion of a bomb in a Volkswagen parked beside it.

Among the Oakeley Vaughan victims were Lester Piggott, the greatest of postwar British jockeys, and Earl Alexander of Tunis, son of the war hero whose armies defeated Rommel in North Africa, an aristocrat to his fingertips, who has lost a fortune made in communications companies to the malfeasance of Lloyd's underwriters. Charles St. George had recruited both, and when the first cash calls came he made them whole out of his own pocket, taking in return a pledge that they would not sue Oakeley Vaughan or Lloyd's. But the first call was, as usual, nothing but a small sample of what was to come. In 1988, pressed by its Names' lawsuit, Oakeley Vaughan became the first Lloyd's agency in history to seek court protection for an orderly liquidation.

Lord Alexander, who had been recruited not only as a Name on the syndicates but as a director of Oakeley Vaughan, proved an implacable antagonist, with a forum for his antagonism in the House of Lords. In 1989, he tabled a question in the House, asking what the government planned to do about the emerging mess at Lloyd's. Lord Young of Graffham, chairman of Cable and Wireless, one of several corporate directors Margaret Thatcher had brought into the British government, replied that "there is no question of any further Government enquiries into self-regu-

lation in the Lloyd's market." (Tory governments have been un-
flinchingly at Lloyd's side since the troubles began. In December
1991, as the Lloyd's story became increasingly ugly, Prime Minister John Major spoke at the opening of the new C. E. Heath
brokerage offices, and noted that as freedom of trade in financial
services came to the European Union, "we do have in this country one priceless advantage over actual and potential European
competitors. And that priceless advantage which we should never
spurn or lose is the international fame and standing of Lloyd's of
London." He really did.) And Lord Alexander was still there in
1993, reinforcing Lord Peston's call in the House of Lords that
the government should take over the regulation of Lloyd's. "A
consequence of self-regulation and non-accountability," Lord
Alexander said, expressing with admirable economy the central
argument of all the Names' cases against Lloyd's, "is the viola-
tion of the law of agency. . . . When a conflict of interest arises
between a name and the Lloyd's agent betrays the name."[3]

●

During the time when the Sasse and Oakeley Vaughan matters
were being swept under the rug, the leaders of Lloyd's were publicly worried about the suspected misbehavior of others in the
market—specifically Ian Posgate and Christopher Moran, younger
men from middle-class backgrounds who were bold, colorful, apparently very successful, and disrespectful of their elders and bet-
ters. Posgate had announced himself a Cambridge graduate with
first-class honors in mathematics (Bertie Hiscox says it wasn't
true), and loved to display his ability to do the numbers for an insurance policy in his head. He took big risks for big premiums, and
when he had a run of luck—which he did in the 1970s—his syndicates closed with big profits for their Names. These were James
Bond years: The market nicknamed him "Goldfinger."

But the profits for the Names were not as big as the profits for
Posgate, who made interest-free loans to himself from the premium trust fund—and when caught scornfully proclaimed that

whatever might be wrong about such behavior, everybody did it. Like Sasse and Oakeley Vaughan, he also accepted premiums well beyond the limits of his Names' capacity. In 1970, when Lloyd's attempted to take away his right to act as an underwriter on the floor, he was able to fight off the Committee, though he grudgingly accepted an insistence that he become an employee of one of the larger companies—Alexander Howden, another of these three-headed monsters that recruited Names and broked business as well as operating syndicates.

Posgate was popular in the Room as well as with the external Names, lots of rakish charm. As active underwriter for both Howden and a managing agency he controlled (Posgate and Denby), he wrote, in 1981, 10 percent of all the business done at Lloyd's. In that year, to the disgust of the old-line leadership, he was elected by his peers as one of the Committee that ran the Society of Lloyd's. The next year, he was in trouble again, was dismissed from the Committee and later suspended from Lloyd's, having dodged several bullets that might have produced his expulsion.

Moran by contrast was an underwriter and a Names' agent whose Names made money, and his showmanship was the design of policies with a heavy gambling component, like tonners, which he was skilled at placing with some of the less attentive underwriters. He also liked to park his green Rolls-Royce with its CJM license plate either right at the front door or in the chairman's reserved parking space. A "black Irishman," he was (and is) a compact, handsome man, with a gift of gab and tremendous energy. Because he was in effect his own principal in some of the gambling policies he broked to the underwriters, he was unpopular everywhere Posgate was popular—so unpopular, indeed, that in 1982 he became the first member ever to be expelled from Lloyd's by a vote of two consecutive general meetings of the membership. This was a remarkable accomplishment for the leadership, given that the Lloyd's Act then in force permitted expulsion only if more than 80 percent of the Names at the membership meeting agreed. Moran was saved from worse punishment by his solicitor, Lord

Goodman, and not only survived but flourished—recently he was listed among the 500 wealthiest Englishmen, with assets between $60 and $200 million. He kept his cufflinks.

It was the difficulty of ridding Lloyd's of Posgate and Moran (Sasse had left voluntarily, if under pressure) that persuaded the Committee that it needed some statutory authority to keep out of the Room the people the leadership didn't like. Under the Lloyd's Act of 1871, significant decisions affecting Lloyd's had to go to a membership meeting. In 1871, when there were only 675 Names, all of whom knew one another or some members of one another's families, such town meeting rules were appropriate. By 1979, with 17,279 Names (only 513 of whom came to that year's annual meeting), such governance was useless, especially for purposes of market regulation. Expressing himself quite confident that nothing of any great moment would come of the matter ("I do not expect any fundamental changes in Lloyd's rules and regulations, just an updating in the existing practices and rules"), Lloyd's chairman Ian Findlay asked Sir Henry Fisher to chair a working party to look into how the market was functioning.

Fisher was a man of great distinction, at the heart of the establishment. His father had been archbishop of Canterbury; he had been a high court judge and the warden of an Oxford college. His committee included four people from inside the system (a broker, a Name's agent, and two underwriters), plus a banker and a journalist turned foundation executive. Their 1980 report, *Self-Regulation at Lloyd's,* has been dismissed as mostly a slap on the wrist for the existing order, and Fisher's letter of transmission does include the fulsome tribute "that the recent problems at Lloyd's should not be allowed to obscure the very great success which Lloyd's, despite its antiquated constitution and the restricted powers of regulation of its community, has achieved over so many years and the high reputation in which it is held worldwide."[4] But in fact the Fisher report, read carefully, telegraphs many of the disasters that were to strike the market in the years ahead.

"There should be a Bye-law," Fisher recommended, "forbidding the incorporation of any clause in an Agency Agreement purporting to exclude or limit the Agents' legal liability. . . . All Underwriting Agents should carry Indemnity Insurance. . . . The Committee should have power to intervene at any time if it becomes apparent that an Active Underwriter is not capable of performing his duties satisfactorily. . . . The Council of Lloyd's should take steps to discourage reliance by Underwriters on the services of Brokers in the settlement of claims. . . . Continued and unremitting efforts should be made to devise and introduce an effective scheme for ensuring early detection of Premium Income Limit excesses."[5]

The Fisher committee worried that underwriters would "be required to place the interest of Lloyd's above the interest of their Names."[6] They feared that at a time when Lloyd's was seeking to increase membership, Names might make a business of recruiting other Names, and demanded that sponsors reveal "whether they are to receive any commission or other remuneration for the introduction."[7] They thought Names didn't "always" get enough information about the syndicates their agents suggested they join, and that too few agents understood "the obligations which the law imposes on every Agent for reward, i.e., that he and his employees a) will act in what they honestly believe to be the interest of the principal [the Name]; b) will exercise reasonable skill, care and diligence in conducting business on behalf of the principal."[8]

Fisher proposed that "the Council should forbid clauses in Agency Agreements which give the Agent wide discretions or unilateral power to vary their terms."[9] He warned that Lloyd's should police possible gouging by Names' agents, taking advantage of their Names: "The Council might also wish to control the items which can legitimately be included in Syndicate expenses and those which should be borne by the Agent out of the Agency fee."[10] The committee saw the danger of allowing brokers to handle premiums on their way to the underwriter, "particularly . . . when interest rates are high and the benefit to Brokers of retaining premiums is significant."[11] They urged that syndicate auditors be permitted to issue "qualified" statements—rather than simply accepting or rejecting what the underwriter had done—when commenting on reinsurance to close.[12]

What Lloyd's wanted was power to discipline the brokers and underwriters the leadership didn't like. To gain that power, Lloyd's would need a new act of Parliament, for the old act was what enshrined the rules requiring an 80 percent vote of at least 100 members at a special meeting called for the purpose before anyone could be expelled. Disciplinary powers could not be effective if the individual to be disciplined could sue Lloyd's, so immunity from suit had to be part of the new act. The Fisher report was used as the lever to prod Parliament to deliver a new Lloyd's Act.

In return for the new powers, the old Committee of insiders that ran Lloyd's was prepared to accept Fisher's recommendation for a Council including both external Names and public members that would be the policy-making body (with a continuing Committee that would handle day-to-day affairs, leaving the Council essentially a figurehead). And, with great reluctance, the leadership was also prepared to accept an act that forbade any further acquisition of underwriting agents by brokers, and gave the Council power to force brokers to "divest" themselves of the managing agencies they already owned, after a grace period of five years.

The rest of the Fisher recommendations would be left to the discretion of the Council, which meant that nothing would be done about most of them. One that *was* accepted was a requirement that both Names' agents and companies that ran syndicates must carry "E&O" [errors and omissions] insurance, the equivalent of American malpractice insurance, to cover a loss as great as the full premium accepted. In 1985, as part of the general celebration following upon the resignation of the first professional manager the market had ever had (hired originally at the insistence of the Bank of England—see below), the required coverage was halved. And in 1991, after the extent of misbehavior at Lloyd's had become relatively common knowledge, the bylaw was canceled in its entirety. Dr. Alexander Munn, a burned Name, told a 1993 meeting of the membership that after the Names' agents had lost their insurance, David Coleridge, then chairman of Lloyd's, told him that " 'members' agents' mandatory coverage was dropped because it was not available. Managing agents' E&O cover will only remain mandatory as long as it is available.'

"It is quite extraordinary," Dr. Munn continued, "that in the world's foremost insurance market, whose proud boast is that it will insure anything, [where] there is no such thing as a bad risk and only a bad premium, . . . so many of Lloyd's professionals just cannot get E&O cover. . . . Lloyd's professionals will not insure other Lloyd's professionals because they know only too well how incompetent, dishonest and negligent so many of them have been. It takes one to know one."[13]

British legislation encompasses the idea of a "private" act, which governs only one limited group of citizens. In November 1980, the Lloyd's bill was introduced on that basis at Lloyd's request, and referred to a select committee. It had a much harder time than the Lloyd's committee had expected. Lady Middleton and her colleagues in the new Association of Lloyd's Members lobbied strongly against giving immunity from suit to Lloyd's Council members and Lloyd's as an institution. They were supported by Ian Posgate, whose obvious self-interest did not diminish his effectiveness. Here Lloyd's found unexpected allies in the Labour Party, because the leadership of trade unions also had immunity from suit, which the Conservatives were thinking of taking away. The recommendation for rapid divestment of managing agencies by brokers, however, was a different story. Parliament was not going to accept wishy-washy we'll-look-at-it-later language when the insider members of the Fisher Working Party were themselves firm on the subject. As of 1987, three broker groups (all of which owned underwriting agencies) placed 41 percent of all the premiums paid at Lloyd's; twelve groups, almost all of them owners of underwriting agencies, placed 68.4 percent. The eight largest underwriters were all controlled by brokers, and accounted for 59 percent of all the premium income in the market. With this kind of concentration, divestment looked essential.

The select committee of Parliament also felt strongly that there should be a "divorce" of the names' agents and the managing agents who ran the syndicates, because that inbred relationship was even more likely to produce conflicts of interest than the ownership of underwriters by brokers. Unfortunately, this subject had not been covered by Fisher, because he and his committee started from an assumption that the law of agency properly interpreted would assure that the interests of the agents and the interests of the Names remained congruent. When the 1981 annual meeting of Lloyd's Names opposed any steps toward divorce, Parliament backed away.

The new chairman of Lloyd's, Peter Green, whose father had been one of the triumphant underwriters of the 1950s and 1960s, worked hard for the bill. After it passed, he was knighted for his services to Lloyd's and awarded the Lloyd's Medal, which has been given only twelve times in the history of the institution. But the man who really took it through Parliament was Lord Marcus Kimball, a Name, a hunting-fishing-shooting squire, and a parliamentary operator who knew how to work the lobbies. "Kimball," says Alan Smallbone, "would go up to a Tory M.P. and take him by the elbow and say, 'On this Lloyd's bill, now, we're counting on you,' and the man would say, 'Is there something wrong with the bank?' [one of the four giant British banks is called Lloyd's, no relation to the insurance market], and Kimball would say, 'No, the insurance market, and we need you,' and squeeze the elbow, and the thing would be done."

In the end, the Lloyd's Act gave the newly formed Council the power but not the obligation to regulate the market. The obvious truth, which everybody was too polite to point out, was that the Council would not want to regulate the market. Presenting Lloyd's case for a new act to the select committee of Parliament, Lloyd's retained counsel Peter Boydell, Q.C., who opened his formal statement with the words, "This bill is concerned with the proper running of the coffee house."[14]

Except for the annual solvency audit, which had to be reported to the Department of Trade and Industry, the Council was not in fact accountable to anybody. There could be a "judicial inquiry" if the DTI wanted one, but it never did. Thus the first rule of effective self-regulation—that the self-regulator must be forced to justify its actions to a governmental body on demand—was violated from the beginning. And the "panel" of auditors chosen by Lloyd's worked under codes and conditions set by the Council, not by their own "self-regulatory" association of accountants.

Ian Hay Davison, who would serve for three years as the salaried chief executive officer of Lloyd's after sixteen years as managing partner of Arthur Andersen in England, exposed the fallacy: "Despite their title, the panel auditors were not in fact charged with carrying out an audit at all. . . . Agents, underwriters, Names and the committee were all under the misapprehension that the work done by the panel auditors was an audit, in the commonly accepted sense of that word: an independent opinion on the veracity of a set of accounts. But it was not. . . . The accounts of an underwriting syndicate, and the determination of its profits, depend upon how much reserve is necessary to close the accounts. The figure for this reserve is provided by the underwriter in the form of the reinsurance to close. Some of the panel auditors were still living in the days . . . when auditors accepted a certificate of stock 'at director's valuation': they did not consider it part of their duty to *audit* the reinsurance to close, yet the result of the syndicate for the year of account was wholly dependent on this one figure. Under these circumstances it is no surprise that some of the auditors missed the scandals and failed to point out the impropriety of what was going on."[15]

And under those circumstances, it is also no surprise that the Names who lost the billions of dollars in improper reinsurance the managing agents arranged to close their syndicates are now suing the auditors as well as the underwriting agencies and the Names' agents.

While the Lloyd's Act was wending its way through Parliament in spring 1982, the greatest scandal Lloyd's had ever known was rising to the surface. For some years, and despite grumbling in the market, the giant international U.S.-based insurance brokers had been acquiring controlling interests in Lloyd's brokerage operations (and thus, pre-divestment, Lloyd's underwriting agencies). In January 1982, Alexander and Alexander acquired Alexander Howden, one of the largest operations at Lloyd's, for $300 million. Howden's existing management, chaired by Kenneth Grob and driven by Ian Posgate (who had one-quarter of the entire Lloyd's membership as Names on his syndicates), continued to run the company. They were leaders of the opposition to divestment, and gave evidence before the select committee of Parliament—evidence that under hostile examination by Lloyd's counsel included information Lloyd's had gathered from Alexander and Alexander's submission about their acquisition to the Securities and Exchange Commission in Washington. Lloyd's counsel Boydell drew from Grob (who at first denied the facts, then recovered his memory) figures indicating that Howden had reinsured 56 percent of Posgate's underwriting through its own brokerage into insurance operations Howden owned outside Lloyd's, in various tax havens. Thus Howden got the profits on the underwriting, the profits on the reinsurance brokerage, and the profits on the reinsurance underwritings. And those profits on the reinsurance underwritings, being outside the Lloyd's market, obviously were not going to the Names.

Grob was another of these outsiders. Trained with Peter Green at the Janson Green box, he had become the most rapacious of the Lloyd's raiders in the 1970s, growing the revenues of the old (1812) established Alexander Howden firm at a rate of almost 40 percent a year. During the Lloyd's hearings, it became common knowledge that he had won the brokerage for the insurance on Qantas Airways by promising its management to get them the same policy they'd had for half a million dollars less, a promise that seemed to verify the Fisher report findings that broker control over underwriters distorted market conditions. He was known in the market as "the Grobfather" because of his ability and willingness to make people offers they couldn't refuse. His Cap Ferrat home on the Riviera, which he had bought from Gregory Peck, was one of the most pretentious in France, a feature of every guided tour, and he had a significant collection of impressionists and modern art. (Later investigations would reveal a note from Posgate to Grob, informing the Grobfather that he had just given a Howden broker a reinsurance order worth $450,000 in premiums, and asking, "Can I have a picture?" The word "picture" was then crossed out, and the word "car" was substituted; that would be some car.)

By the July Fourth weekend of 1982, accountants Deloitte, Haskins and Sells had informed Alexander and Alexander that there was a large hole in the Howden accounts, that a good part of the reinsurance premiums paid to Howden's external companies had simply been siphoned off by the agency's owners for their own benefit. Alexander and Alexander was stuck with its purchase, but had a loss of hundreds of millions of dollars on the transaction. This was taken from income for tax purposes in the United States, and the Internal Revenue Service said that stupidity did not create tax deductions: Alexander and Alexander could take its loss only from capital gains on other transactions, and only when it actually sold the Howden operation or liquidated it. The appeals through the system took eleven years, but finally, in October 1993, the IRS agreed that the losses Alexander and Alexander had suffered in its acquisition of Howden were not a consequence of commercial misjudgment but the results of a theft.

The Lloyd's Act was still almost three weeks short of its final passage. The revelation that a major fraud had been perpetrated by some of the market's major figures would surely have changed the attitudes of lawmakers to "self-regulation at Lloyd's," and the Lloyd's bill would have been returned to committee for major repairs. It is just barely conceivable that Lloyd's was still in the dark about what Alexander and Alexander had learned, though Hodgson reports that Green had been told on July 12. Davison reports that it was "1 September 1982" (six weeks after the royal assent had been given to the Lloyd's Act) that "A&A gave Lloyd's the first news of Deloitte's discovery." What *is* certain is that Peter Green had known in early 1982 of a fraud perpetrated by another underwriter (Peter Cameron-Webb: see below) and had on the basis of his own questioning of those concerned concluded that there was "no evidence of dishonesty"—and also that the government and the public were entirely in the dark on all these matters until September 19, when Alexander and Alexander brought suit against Ian Posgate and the four top managers of Howden.

It soon developed that there were wheels within the wheels. One of the larger underwriters, also trained at the Janson Green box with Lloyd's chairman Peter Green, was an affable sportsman named Peter Cameron-Webb. His partner was Peter Dixon, an accountant who counted Peter Green among his clients. The PCW syndicate was owned by J. H. Minet and Company, an incorporated broker with shares in public hands, including some in St. Paul, Minnesota, where a local insurer held enough to put a man on the Minet board. But PCW had given its reinsurance brokerage to Howden, which had placed the policies with reinsurance entities Cameron-Webb owned personally, in Gibraltar, the Isle of Man, and Guernsey, all parts of the British Empire where British tax and some other laws were not imposed. The immediate result of this process was the removal of about $60 million from the pockets of PCW Names to the pockets of Cameron-Webb himself.

Among the few other beneficiaries was John Wallrock, a former naval captain, chairman of the board of Minet, and Minet's delegate to the PCW board. Wallrock's defense was that everybody did it, and Lloyd's top management had known about it all along. As Green had found no evidence of dishonest intent in the very similar arrangements Cameron-Webb had made with another captive reinsurer the year before, it was considered unwise to let him be the investigator of the new allegations. There wasn't much Lloyd's could do about Cameron-Webb, anyway; he had retired from the Room at the end of 1981, and had left the country, sailing away in his own oceangoing steam yacht, building himself a splendid residence in Florida near Miami. For reasons that have never been satisfactorily explained, the Serious Fraud Office delayed requesting his extradition from the United States until a day after the statute of limitations on prosecuting his alleged crime had expired. Peter Green had accepted Cameron-Webb's retirement from his own syndicates. Presently, having been exposed as the proprietor of a dubious reinsurance scheme in the Cayman Islands, Green (now Sir Peter, having been knighted for his contribution to Lloyd's) resigned himself.

Before Sir Peter's departure, the Lloyd's Act being in place and nobody having supervisory authority over the Society, Gordon Richardson, the governor of the Bank of England, had intervened to improve the management of the market. He told Green to hire Ian Hay Davison, retired head of Arthur Andersen in England, first to perform an accountant's report on Lloyd's audits, and then as Lloyd's first-ever salaried chief executive officer. As an accountant, Davison looked first to the influence of the tax law on people's behavior, and he found what he was looking for.

The thievery had begun in the 1970s, when tax rates on passive income (interest and dividends) earned by British nationals topped out for the very rich at 98 percent. Placing money abroad, if you could get it out, would greatly reduce taxes. The Inland Revenue (United States: Internal Revenue) considered the reserves built up by insurance syndicates or Names to be profits, over a small allowance for the purpose of reserving for claims to come, and wanted to tax them. Reinsurance purchased abroad escaped the Inland Revenue and built reserves that could keep earning income, which would not have to be taxed until repatriated.

"Typically," Davison wrote with some distaste, "the terms of such a 'funding,' or 'banking' policy were that the claims under the policy could not exceed the premiums, plus the interest earned by the insurance company on those premiums, less a commission to the reinsurers. The reinsured could determine when a claim was due. . . . These arrangements were capable of increasing degrees of refinement in which, in some cases, the line between permissible tax avoidance and criminal tax evasion became somewhat blurred. . . . [C]oncealment was easy. . . . [A]s the reinsurance premiums were paid away from the syndicate and not accounted for or audited, they provided a fund from which dishonest agents could steal, and in a few notorious cases that is what they did. Thanks to the modern practice of Names spreading their interests, and their risks, among many syndicates, many managed by agents other than their own, such doubtful arrangements ultimately affected *92 per cent* of the Names."[16]

Actually, the overseas arrangements were themselves largely refinements of practice long accepted at Lloyd's. As noted, syndicates could reinsure their risks horizontally (a number of different underwriters on the original slip, each taking a share of this policy) or vertically (covering themselves for losses above a certain amount). They could also buy "reinsurance" selectively after the original policies had been issued. It was good business for the Names if underwriters who had stuck their necks out when signing an original slip later laid off on others at a profitable price what had come to seem the more dangerous of their risks. But the underwriters could also reinsure the safest of their risks, paying to another syndicate money that was otherwise sure profits for the Names on the first syndicate. Such sure-thing syndicates were called "staff syndicates," because they were for the benefit of the managing agent's employees, or "broker syndicates," because membership in them was made available to the brokers who brought the parent syndicate important business, or more generally "baby syndicates," because they normally were very small, with only a dozen to thirty names. In 1982, the second most profitable syndicate, taking the ratio of premium to earnings, had only three Names—Henry Chester, Mrs. Henry Chester, and a friend of theirs. What made this especially interesting was that Henry

Chester had been the underwriter Peter Green asked to do the first investigation of the Oakeley Vaughan syndicates.

These baby syndicates were especially easy to set up when one active underwriter wrote business for two or more syndicates, as Posgate and Cameron-Webb had done. An underwriter with several syndicates insuring the same risks could also benefit one of them by taking the entire deductible on the reinsurance program for another one, allowing the favored syndicate to collect on its reinsurance from the first loss. Among Davison's accomplishments was the adoption of a "code of practice" that railed against such cheating, but a code of practice is not a bylaw and is not enforceable unless people wish to enforce it, and there is little evidence that Lloyd's has so wished.

After Green's resignation (forced, it is believed, by the Bank of England), the Lloyd's council chose a chairman from the ranks of the brokers—Peter Miller, who had been a barrister before he became involved with Lloyd's. Miller was not prepared to accept Davison's status as chief executive officer—indeed, he told a meeting of the Society that he considered the relationship between him and Davison to be comparable to that of minister and senior civil servant in a government bureau. Miller had himself been a member of a baby syndicate. He is a very handsome man, neatly groomed and trimmed, not unlike David Rowland, but with more regular features—quite perfect, yet not at all feminine. I met him at a lavish reception for Names in New York City, before Lloyd's time of troubles, when my agents thought nothing of taking four large rooms at the Pierre for their shindig. Miller was lionized by everyone as the brilliant leader for the future who would easily correct any minor flaws that had survived Davison's work.

According to Jonathan Mantle, Miller was asked on a BBC television show how working members who made money out of discreditable practices could be expected to police the market. His reply was "Isn't that the very heart of self-regulation?"[17] Gordon Richardson had been replaced as governor of the Bank of England by Robin Leigh-Pemberton, who was among other things a Name at Lloyd's, and in 1985 Davison left, which pleased Miller, who then replaced him with the far more malleable Allan Lord, who *was* a senior civil servant.

●

The need to resolve the Cameron-Webb matter came on Miller's watch, and he made a dog's breakfast of it. In summer 1984, he estimated the losses on the PCW policies at $60 million, which by coincidence equaled the amount Lloyd's had recovered from Cameron-Webb's Gibraltar operation plus the sums Howden as broker and Minet as parent of the syndicate had agreed to contribute to a fund for victimized Names. PCW Names were told that this money would be available to them, pro rata to their exposure, and those that didn't have that kind of cash available to them would be able to continue underwriting (making those beautiful profits in the future) only if they took the settlement.

From the point of view of their agents, it was urgent that they did—because otherwise they would have had a suit against the agents for negligence in entrusting their money to Cameron-Webb—so the agents exhorted them to sign up. Nearly all of them did, including the Conservative Party deputy leader and novelist Jeffrey Archer, the duchess of Kent, and the Saudi operator Adnan Khashoggi. Lloyd's had billed Khashoggi for $30 million. A businessman I know asked Khashoggi's secretary what he thought of Lloyd's, and he said, "Don't mention Lloyd's, or he will kill you."

The settlement covered the PCW Names through the losses recognized in mid-1984, but did nothing for their future. Miller pretended, may have believed, that there were no problems in the future. But it soon developed that the future was catastrophic. PCW had written or reinsured a number of product liability, medical malpractice, and employers' liability policies for American insureds, who were being drained to death in the American courts. New claims arrived every week, and after the payment of the $60 million to the Names in 1984, there were neither reserves nor reinsurance payments to meet them. A year after the settlement offer, Names were confronted with enormous cash calls. "[F]or the first time," Davison wrote later, "many at Lloyd's realized what unlimited liability really meant.

"The direct Names had a number of particular grievances: Cameron-Webb had a policy of advising his Names to concentrate their underwriting on his own agency's syndicates so they lacked any chance of covering their losses with profits elsewhere; he had strongly discouraged his Names from taking out stop-loss policies and when they did the cover provided was inadequate [a ludicrous understatement: Cameron-Webb wrote stop-loss policies for his Names in his own syndicates, thereby getting further commissions from them, and when his syndicates lost money the stop-loss policies turned out to have been ambiguously worded and unenforceable]; many Names suspected that the new losses had arisen through fraud. . . . Lloyd's itself had been less than helpful, as they saw it, with the solvency deadline and they were not sure that Lloyd's was on their side rather than that of the members' agents or brokers concerned. . . . The Names in question faced losses of up to five times the premium income they had written on the syndicates. Not surprisingly, in view of the uncertainty, they refused to pay, and a large number of them were suspended in August and September 1985."[18]

In May 1984, shortly before negotiating the offer of funds from PCW's Gibraltar accounts, Howden and Minet, chairman Miller had written the membership a letter reminding everybody that "the Lloyd's Central Fund is maintained for the benefit of Lloyd's policyholders in order to ensure that valid claims are paid in the event of the default of an individual Name. The Central Fund is not available to mitigate any hardship suffered by Names in meeting their several obligations." In June 1985, he made a speech at the annual general meeting of members stressing "that the incompetent or even wrongdoing agent is still the agent of the Name. . . . The one thing the Council cannot do is to provide some sort of financial lifeboat [the British term for what Americans call "bailout"] and thus depart from the principle that we each individually have to respond for our share of losses if, unhappily, they occur."

This did not persuade the PCW Names to pay: Lloyd's in the end had to earmark all the Central Fund to get the Names through the solvency test, and now faced the embarrassment of having to sue the Names to extinguish the earmarkings of the Central Fund in a lawsuit where the defendants could bring out to a still mostly uninformed public and Parliament the enormity of the regulatory failures that had facilitated Cameron-Webb's fraud.

By fall 1985, Miller announced that the council "is determined that the Names on these syndicates should receive justice," and the next year the talk was entirely of settlement, to avoid "five or more years of litigation here and perhaps in the United States, which would be expensive, of no assistance to our good name, and might well cast doubt on our ability to deal with our own problems within the framework of the Society." By then, the PCW Names had distinguished lawyers, including Lord Goodman, an enormous man with an enormous if slow-moving presence, perhaps the most admired solicitor in London, chairman of, among other things, the Arts Council that distributed government largesse to national institutions, and adviser to Prince Charles.

The first compromise was to lend the PCW Names the $350 million they needed to maintain their solvency at Lloyd's (more than depleting the Central Fund, which then totaled $300 million), the loans to continue, without interest, pending a solution. The solution when it came left Lloyd's with an Old Man of the Sea on its shoulders. Despite the proud boasts of "each for his own part and not for any other," the Society as a whole would assume three-quarters of the total losses of the PCW Names as recognized at the end of 1985. For putting up the remaining 25 percent, Peter Miller pointed out in his letter to the affected Names, "Members' exposure on the PCW Syndicates is FINALLY TERMINATED."[19] Perhaps this "cap" on losses, a beneficence never offered to the losers of the 1990s, was facilitated by the fact that the chairman was a member of no fewer than five of the syndicates in question.

A new reinsurance syndicate, given the number 9001, was formed with the chairman and a deputy chairman of Lloyd's as its only members. It was reinsured by a Lloyd's-owned reinsurance company called Lioncover that was capitalized with $80 million from the Names' agents who were defendants in the suit and their E&O insurers, $64 million from Lloyd's itself, and $50 million from the Names. Money was also scrounged from what remained of the PCW syndicates, including $36 million from the newly formed Feltrim Syndicates, which presumably were taking over the better PCW risks but were in fact on the hook for many of the overelaborate reinsurance policies we shall examine in Chapter 7. Lloyd's hoped to raise whatever else might be necessary through lawsuits against Cameron-Webb. Lots of luck.

Lioncover is what Ross Perot would call the crazy aunt in Lloyd's attic. Its losses, all borne by all the Names together through the Central Fund, ran from 1987 to 1992 at a rate of about $50–$80 million a year, then jumped to $165 million in 1993. In 1994, they were back to an admitted $50 million. Chatset's 1993 *Guide to Syndicate Run-Offs* estimated an "ultimate shortfall" of about $1.125 *billion*, all of which will have to come out of the pockets of continuing Lloyd's Names, year after year. The Names hear that Mr. Cameron-Webb, meanwhile, continues to go shopping on New York's Fifth Avenue in his chauffeur-driven Rolls-Royce and keeps his gorgeous homes. His sidekick Peter Dixon has a greatly envied horse spread in the best hills of West Virginia (where he was also "Master of the Beagles"). Names must expect an average loss of about $10,000 a year *each* for the foreseeable future to pay the bills of Lioncover.

●

What is most striking about the PCW endgame is that the Lloyd's Policy Signing Office anchor was on every one of the PCW policies that produced such gigantic losses—but Lloyd's had not the slightest idea that this Godzilla was loose in the Room. When the $60 million settlement offer was made in 1984, Peter Miller honestly believed that this would essentially take care of the problem, and when Lioncover was established, members were told that its reserves would be adequate to avoid any future "mutualization" of the PCW losses. Though it was known that Cameron-Webb typically took 100 percent of the risks offered him, so that no other underwriter saw what he was doing, it simply had not occurred to anybody that an underwriter who was going to steal the premiums he paid to reinsurance companies he owned himself would not care about the risks in the policies he wrote—indeed, he would seek volume for its own sake, in order to maximize his personal return. And he would write policies that required the least current payout and thus the greatest possible reserves—"long-tail" liability policies where the claims might not come in for years—because he was going to steal the reserves.

The only people who knew how deep a hole Cameron-Webb had dug were the brokers who had brought him the policies, and they had no reason to advertise their knowledge. Many of them had been beneficiaries of PCW's baby syndicates, or had been paid brokerage commissions to place PCW reinsurance in what were only later revealed as Cameron-Webb's own shell companies (though surely some of the brokers had an inkling, viz. Howden's decision to contribute to the original settlement with the Names in 1984). There was certainly nothing in PCW's reports to alert Names, whose profits had been kept high by the simple device of underestimating the reinsurance to close premium that should have been required to get them out of the liabilities they had in fact incurred. As Ian Davison knew, auditors would question underwriters' assessments of the necessary RITC only when the smell was so bad an insensitive nose would find it offensive in another room. And because it was only the brokers who knew the extent of a syndicate's liabilities (and no one broker knew them all), an underwriter himself had no check on native optimism.

By 1982, Lloyd's was no longer an accident waiting to happen: The accident had happened. For Fisher and Davison, that accident was a legal and moral one: the apparent loss of any sense of what it meant to be someone's *agent.* In the cold light of history, however, the accident was commercial: Lloyd's was already in terrible trouble, and en route to making its troubles even worse. A case can be made—we shall make it—for the proposition that key members of Lloyd's had heard the roar of the waterfall toward which their boat was drifting. But the vast majority of the membership and no small portion of the leadership didn't have a clue. They were embarrassed by the scary stories, but invincible ignorance kept them confident, happy—and careless.

CHAPTER 6

THE ROT
IN THE FOUNDATIONS

Insurance is a business where the sins of the fathers may be visited upon the sons—and not unreasonably so. The social function of insurance is not only to spread risks, but to minimize them. Few shipping insurers would write policies on hulls not approved by The Salvage Association or some other inspector of vessels. A manufacturer of electrical equipment wishing to obtain product liability insurance had better get a seal of approval of his products from Underwriters Laboratories—and sensible customers look for the UL label on the machine. Fire departments count on fire insurance companies to do much of the work of enforcing fire codes.

In the case of asbestos poisoning, the mining companies that pulled the stuff out of the ground, the manufacturers who processed it, the builders and shipbuilders who used it, and the insurance companies that underwrote their liabilities to workers and users all behaved disgracefully, for decades after everybody involved with the substance knew it was terribly dangerous.

According to a statement by Kenneth W. Carlson to a House of

Representatives hearing in 1975, a French *inspecteur de travail* wrote a report on fifty deaths from exposure to asbestos dust as early as 1906.[1]

The first workmen's compensation laws to mention asbestosis as a work-related illness passed in Iowa and Illinois, over the opposition of the industry, in 1913.

In 1918, a bulletin of the U.S. Labor Department reported that American and Canadian insurance companies refused to write life insurance on asbestos workers. The *British Journal of Medicine* in 1924 carried a report on a thirty-three-year-old woman whose lungs had filled with asbestos dust, causing her death, and four years later reported on eleven autopsies showing asbestosis as a cause of death.

In 1934, Dr. Roscoe Gray, surgical director for Aetna Life Insurance, published his *Attorney's Textbook of Medicine*. "Asbestos particles inhaled into the lung," he wrote, "produce an exceedingly severe and perhaps fatal inflammation. This condition, called asbestosis, is not so important as many other forms of mineral irritation of lung tissue, because of its infrequency. However, it will become more prevalent as the industry grows. . . . Since asbestosis is incurable, and usually results in total permanent disability followed by death, care and caution should be used before a claim is assumed. This is a very serious disease and practically incurable. Particles once ingested continue their slow, insidious, tissue destruction through years, even though exposure may long have terminated. . . . Death usually occurs within a year after the patient can no longer work."

By the 1930s, the asbestos products manufacturers were leaning on academic and medical researchers to downplay any findings of harmful effects from breathing asbestos fibers. They fought state legislation making asbestosis a compensable disease under worker's compensation statutes. They launched their own alleged study of asbestos risks at the Saranac Laboratory, under an agreement by which all the results of the study belonged to the manufacturers who sponsored it, and nothing could be made public without their consent. In 1936, they opposed any release of data from a U.S. Public Health X-Ray Survey to keep information from all the "shyster lawyers and doctors in the country." Interestingly, one of the things the manufacturers appreciated about *Asbestos Magazine* in the 1930s was that it had "been very decent about not reprinting the English articles" on the subject of asbestosis. The fact that the people who worked for them were coughing their lives away was not the sort of thing the officers of these companies wished to be known.

The early cases brought by workers against their employers were almost all from the asbestos textile makers, and they were all settled without trial. During World War II, asbestos was heavily used as an insulating material in both merchant ships and warships. By the 1950s, it was clear within the industry that a major calamity had occurred.

In 1959, the medical director of Johns Manville wrote to a senior staff member that in his review of thirty longtime shop floor employees he had found twenty-one cases of lung cancer.

In 1963, the cat came noisily out of the bag: The *Journal of the American Medical Association* published a long article by Dr. Irving Selikoff of New York's Mount Sinai Hospital describing an epidemiological survey of insulation workers and their susceptibility to asbestosis, lung cancer, and mesothelioma. A year later, Johns Manville for the first time included a health warning on packages of its asbestos insulation and asbestos tile.

Asbestosis is a disease that takes from twenty to thirty, even forty, years to manifest itself. At the time of Dr. Selikoff's paper, there had been only a few dozen cases brought to court (though there had been some thousands of cases seen by doctors). Manufacturers and users of asbestos products, who had done little other than minimal dust control to improve the safety of their workplaces, argued that before 1964 they were ignorant of the damage that could be done by asbestos fibers; insurers said they had no more information than the manufacturers and users. All of them were lying, as was quickly demonstrated when the lawyers for the victims gained access to various corporate files in the process of preparing their cases.

Properly handled, installed, and maintained, asbestos was a useful insulating product, and it could be handled safely by trained and rather elaborately equipped workers. Improperly handled, installed, and maintained, it is a killer. Certainly from the 1930s, the manufacturers and users of asbestos—and their insurers—knew that by treating asbestos as a harmless product they were endangering the health of the people who worked for them. They knowingly permitted tens of thousands of people to be put at risk of a horrible disease and a horrible death, because they were unwilling to spend the money to protect them. Names who are outraged at their agents, insurers who are furious at the U.S. court system for ludicrous punitive awards and greedy lawyers, might pause a moment in their rage and fury and direct just a little of their emotions at the companies that cast aside their workers to keep their prices down and their profits up. There seems to be something crazy about asking twenty thousand Names at Lloyd's, who became underwriters forty years after the asbestos manufacturers did their dirty work, to make the shipworkers and insulators and textile weavers whole. But from the point of view of the people whose loved ones are dying from asbestosis, there is nothing crazy or even unfair about asking the heirs and assigns of the manufacturers involved—and their insurers—to share in some degree their victims' suffering.

●

Prior to Dr. Selikoff's paper, most doctors treating men who were dying from lung cancer did not associate their patients' disease with the asbestos they had inhaled on the job. The victims themselves did not know they might have a right to compensation from their former employers. And lawyers, seeing these matters as worker's compensation claims (where awards were stingy and legal fees tightly controlled), had no idea of the bonanza that was opening up for them. But insurers stood, all unaware, at a conjunction of increasing numbers of asbestosis cases, increasing publicity for research on asbestosis, and greater sophistication in the creation of product liability claims. The carnage was going to be something awful to see.

One of the first to hear the train coming down the tracks was Ralph Rokeby-Johnson, active underwriter of Sturge 210, a beefy sportsman well regarded throughout the market—even by burned Names. "I knew Ralph," says Washington lawyer James Patton. "Very likable, very bright." His specialty was American industrial risks, which accounted for at least three-quarters of his business, and he kept up with the news. The syndicate itself went back to 1920, and was one of the largest at Lloyd's, considered either in number of Names or in "stamp capacity." It was also one of the most respected. In 1958, Sturge had been the manager for the reinsurance of the Roylance syndicates, property of a former chairman of Lloyd's who had been optimistic about American tornado risks, in a maneuver that in effect spread through the entire market the losses the Roylance Names were supposed to pay alone as sole traders.

As early as 1972, Rokeby-Johnson is reported to have told a golfing companion that liability for asbestos products was going to revolutionize and perhaps destroy the insurance industry, worldwide. In 1974, he acted on this insight, commissioning C. T. Bowring, in those days both a broker and a syndicate manager, to find a reinsurer to take as much as possible of the risk Sturge had under insurance contracts that went back forty years and more. Specifically, he wanted coverage on the years prior to 1969, all of which were now reinsured to close in his own syndicate, which meant that risks for a generation of asbestosis could conceivably fall on his current Names.

Rokeby-Johnson was willing to pay handsomely for this protection. In a year when the premium income of Sturge 210 totaled considerably less than $200 million, Rokeby-Johnson offered to pay $60 million to get out from under *potential* liabilities for a period that had ended five years before. The deductible was $20 million; everything above that amount was to be paid by the reinsurers. The formal structure was a "stop-loss contract": The claims would come to Sturge, which would pay them, then claim under the contract from its reinsurers. Bowring was vain of its American contacts, and presently earned the right to vanity: Hadey Wakefield, one of its senior brokers, sold the policy to two American insurers—Fireman's Fund in San Francisco and Kemper Insurance in Chicago. Other Lloyd's syndicates still had exposure to asbestos liabilities in the United States, but by far the largest piece of it had gone home to America.

By 1979, straight-line projections of the number of asbestos claims and the award per claim were striking terror in the insurance market—and there was some evidence that the reality would be much worse than the straight-line projection. On November 11, Myron Dubain, chairman of Fireman's Fund, met with Bob Ballantyne of Bowring to discuss what was happening with the Sturge business, and Ballantyne "summed everything up by saying that Sturge were writing the worst possible stuff at the worst possible time."

In May 1980, the American law firm of Lord Bissell and Brook made a report to companies in the London insurance market about the situation at Johns Manville, the largest miner and fabricator of asbestos products in the United States. "There are numerous well informed people who profess to believe," the firm wrote, "that the claims filed to date represent only the tip of the iceberg in this asbestos litigation. The Secretary of Health, Education and Welfare of the United States [Joseph Califano] recently stated that 67,000 people each year will die from exposure to asbestos during the next 30 years. We know that between 8 and 11 million workers have been exposed to asbestos in the United States since the beginning of World War II and that of these 4.5 million people have worked in shipyards. Most of these shipyard workers were heavily exposed to asbestos and it is estimated by HEW that a third of those heavily exposed have died or are likely to die of asbestos-related cancer. . . . We recommend that each Underwriter on the First and Second and Third Excess of Loss Treaties be shown this Report. We also strongly recommend that each Underwriter take all of these factors into account in determining the loss reserves to be posted on these claims."[2]

Rokeby-Johnson suggested to the Committee that Lloyd's itself should take a look at the problem, and an "Asbestosis Working Party" was formed, chaired by Ted Nelson of the K. F. Alder managing agency. The other members included Rokeby-Johnson himself and Robin Jackson of the Merrett agency, Rokeby-Johnson representing the alarmist view and Robin Jackson, the unworried. On August 5, 1980, the working party sent a letter to the insiders in the market urging that syndicates that had written general liability policies for American businesses should put aside a reserve of $75,000 for each anticipated claimant. Names did not learn for ten years that any such letter had ever been written.

In early 1981, the Johns Manville company annual report revealed some troubling statistics about the growth of claims. In 1978, the company said, it had been named as a defendant in an average of 65 cases per month; in 1979, the number of new cases brought against the company had risen to 141 per month, and in the first three-quarters of 1980, to 194 a month. In the fourth quarter, there were 304 new cases each month. "The ultimate liability of the Company after application of available insurance cannot be estimated with any degree of reliability," the annual report concluded. "No reasonable estimate of loss can be made and no liability has been recorded in the financial statements."

Later in 1981, the Commercial Union Insurance Companies published a report entitled *Asbestos . . . a Social Problem*. Its authors concluded that "the proliferation of asbestos litigation and the money that must be expended for legal costs and damages threatens the financial stability of many of the insurance companies that are presently defending and indemnifying the various asbestos defendants. . . . [T]he nature of the problem necessitates federal legislative action to devise and implement a system that adequately and equitably addresses the needs and interests of asbestos victims, the asbestos industry and insurance companies."[3] This was an effort to influence legislative process in the United States, and although Commercial Union had an operation in the United Kingdom, the report was not circulated in Britain. On June 1, in another burst of sunshine on the television news shows, Mount Sinai's Dr. Selikoff reported the results of his follow-up study, and issued an additional 650-page report to the Labor Department, detailing the horrid effects of exposure to asbestos.

In autumn 1981, the Lloyd's panel auditors, who would have to approve the reinsurance to close before the 1979 syndicates could declare their year ended and pay off their Names, met to discuss with the members of the Lloyd's audit committee the question of the reserves that would be set aside (which was also, of course, the premium that would have to be paid for an RITC) to pay out the "long tail" of liabilities deriving from asbestos exposure. Deputy chairman Murray Lawrence, according to Lloyd's notes on the meeting, told the auditors that a data bank was in the process of preparation, containing "details in respect of the 10 or 12 major assureds with all years of cover. The loss adjusters would then be able to make some estimate of underwriters' lines on such risks." Though the data bank would include only direct insurance by Lloyd's syndicates, "it would be possible . . . to give a rough estimate as to the exposure in respect of reinsurance business."[4]

Exactly how that estimate was to be derived was not, apparently, discussed. Robert Kiln, chairman of the audit committee, warned that he did not wish to see anything from that data bank mentioned in the "Instructions" to the auditors, which was their annual charter for assessing the solvency of Lloyd's syndicates.

In January 1982, the auditors pointed out at a similar meeting (this one including Ted Nelson as chairman of the Asbestosis Working Party) that they had been given no instructions with reference to weighing the desirable reserves against future asbestosis claims. On February 16, Don Tayler of the working party sent underwriters with asbestos exposure a letter to tell them that his group was setting up a central source to hold information about asbestos claims and lawyers' advice with regard to them. This was no help for the accountants. A week later, half a dozen of the largest auditors wrote a formal request for instructions to Lloyd's, pointing out that the syndicates seemed "unable to quantify their final liability with a reasonable degree of accuracy." Clause 3 of Lloyd's Instructions read " '... if there are any other factors which may or may not affect the adequacy of reserves, then the auditor must report to the Committee and obtain their instructions before issuing his syndicate solvency report.' We consider that the impossibility of determining the liability in respect of asbestosis falls into this category and we accordingly ask for your instructions in this respect."[5]

So the auditors and the Lloyd's officials met again on March 9, the audit committee now represented by the Henry Chester who had found nothing significantly wrong when he investigated Oakeley Vaughan for Peter Green (and who was on one of the most profitable and most private baby syndicates). Ted Nelson from the Asbestosis Working Party thought the people who saw new claims from victims in the millions were being scaremongers, and that fifty thousand might be a reasonable guess for the number of suits that would be brought in the next decade. This was frightening enough: At the previously suggested loss of $75,000 per claim, the total would be $3.8 *billion*, of which Lloyd's as the home for the largest reinsurers of these risks might be stuck with a third or more. Accepting Tayler's number, Ken Randall of Lloyd's agents supervisory department suggested that when asbestosis liabilities formed 10 percent or more of a syndicate's accounts, the year should not be closed. Chester, to give him his due, then pointed out the danger that some syndicates—and some outside companies, too—were shedding their asbestosis liabilities onto other Lloyd's syndicates, concentrating and multiplying the risk to the market. He added that "consideration was being given to asking the market to stop writing such reinsurances in the open years."

None of these discussions, of course, was made part of any public record or conveyed even to market insiders. One of the insiders, however, underwriter Colin Murray, got wind of what was afoot and wrote angrily to Murray Lawrence. Premiums to be paid for reinsurance to close, he argued, were "based mainly on subjective judgment. . . . Ultimately the Underwriter is surely the best judge through his knowledge and experience." In a postscript to the letter, he added: "I hope also that Panel Auditors will enjoy a restoration of courage. Let them if need be look for this to their forebears and think of Bannockburn, Crecy or the parting of the Red Sea (dependent upon ancestry)."[6]

Finally, on March 18, Lloyd's gingerly advised the auditors and the underwriters. Auditors were informed that Lloyd's had "decided that it is inappropriate to specify a minimum IBNR [incurred but not reported] loading to apply across the Market; the IBNR loading is regarded as a matter for Managing Agents to solve depending upon the particular circumstances of each syndicate." Deputy chairman Lawrence wrote to the underwriters, warning that reserves should "fairly reflect the current and foreseeable liabilities of all syndicates. I should stress that the responsibility for the creation of adequate reserves rests with Managing Agents. . . . Where the reserve for Asbestosis represents a material proportion of the total reserves of the syndicate, Agents should consider whether or not to leave the account open."[7]

Ken Randall, who drafted the Murray Lawrence letter, has admitted that it was a cop-out. "At the time that the 1979 account was being closed," he said in 1989, "there were two practical alternatives available to underwriters with an asbestos involvement. The first was to make full provision for the losses in line with information then available which would have resulted in many syndicates remaining open and some going out of business. The alternative was to roll the losses forward so that claims arose in the future and future Names had to pay. This involved massaging the audit at December 1981."

Randall, the notes of the 1989 meeting continue, "was concerned [in 1982] that there was serious inconsistency between the instructions that we contained in the letter which were expressed in strong terms and the practice subsequently in the Market." John Donner is a Name's agent turned scourge of Lloyd's with reference to asbestosis questions, wearing a huge black wide-brimmed opera hat and an opera cape to Lloyd's meetings, and making his presence felt. At this 1989 meeting, he "suggested that the letter was intended to give the impression that all was in order whereas this was not the case; many underwriters had already decided to close '79 using figures that did not reflect what they knew about the risks, the liabilities for which they were supposed to be properly reserving."[8]

April 30 was the statutory deadline for delivering solvency audits as of December 31 of the previous year, and between the Lloyd's letters and that date the awful truth became totally inescapable: Johns Manville, largest of the American asbestos producers and fabricators, published an annual report for 1981 admitting that "no reasonable determination of loss can be made." Manville's accountants had qualified their statement the year before; they did so again, even more vigorously this time. Nevertheless, virtually all the 1979 syndicates with asbestosis liability got a reinsurance to close from *somebody*—and many of them thereupon paid their Names a supposed "profit" from underwriting in a year when some of the experts knew the real results would turn out to be significant losses. To the extent that the Names on the 1980 years of these syndicates were the same as the Names on the 1979 years, they were neither winners nor losers from the decision to pretend that reserves were large enough to pay off future claims. But to the extent that new Names signed on for the first time in 1980, they were placed in great peril nobody ever told them about; to the extent that 1979 Names got out of Lloyd's and went home with their profits (or died, leaving a nice estate to their heirs), they were very lucky.

●

While these events were playing out in the Lloyd's market, developments across the Atlantic, in commerce as well as law, were directing Lloyd's future in unsuspected ways. Following the fashion for financial conglomerates, the credit card, travel agency, and banking giant American Express had acquired the San Francisco insurance company Fireman's Fund in 1968, and then in 1981 the New York stockbroker and investment banker Shearson Hammill.

The acquisition of Fireman's Fund looked like a dubious proposition in 1981, and the acquisition of Shearson gave American Express a vice-chairman, Sanford Weill, who had built a major nationwide stock market house largely on a nose for trouble. On his first cursory look at the prospects for Fireman's Fund, Weill noted that there was one contract and one only in the portfolio that left Fireman's Fund subject to unlimited liability, and that was the stop-loss contract with Sturge, covering the Lloyd's syndicate's general liability risk—in practice, asbestosis. Fireman's Fund's contact man with Lloyd's was then a compact, handsome, serious-minded but informal young underwriter named Jay (officially, Joseph) Brown, who later became president of Fireman's Fund and at this writing is chairman and CEO of Talegen, the successor to the Crum and Forster insurance companies. The Talegen main office is in Seattle, which Brown likes because he comes to work in chinos and a short-sleeve shirt. "Fireman's Fund," Brown recalls from his office on the Seattle waterfront, "had been an incredibly heavy buyer of insurance from Lloyd's since the 1906 earthquake. It was a positive relationship. Every reinsurance relationship has bumps along the road, but this one was healthy."

Brown had come to work for Fireman's Fund in 1974, and had been sent to Lloyd's to sit on a box and learn just how they did business in London over the winter of 1978–79. (This was an exchange relationship, in which the Murray Lawrence agency sent Richard Keeling to San Francisco to work at Fireman's Fund for an equivalent period.) "The Sturge stop-loss contract had begun to develop problems in 1976," he says euphemistically. "We tried to buy unlimited stop-loss insurance for ourselves, but there was no market. So we started buying specific coverage, retroceded [the term of art for reinsuring reinsurance] around the world, to protect ourselves. In 1980–81 it began to look from the reports we were getting from Sturge that the retrocessional coverage would not be enough. It became evident to some of us that the Sturge contract could develop adverse consequences."

C. T. Bowring had broked the asbestos contract into Fireman's Fund, and the broker involved, Hadey Wakefield, was still there, head of the North American division. But in the meantime, Bowring had been acquired by the American insurance agency Marsh and McLennan, which had its own relations with Fireman's Fund. Marsh put Bowring under pressure to keep Fireman's Fund happy. "We asked Hadey," Brown reports, " 'You know this risk from six, seven years ago? Will you prepare a history?' We thought they probably understood the risk better than we did."

Wakefield took a proposal to the Outhwaite and Merrett syndicates, to place a cap on Fireman's Fund's asbestosis losses, and it was accepted by both the marine and nonmarine sections of these agencies in late 1981. The active underwriter on Merrett 421 who signed the slip was John Emney, Merrett's expert on American risks. Emney told the Lloyd's internal review committee who investigated the losses on Merrett 421 that the proposal went through several drafts before an acceptable statement of the risk was found. It was, Emney said, "a highly political issue . . . more an exercise to get Bowring's out of the shit than to place a risk—if you will pardon my French."[9]

Informed of this statement, Stephen Merrett huffed and puffed. "We were aware," he told the investigators, "that the Fireman's Fund were putting very heavy pressure on Bowring's with whom they had a very, very long relationship to do something to ease the problems that the Sturge contract had created for the Fireman's Fund. But in no sense, to my knowledge, was it argued overtly that we should write this account for the sake of Bowring's. I would state quite categorically that I gave John no understanding, to the best of my recollection, and certainly no instruction, that he should write that contract."[10]

To make sense of all this probably requires an appreciation of the position of Stephen Merrett at Lloyd's. First, he was his father's son: Roy Merrett had been one of the most successful and admired underwriters in London. Roy Merrett had started as, to take the favorite phrase, a "barrow boy," whose first job in insurance had been as a teenage "policy pusher," taking the agreed-upon documents to clients to get the right papers signed by the right people. Promoted from such chores to broker, he became an underwriter in the 1930s, with a syndicate of four Names, one of whom promptly died. He spent part of World War II in Portugal, arranging insurance for the Portuguese merchant marine at the urging of Britain's Ministry of Economic Warfare. In 1957, he led a delegation to Indonesia to negotiate (successfully) the release of some forty Dutch ships held by the recently independent Indonesian government; in 1965, he was in charge of Lloyd's negotiations with India and Pakistan to secure their mutual release of each other's cargo ships.

Six years after Roy Merrett's death, in 1985, The Merrett Group published a fiftieth anniversary booklet commemorating its birth in 1935. The frontispiece was a quote from the founder: "There can hardly be another business where flattery can sometimes be used to such financial advantage by an unscrupulous broker," he had said, "and with such disastrous results to an unwary underwriter." The booklet bore the title *Something Quite Excellent*, presented as a calling card on a silver salver. On its last pages appeared the bromide that "between now and the end of the twentieth century the industry will change, for better or worse. However, the basic principle must still be what it has always been—the premiums of the many must be sufficient to pay the losses of the few. Underwriters have still to rely on the golden principle of good faith. . . . Stephen Merrett now carries on the family name into the coming years at Lloyd's. No doubt in another fifty years, in the year 2035, a future generation of underwriters and their associated Names, will be looking back at a century of growth. . . ."[11]

Stephen had come to Merrett Underwriting in 1963 from Exeter College, Oxford (making him one of few Oxford or Cam-

bridge graduates on the floor), after an eighteen-month apprenticeship at Minet. By 1965, he was a Name, and by 1971, he was an
underwriter. He made his personal reputation on the floor in an
interesting way, by insisting—almost alone among the London
underwriters—that the blowing up of aircraft by Arab hijackers in
1970 was a loss to be recompensed to the airlines by their "all
risks" policies written by American insurers rather than their
"war risks" policies written by Lloyd's. The Lloyd's syndicates had
offered to pay 60 percent of the losses, but the Americans refused,
insisting that guerrilla action was war, and Lloyd's should pay the
lot.

Merrett argued that the American courts would not regard ter-
rorism as an act of war, and would hold the American insurance
companies liable. As there seemed little to lose by taking this tack,
the kid was given his head. He worked with Lloyd's American
counsel in preparing the case, and testified in court in New York,
where a federal judge in February 1973 accepted his arguments
and loaded the entire burden onto the American companies. Merrett and the seventy-one other insurers of Pan Am aircraft had ad-
vanced the airline more than $8 million in the course of the
proceedings, and the refund by the American insurance companies
was the largest ever received by Lloyd's underwriters. This episode
gave Merrett a reputation, and a self-image, as an expert on what
American courts would do.

And in the asbestosis cases there was—by late 1981, it might be
more appropriate to say there had been—an argument that the
courts would not demand payment from insurers with policies
covering the employers of the victims only in long-past years. The
policies themselves spoke of insuring against "occurrence," and
there were various ways to define "occurrence." The two prime
contenders were "manifestation"—the year in which the victim
got sick—and "exposure"—the year or years in which he made
contact with the asbestos fibers that were now destroying his
lungs. If the courts would rule that the insurance companies were
liable only for the year in which the employee fell sick, then the

premium for reinsurance of old years was found money—very few people were going to claim in 1982 or later that they had become sick in 1969 and had not reported it. If, however, the courts held that the company responsible was the one that first put this former employee in contact with an irreversible asbestos poisoning, then the deluge of claims that Johns Manville's accountants anticipated was going to decimate any insurance company that carried asbestos risks.

One American law firm—Mendes and Mount, of New York, often employed by Lloyd's—had projected a happy future for the insurers. "Reservations from a manifestation approach," the firm wrote in a letter to a Lloyd's client in January 1980, "would at most be minimal . . . for we doubt that there are any cases alleging manifestation dates arising during the period of Underwriters' coverage. Thus, we do not deem it necessary for Underwriters to establish manifestation reserves." Twenty months later, however, the handwriting was on the wall: On October 1, 1981, the District of Columbia Circuit Court of Appeals ruled in *Keene* v. *INA* that every employer who had ever put an employee in contact with asbestos was liable to him for his lung cancer, and every insurer that had sold a policy to any such company was jointly and severally liable—that is, on the hook *for the whole amount.*[12] INA had taken the case to the Supreme Court, but this was not the sort of thing the Supreme Court was likely to consider. On July 16, 1982, Ralph Rokeby-Johnson wrote a letter to Bowring about the Fireman's Fund involvement: "We are all concerned," he noted, "that the run-off of our old years should at this late stage now look so bad; happily, we are dealing with professionals who know from their own experience that no one could have foreseen in 1974 what has now occurred."

Stephen Merrett had put the first toe in this water in 1979, when he wrote a limited reinsurance on general liability prior to 1970 for a Lloyd's syndicate with minor asbestos exposure. The occasion was the formation of Syndicate 421, an "excess of loss" reinsurance syndicate. In 1984, Merrett described the situation as one "where the amount of risk being transferred to us as reinsurers was very small, and the reward wholly justified the risks although the profit was not exceptional—in other words, safe, low- margin business. During 1981, a number of proposals were made to us of a quite different kind, and some of them were accepted after careful consideration. The basis of these contracts was that we would take on the unlimited liability of other syndicates in respect of years which had been 'closed' for some time—mostly for 1975 and before—at our evaluation of the risk that the claims known to be outstanding in those accounts, and other claims not yet reported, might exceed by a substantial margin the level that the syndicate's managers and their auditors expected them to reach.

"It is apparent," Merrett added in his 1984 statement, "that although a cautious view was taken of the likely development of the accounts as then perceived, the contracts were not given the searching scrutiny they should have been given and there was insufficient consideration both of the 'worst case' development possibilities and the way in which in those circumstances the aggregate exposure of the syndicate to the book of business would be too large a part of the whole."[13] The category was known within The Merrett Group as "special risks."

The Fireman's Fund retrocession was clearly one of these "special risks." Merrett in various syndicates wound up with half of it. The other half Wakefield placed with Outhwaite 317/661; indeed, Outhwaite led the slip, having signed before Merrett and set a price Merrett accepted. This was a marine syndicate with an "incidental nonmarine" adjunct, run by Richard Outhwaite, who was an alumnus of the Merrett box. He had been Roy Merrett's fairhaired boy, a second son to him after Merrett's own first son, Neville, decided that insurance was not for him. Once Merrett's *real* second son arrived on the scene, Outhwaite's days at Merrett were numbered, though the old man was known to have made major efforts to keep them working in tandem.

Going out on his own had been a very successful step for Outhwaite, whose syndicate had become one of the most sought after and exclusive at Lloyd's. Unlike Stephen Merrett, who was aloof and complicated, more at ease, it was said, with women than with men, Outhwaite was soft-spoken, boyish beyond boyish years. Ruined Name Clive Francis, who was the first "administrator" of the Names' action group formed to sue on the Merrett losses, argues that these two men had remained bitter rivals, and took so high a proportion of the asbestos risk from older years (only a handful of other syndicates took any of it) because they were competing for what might be high-profit business.[14]

There is, perhaps, another consideration here. Autumn 1981 was a crucial period in the progress of the Lloyd's Act through Parliament. PCW had reared its hideous head and been driven temporarily back into the ground. Lloyd's was determined to present itself as a carefully run institution that took good care of both its policyholders and its Names. Leaving a syndicate open at the end of its three-year term was then an extraordinary event. Between them, Merrett and Outhwaite wrote reinsurance for all or some of the losses that might lie in the future for about fifty syndicates, which permitted some of the more timid auditors to give these syndicates a solvency statement that might otherwise have been denied. Both Merrett and Outhwaite were young and ambitious.

In fall 1993, Stephen Merrett said bitterly in a personal interview that he had been willing to insure other underwriters because "I trusted the regulators. I believed they knew what they were doing, but they didn't regulate. Insurers were entitled to believe Lloyd's was seeing to it that these were proper businesses. Lloyd's had a review department, which was supposed to report to the committee when an agent was failing to manage a department properly." He had been shocked to find out about the improprieties that had been permitted in the market.

The easy interpretation of this comment is the cynical interpretation. Merrett had been on the Lloyd's committee since 1981, and speaking of his surprise at the incompetence of some Lloyd's underwriters, heavy lids under a mop of gray hair, he *did* sound like Claude Rains in *Casablanca,* who professed himself shocked by the very idea that there was gambling on Rick's premises. But Merrett might also have in his mind certain implied warranties that his seniors at Lloyd's had given him in 1981, the year he was first elected to the Committee, in connection with his willingness to reinsure other Lloyd's syndicates and drive the wolves of unfavorable publicity from the door while the Lloyd's Act was pending in Parliament.

"Special risks" in any event was a business that was guaranteed to make an underwriter look good—for a while. The beauty of these "run-off" contracts, after all, was that the premium came in now and could at the underwriter's discretion be used to beef up current profits, while the payments on losses would dribble out slowly over a long period of time. Indeed, on many of these contracts, the very fact of losses might take a long time to travel the distance from the dinosaur's tail to his head, because the successful claims would be paid first by the company involved, which would then get the money from its insurer, which would in turn get the money from its reinsurers, which would then turn to the retrocessionaires. Thus the premium would remain in the hands of the Outhwaites and Merretts for a long time after the money was constructively gone, and would earn income for them—at interest rates that in 1980 and 1981 might approach 15 percent a year even on short-term paper.

Merrett obviously saw fairly quickly that he had made a mistake. In 1984, his Names' agency withdrew all Merrett Names from the Outhwaite syndicates. "Our concern," he wrote to the manager of the Outhwaite agency, "has focussed upon the 'run-off' protection written, which we believe will throw up losses for which reserves will have to be established. . . . We are concerned that should there be a significant further deterioration in this part of the account, it will mirror a deterioration in the share of the original business that was written in our own . . . syndicates."[15] In April 1985, in a letter to the direct Names (i.e., Names placed by Merrett's Names' agency into Merrett's own syndicates), he wrote that these "contracts were outside the traditional scope of our business and it is quite simply the fact that, in hindsight, they represent poor underwriting judgment." Hadey Wakefield, incidentally, is not to be blamed: He didn't know any better—he was himself a Name on Outhwaite 317.

●

In early 1985, the Outhwaite syndicate sent a message to the Names on syndicates 317/661 that "the 1982 year had resulted in only a marginal profit. This is disappointing as the underlying results of the business have been quite satisfactory. However, the significant increase in advices from the old years arising from Asbestosis and other causes has led us to take what we believe is the prudent step of increasing our reserves very substantially." Some members got checks; most did not, because the small profits were eaten up with Names' expenses. Then Outhwaite learned that Ernst and Young was not prepared to give his syndicate an unqualified solvency statement, and he wrote the Names again to tell them the 1982 year was remaining open. "It is our considered view," he wrote, "that despite the common assumption that an open account usually arises because of a significant loss, the 1982 account will prove to be profitable." As of the Chatset report of November 1993, the cumulative losses on Outhwaite 317/661 had exceeded $400 million, and the loss to Names was more than $90,000 for each $15,000 of premium accepted. Future losses were estimated by Chatset as high as $800 million, though some figure near half of that was considered more likely.[16] (Remember that this syndicate is still paying off on insurance policies written before 1983.) There is no way the 1,400 Names in this syndicate can pay that kind of money all by themselves.

In 1990, a group of some hundreds of Outhwaite Names brought suit against the managing agency and against ninety Names' agencies that had put them at risk in the Outhwaite syndicates. It had almost taken that long for the leaders to *find* the other Names on the syndicates, for the Names' agents, who were after all to be sued, refused to send the action groups' material to the Names they represented, as they do now. Outhwaite's defense was that members "ought to know that the underwriting of insurance business at Lloyd's exposes them to the risk of unlimited liability," and that "because of the relationship between premium and risk, the greater the opportunity of profit, the greater the risk of loss."[17]

In 1992, the Outhwaite case actually came to trial, complete with testimony most embarrassing to Lloyd's by the reinsurance expert at Munich Re. Before any more evidence of incompetence could be exposed, Merrett as the lead underwriter on the Outhwaite "E&O" slip (malpractice insurance) made a settlement offer of about $175 million, which covered 80 percent of the then known losses *of those who had sued.* (It was in connection with these negotiations that Merrett kept the lawyers waiting past midnight while he went to the opera and hobnobbed with the queen.) People who had not joined the lawsuit got nothing. "This was not," Peter Middleton said in 1994, "Lloyd's finest hour."[18]

It soon developed that Lloyd's did not in fact plan to give any actual cash even to those who had sued—the settlement would be good only for credits in the Names' accounts, to be held against the payment of subsequent losses, either in this syndicate or others. After an uproar in the press, Lloyd's more or less relented, letting some of the money be paid out to the Names and more to be used for the purchase of stop-loss insurance, then still available. (Later, the case of *Napier* v. *Kershaw* established that Lloyd's charter did not give it the right to sequester awards made to victims of negligence by Lloyd's underwriters. Lloyd's would, however, as we shall see, try again.) Unfortunately for the Outhwaite Names, the losses identified in early 1992 were a fraction of the losses 317/661 would ultimately rack up—and they remained liable for those.

Some at Lloyd's believed that Merrett should have thrown in the towel on his own syndicates in 1984 or earlier, admitting that there was no way to quantify the losses that would come from the retrocessions written in 1981 and 1982 and thus no acceptable procedure for arranging a reinsurance to close. Instead, Merrett not only soldiered on, but immensely expanded his syndicates. Merrett 418 went from less than 2,800 Names in 1984 to more than 4,000 in 1985, the year in which I and Supreme Court Justice Stephen Breyer and about 200 other Americans were permitted to join. Clive Francis, while manager of the 418 Action Group, argued that Merrett was hoping to grow his way out of his troubles.

But evidence emerged in the trial of the Merrett 418 Names case in spring 1995 that the closure of the 1982 syndicate had been the subject of a discussion at the chairman's office in spring 1985. Lloyd's chairman Peter Miller, CEO and deputy chairman Ian Hay Davison, and deputy chairman Murray Lawrence apparently met with Merrett and advised him that he could and should write a reinsurance to close for his 1982 syndicate, which had taken on the asbestosis risks. Lloyd's resisted calls by counsel for the Names to produce notes or memos that may have changed hands with relation to that meeting. Those who claim that the recruitment of 1,200 new Names for Merrett 418 (1985) was an innocent act of honest commerce now bear the burden of proof. One should also remember that Merrett did not cut and run himself: He had the largest premium limit on his own syndicate from beginning to end, with well over $400,000 in premium capacity on 418.

One part of Merrett's strategy was to void the reinsurance contracts he had written for other insurers, mostly at Lloyd's. Claiming in 1990 against Pulbrook 334, which he had reinsured on general liability in 1980, Merrett argued that its underwriter was aware of a coming flood of asbestosis claims but failed to disclose its knowledge when buying the asbestosis policy. After Merrett had taken over the Pulbrook group in 1987, an arbitration panel voided 418's policy reinsuring 334, but excoriated Merrett, finding that his role in the writing of the reinsurance policy "bordered on conduct which could be described as grossly negligent."[19]

Working at it, challenging everybody at every turn, Merrett was able to secure a considerable reduction in the claims that could be made on him by his "cedants"—the companies that had "ceded" their risks to his syndicates. Both Outhwaite and Merrett came to Fireman's Fund with, says Jay Brown, the man to whom they came, "all sorts of arguments about why they shouldn't pay. They insisted that our presentation had been insufficient, that we knew more about asbestos than they did. It was interesting. A syndicate at a box ninety feet away from them had written these policies, but we were supposed to know more than they did.

"But one of the things I've learned in twenty years of buying reinsurance is that people honor their contract only until it becomes painful. When people are threatened with bankruptcy, their behavior pattern changes. If you've paid ten million for a policy, he'll pay twenty million, thirty, maybe even fifty—but once it gets beyond the realm of what was thought possible he will fight. We decided we would settle with Outhwaite and Merrett and then turn to Sturge. I negotiated a settlement with Outhwaite and Merrett, in 1988–89. Outhwaite was in the papers every day, asking big-time money from his Names. Merrett was still reporting profits . . ." In fact, when Merrett finally, grudgingly, left the 1985 year open, his initial report to his Names was that he was doing it in hopes of *greater* profits for the year, because he was anticipating a reduction in the reserves he had taken against retrocessions he hoped to void.

The terms of the settlement with Fireman's Fund are a matter of general knowledge, thanks to the loss review Lloyd's experts performed on Merrett 421, which had a piece of the contract. The deal was not actually concluded until 1989. Its central features were that Merrett paid Fireman's Fund $85 million in four stages in return for Fireman's Fund accepting the first $160 million of losses as a deductible. Meanwhile, Brown, in his own words, "was leaning on Bowring's: 'I've had to cap my liabilities, and now you have to go with me to put a cap on our liabilities to Sturge.' We had lots of lawyers," Brown adds rather dreamily, "and evidence that Sturge hadn't handled some of this too well. From Sturge's point of view, the question was 'Do you risk going to court and losing massive amounts of the coverage—or do you cap the other guy's losses?' "

Clyde and Company, London solicitors, advised Sturge on February 24, 1989, that the Lloyd's firm had made a serious error in billing Fireman's Fund and Kemper for losses that had been covered by reinsurers in place before the deal with the Americans had been struck. Those reinsurers had become insolvent and hadn't paid, but the Americans argued that their contract did not give Sturge the right to load such losses on them. There was a lot of money involved, probably as much as $90 million. The last thing Sturge needed in 1989, when it was in the throes of selling stock to the public, was a $90 million loss. So Sturge took back the asbestosis liability as part of a complicated contract that excused them their debts.

On May 8, 1990, representatives of Sturge and Kemper, including their lawyers and accountants, met to study the progress of an audit. The minutes indicate it was a cheerless meeting. Sturge's syndicate, one of the Kemper people said, could not be audited. "Reports could not be obtained by year and layer. The system did not show claims as against recoveries. Files were not available. The process had to stop. The only way would be to take the cards [old-fashioned IBM punch cards]—it was not known whether they were available—and to put them on the system. . . . [Kemper] had requested 220 claims files and had got 96. These are the bigger paid claims. Some were incomplete as they lacked slips and wordings. You could only get what the broker gave you. . . ."

Brown estimates that, in total, Fireman's Fund lost about $300 million on its deal with Sturge, reduced to a net of perhaps $60–$70 million after the receipts from Merrett and Outhwaite. Sturge has not yet begun counting, but the losses have already been enough to kill off the willingness of Names to continue backing the Sturge syndicate in which they are concentrated, forcing its demise. And everybody in London seems to expect more defections from Sturge, which could put the managing agency out of business. Chatset in autumn 1993 thought the Sturge losses might reach $1.2 billion.

Ralph Rokeby-Johnson, who had broked the original reinsurance contract out to Fireman's Fund in 1974, retired from Sturge in the mid-1980s, sold his stock, and retired to America, though he remained a Name on Sturge 210 and Outhwaite 317. Some at Lloyd's see a rich irony in his inability to escape the asbestos risks he laid off on Fireman's Fund in 1974. When he left the United States to live in South Africa after the political settlement there, he put his Rancho Santa Fe house on the market, at an asking price of $14 million. Perhaps there is no need to feel sorry for him.

●

Merrett's judgment was confident and ultimately wrong in other areas where he was a lead underwriter of American risks. Almost a fifth of his premium income in the years 1986–90, for example, came from "professional indemnity" insurance, described as "dominated by the Accountants' book, followed by Lloyd's Brokers, Underwriting Agents, Lawyers, Medical Malpractice and Directors and Officers. Whilst there are substantial outstanding issues to be resolved," he wrote in 1991, reporting on the 1990 year, "most particularly with regard to the Savings and Loan potential of the 1988 year, it is my view that given the whole professional indemnity account that we write, it is reasonable for us to anticipate an overall profit taking the three years as a whole, and quite possibly on each year separately. The degree to which the terms and conditions of these insurances have been improved for insurers since 1985 is very substantial."[20]

The next year was just a touch less optimistic: "There has been some deterioration in the years 1986–88. . . . For 1990 current indications suggest an overall profit in this area, with a greater profit likely to develop from the 1991 account."[21] In general, Merrett noted, refuting what he considered fear mongering by Chatset (he had hesitated to do so, he wrote, because public discussion of such matters worked "to the overall detriment of the Lloyd's market"), Names who had been on 418 since 1983 still showed "an overall profit" of about 10 percent, and even Names who had joined for the first time in 1985, which was 30 percent of all Names in that year, were down only about 17 percent.[22] Such boasts of achievement were not to be heard again, as the deterioration of 1985 accelerated and subsequent years failed to generate the predicted profits.

In 1993, Merrett's enthusiasm for professional indemnity insurance had dropped a lot: "We have seen very serious deterioration in the years 1986–89. . . . The general issue of how much can be extracted from the accounting firms (and their insurers) is a highly political issue with considerable ramifications for both. . . . I can only apologise for the awful and fundamental change in the result from that predicted at the end of January."[23]

By 1994, both 1990 and 1991 were in run-off and couldn't be closed, and the reason was professional indemnity: "Our main exposure is through a contract which provided indemnity for the very large accounting firms, and some of the large law firms in the United States," Merrett wrote in his last report as a Lloyd's underwriter. "This substantial book of business has been led by syndicates managed by Merrett Underwriting Agency Management Limited for many years. Syndicate 418's participation was small at the beginning of the 1980s but after a very substantial reorganization and re-rating of the programme it appeared that there were real opportunities for profitable participation, and the participation was increased. . . . [R]isks were placed annually for three years, so that each year if the experience had been significantly different from that expected, either party could propose changes. In the absence of agreement on those changes, the contract would continue on the original basis for a further two years.

"In practice, after severe adverse development, insurers were faced with the challenge of either securing customer agreement to a steep increase in pricing, or having to put up with two further years at prices which then looked inadequate. . . . In hindsight, one can feel let down by the failure of both the accounting firms and our legal advisers to recognise more quickly the seriousness of the adverse development in the information of claims development provided to us."[24] All this, mind you, *before* Merrett began to calculate the possible costs of the malpractice (E&O) insurance he had written for his fellow Lloyd's agents, at the incredible risk of his Names.

The fatal aspect of the old years' general liability contracts and their reinsurance turned out to be not the asbestos cases but the more general "toxic torts," especially industrial pollution. Here again, there are questions to be asked of the underwriters about what did they know and when did they know it, for the pollution of Love Canal in upstate New York was well publicized in 1979, and by 1981 the Hooker Chemicals and Plastics Corporation had already been held liable for a billion dollars or so in damages to the people who found their homes built on a dumping ground for hazardous wastes. In December 1980, Congress passed the Comprehensive Environmental Response Compensation and Liability Act (CERCLA), which established a "Superfund" to clean up industrial waste sites. Polluters would be forced to pay on a basis of strict liability—that is, whether or not what they had done had been legal at the time, they were now liable to pay for cleaning it up—and however small their share of the total responsibility, they could be held liable for all the costs that couldn't be shaken from the pockets of the polluters who had caused greater destruction.

Here again there was a strong defense for the insurance companies. Most policies had been written to protect industrial plants against suits from others hurt by "accidental" discharge of wastes. Most cleanup sites in the Superfund program had been polluted by companies that systematically and deliberately put their waste wherever the costs (to themselves) were lowest. Again there arose the question of the social function of insurance: Should insurance companies have insured clients that were making the land and water around them toxic? And whatever the law (and, as Lloyd's syndicates complained, the English language) might say, U.S. courts empowered by CERCLA were going to make the polluter pay. In turn, the polluter was going to make his insurance company pay. If the polluter was already bankrupt, his insurance company would still pay; if his insurance company was bankrupt, any other insurance company that had insured any other owner of this property was going to be in court. Like asbestosis, toxic contamination was about to become a mother lode for lawyers.

Outhwaite 317 of 1982, Pulbrook 90 of 1982, Merrett 418 of 1985, Sturge 210 of 1990, would be basket cases without asbestos liability, as would many smaller syndicates. Chatset estimated in its 1993 book that three-fifths of their outstandings were for pollution: "Take away pollution and there is a containable problem."[25] The American insurance industry is even more savagely hit than Lloyd's by incessantly increasing bills to pay the government to clean up contaminated areas (which in the end it doesn't do anyway). The Superfund legislation was up for renewal in 1994, and in early 1993, the incoming Clinton administration appointed a committee of industrialists, insurers, municipal officers, academics, bureaucrats, and consumer advocates to seek a consensus on a law that could achieve at least some of the aims of public policy with relation to toxic sites without bankrupting too many people.

The committee came up with a formula that would have loaded the costs of cleanup onto future insurance policies and reduced insurers' liabilities for past years. In summer 1994, under severe pressure from American International Group (AIG: Maurice Greenberg's company—it doesn't have much old pollution liability), the committee backed away from its formula and presented a plan that involved payment by the insurance industry of $8 billion in CERCLA damages over ten years, which would fulfill the industry's responsibility to the government for cleanup costs and presumably save a fortune in legal fees. Under this arrangement, individuals and businesses claiming to have been damaged by industrial polluters could still take their cases to court, but would not participate in the fund. Legislation to carry this compromise into law was among the many casualties of the rushed conclusion of the 103rd Congress, but something like it may well be passed before 1996 by a Republican Congress less solicitous of the trial lawyers. Best estimates in mid-1995 were that a new Superfund law would do Lloyd's some good, but not much—even if it came in time.

For our present purposes, the most fascinating fact about this committee is that its membership included exactly one non-U.S. national: Stephen Merrett. His contribution to the public debate was the comment that it doesn't make much sense to make the soil on which a chemicals plant stood safe for children to eat if it's going to be used for another chemicals plant. As always, it was an intelligent comment—and naggingly offensive to the people who disagreed with him. The problem at Love Canal, after all, had been the residues left by Hooker Chemicals—and the nature of that problem was that the children living on the site were getting sick.

CHAPTER 7

THE WHIRLPOOL

Clive Francis argued that Stephen Merrett expanded his syndicate 418, especially between 1984 and 1985, in the hope that somehow he could grow out of his troubles. Merrett's reply was that, taking a four-year perspective, 418 did not in fact grow faster than the Lloyd's market as a whole. And he was right: While few beat the 40 percent growth in Names that Merrett chalked up in a single year, an actual majority of Lloyd's syndicates grew like Jack's beanstalk starting in 1980, when the Lloyd's leadership first had to face the likelihood of an asbestosis meltdown. For the market as a whole, the number of Names almost doubled over eight years, which meant a rate of 9 percent a year.

A minority of the older, tougher, experienced underwriters ignored this flood of callable capital into their market, retained their limited stamp capacity, built heavy reserves to ensure investment income sufficient to produce profits even in years when the underwriting showed a loss, and continued to write a conservative line of mostly English business, insuring ships, airplanes, automobiles, trade in general, but not one another. The majority of Lloyd's managing agents in the 1980s, unfortunately, behaved otherwise. They hunted around for business they could do, invading one another's specialties, cutting premiums on established lines, and finding new ways to make profits for themselves from overcapacity in their market.

The obvious device was the extension of vertical reinsurance. Before 1980, Lloyd's bylaws forbade syndicates from spending more than 30 percent of their premium income on reinsurance. The diffusion of risk in the market was to be accomplished by limiting participation in a policy—a syndicate was supposed to sign for only a relatively small percentage of the total slip—rather than by taking most or all of a risk and then laying it off with others. If the total stamp capacity of a syndicate was $50 million, its underwriters, using four-fifths of that capacity, might sign onto 400 slips averaging $100,000 of premium each, some larger, some smaller. Brokerage commissions on original underwritings of that nature would be about 10 percent of premium, or $4 million.

In 1980, Lloyd's changed its bylaws to permit syndicates to spend 60 percent of their premium income on reinsurance, and by 1990 more than half the total business written at Lloyd's was reinsurance, most of it within the Lloyd's market. Coupled with the huge recruitment of new Names and new money to Lloyd's, the new rules totally changed the behavior of the foolish, the adventurous, and the inexperienced.

As noted, Lloyd's encouraged its syndicates to reinsure one another. In assessing a syndicate's solvency, Lloyd's gave full weight to a reinsurance agreement with another Lloyd's syndicate, but might insist on a haircut, usually 20 percent, for reinsurance purchased outside the Lloyd's market (after all, the Lloyd's policies were the safest in the world, weren't they?). Usually the threat of a haircut was just a way to keep the business at home, but sometimes, in fairness, the refusal to let a syndicate keep the full value of a reinsurance policy as part of its reserves was entirely justified.

The Devonshire syndicates, for example, looking to buy cheap reinsurance, went to the Korea Foreign Insurance Company (KFIC). That's *North* Korea. KFIC had an office in Paris, which argued to some that it was serious about being in this business, though others might have felt that the whole purpose of the operation was to put North Korean hands on dollars not otherwise available to a rogue state. What had really convinced Devonshire underwriter C. H. Bohling that these fellows were okay was the fact that "a high ranking official from the [North Korean] Ministry of Finance" had deigned to come all the way to London and have dinner with the Devonshire people. Bohling told the loss review committee looking into the losses of his syndicates that he had seen the books and accounts of the Korean Foreign Insurance Company, but he couldn't find his copies. "The Committee questions," its report said mildly, "whether any accounts of the company were ever seen by Mr. Bohling."[1] As it turned out, the North Koreans welshed on about $24 million of reinsurance cover, complaining not unreasonably that the Devonshire people had incompetently failed to keep them informed. The reinsurance was "commuted" to an agreed payment of $2.3 million, which the Koreans agreed to pay, but they didn't.

Reinsurance was the best of business for some of the insiders at Lloyd's. Let us assume that instead of sharing his underwriting risks on the slip with a number of other syndicates, the managing agent with $50 million stamp capacity from his Names takes 100 percent of the risk on $40 million of premiums, and then buys "excess of loss" reinsurance that holds him harmless for losses more than three times his premium on any individual risk. If he has played his cards right—and, after all, he knows more about these risks than the reinsurer can—he can avoid losses and reserves for future losses totaling more than the premium he pays and the income he could earn on that premium if he continued to carry the risks himself. His Names share in that profit—assuming everyone is honest—but the real winner is the broker who has placed the reinsurance, who gets commissions he never would have seen if Lloyd's hadn't changed its rules.

Those commissions for placing reinsurance—not difficult to earn, as insured and insurer are both on the same trading floor at

One Lime Street—have run upwards of 10 percent. (Sarah Gibbs, the superefficient executive secretary of the Gooda Walker Action Group, who knows comprehensively what Gooda Walker did, says that Gooda Walker sometimes paid brokerage commissions of 18 to 20 percent of premium to place its outward reinsurance.) This commission on outward reinsurance is paid (unknowingly) by the Names who backed the original insurers, not by customers for the policies. The managing agents of the reinsurance syndicate get their 20 percent profit commission, plus their expenses, and the Names that back the syndicate doing the reinsurance also pay a profit commission plus fees to their agents. The total receipts to Lloyd's insiders more than double.

By 1990, according to the National Westminster Bank's investment report, the costs for the Lloyd's market as a whole, which included a number of underwriters who continued to play the game straight, had risen to 12.7 percent of gross premiums.[2] In 1992, according to a similar study by Barclay's Bank, total costs at Lloyd's went to 17.2 percent of gross premiums, up from Barclay's estimate of 6.5 percent in 1984.[3] Other estimates are worse.

Nor does the "spiral" stop with a single "excess of loss" policy for the original insurer. The reinsurer may now buy retrocessional insurance, holding him harmless for losses over, say, five times the premium paid by the original insured. And the syndicate that writes the retrocession can then protect itself in a similar manner, and so ad infinitum, brokerage and syndicate expenses and profit commissions being paid to the insiders at Lloyd's at every step of the way. Because there were a limited number of syndicates writing such policies, and they all knew one another, it was by no means unknown for the same syndicate to take different levels of exposure on the same risk, reinsuring other syndicates that were reinsuring it. An intelligent analysis of Lloyd's by Investor's Research Corporation of Jupiter, Florida, performed for the Canadian Names suing Lloyd's, claimed that "by the time a risk passed 9 times from syndicate to syndicate, a premium of £1 million had eroded to £300,000, the rest having gone to brokers and underwriters."[4]

This sort of thing simply did not exist until Lloyd's underwriters in the 1980s, exploiting the new freedom Lloyd's as regulator had given its members following the passage of the 1982 act, invented what came to be called "LMX," for London market excess of loss. As practiced at Lloyd's, London market excess of loss didn't have much to do with insurance as customarily understood. A report to Lloyd's on the reinsurance scandal by Sir David Walker, who had been a vice-chairman of the Bank of England and chairman of the Securities and Investments Board established in Britain in 1986 in emulation of the American Securities and Exchange Commission, noted that "in determining the need for excess of loss reinsurance protection, a primary insurer will make an assessment of the exposures in his portfolio of business. . . . The same base of information is similarly used by the first-tier reinsurer to determine the limits and price of the reinsurance protection that he provides. When that insurer himself seeks protection, he is in turn able to make an assessment of his own book of inward reinsurance business made up of acceptance from a number of different insurers.

"But the transparency of risk was eroded in the LMX spiral as successive reinsurers became more remote from the original insurance assessment and contract. The transfer of risk within the market meant that transparency virtually disappeared beyond the initial levels of the spiral because there was no practicable means available to an accepting LMX reinsurer to establish what size of original insurance loss would trigger a claim under a particular LMX contract. It followed that the only certainly known features of the LMX contract for the accepting reinsurer were the deductible or excess point, the money limit of exposure to the contract, and the premium. . . . [U]nderwriters who were readier to take on LMX business typically questioned the broker only about the premium rate on the previous layer."[5]

Sir David was a member of the Council of Lloyd's, and lacked the instincts of a regulator. The Bank of England's attitude toward its regulatory responsibilities has been not unfairly expressed by an American banker as, "They don't care what you do as long as you don't frighten the horses." Sir David himself had been brought into the Securities and Investments Board to replace its first chairman, Sir Kenneth Berrill, because Sir Kenneth had shown signs of wanting to write rules that would really control the operations of the stock market. Some believe the Walker report is essentially a whitewash—the people involved in the spiral, Sir David is sure, were not the smartest but honest.

"It is apparently quite common for commission to be rebated by brokers," he wrote, "but the committee are aware of no suggestion that such rebates have been applied other than for reducing the net cost of reinsurance for names. . . . The committee are aware that there has been criticism of rates of brokerage and of the earnings of brokers prominently engaged in LMX spiral business. These are, however, market matters, and in that important sense the committee would have no particular competence to express a view on brokerage rates determined in an open market . . . but we do register concern at a process in which the pricing established for brokerage appears to have been quite unrelated to the scale of effort and risk involved for the broker."[6]

The existence of this crazy spiral destroyed what discipline the Lloyd's market had cultivated. It didn't matter whether an underwriter was careful in choosing the risks he would assume, so long as he could lay them off for a good margin less than the premiums he charged. Diversification was and still is the fashionable theory in finance, and men who were intelligent, like Stephen Merrett, could enormously increase their underwriting book and go into risks they didn't well understand because they were protected first by what the economists call the law of large numbers and second by their ability to "arbitrage" the premiums. By spending much but not all of their premium income for reinsurance that kicked in after a relatively low deductible, they could, they thought, guarantee profits whether the business itself was profitable or not.

M. P. A. Wright, underwriter of syndicate 741, wrote in his 1991 report that "during the eighties it was possible to wheel and deal, and by use of reinsurance, produce good profits out of unprofitable business."[7] On the upper reinsurance levels, there was an unwritten and unenforceable understanding between the insured and the insuring underwriters that if losses actually got to that point, and the premium paid for the reinsurance turned out to be significantly insufficient, *future* premiums would be increased to make up for the losses. Where the policies provided for automatic reinstatement after a loss experience, the premium for the reinstatement, especially on the lower levels of reinsurance, might be higher than the original premium.

Through the 1980s, Lloyd's accumulated and thought it profited by a breathtaking collection of risks where the insurer's liability was essentially unlimited, and the syndicates flourished by reinsuring one another. So concentrated within itself did the market become that the same syndicate might well be on different levels of the same risks, insuring, say, first the loss between $2 million and $4 million, then the loss between $12 million and $16 million (the brackets had to grow to justify the premiums). And, of course, you gave the brokerage business on your outward reinsurance to the brokers who brought you the reinsurance business you wrote.

There was an orgy of "reciprocal trading," described by accountant Jeremy Casson in his Lloyd's report on the horrific losses of Syndicates 666 and 268 as "the practice whereby one underwriter will agree to participate on the reinsurance programme of another underwriter who, in return, will write a certain proportion of the first underwriter's programme. It is a long established practice in the international insurance markets and can have many benefits, in particular, if it enables a reinsurance underwriter to participate in business that would not otherwise have been shown to him. However, the benefits are limited if the incoming and outgoing business is the same, or similar."[8]

M. Crowe, the Active Underwriter on these syndicates, gave testimony to Casson: "It was so stupid. It was ridiculous. To get people's covers home people were doing reciprocal exchanges. Depending on the size of the syndicate, someone would say to me, 'I will write $100,000 on you if you will write $25,000 on me.' This sort of thing went on. Again, market practice. No secret. That was one aspect of it, but that was not what I call underwriting. That was called trading. That is a better word."[9]

Eventually, of course, the process came to a halt, when the commission to be made on the premium for the next level of reinsurance was too small to interest the brokers. The game Americans call musical chairs is called "pass the parcel" in Britain. Reinsurance on the top levels looked very profitable for years on end, because claims by insured never rose that high. Walker reported dryly that "it was clearly believed by some underwriters that the highest layers of cover were beyond the reach of any likely loss event."[10] Insurers had been lucky through the 1970s and the first half of the 1980s, with only Hurricane Alicia in 1983 to shatter people's complacency. The windstorms that battered Britain the weekend before the 1987 Black Monday in the U.S. stock market were the first "event" since the *Amoco Cadiz* tanker grounding in 1978 to cause more than a billion pounds of insured damages. The next year the explosion and fire on the Occidental Petroleum oil rig Piper Alpha in the North Sea killed 167 workers and totally destroyed one of the most elaborate man-made structures in history. Both of these went through the top of the reinsurance protection of several LMX syndicates, but did not greatly change the habits of the market. "It is noteworthy also," Walker wrote, "that, despite the losses sustained in the wake of the 1987 storms and Piper Alpha in 1988, reinsurers were still ready to accept LMX business in 1989 at low premium rates, no doubt partly on this assumption that similar catastrophes were unlikely to be encountered in the early future."[11]

Slowly but surely, the advancing claims on Piper Alpha revealed the insane complexity of the LMX market. LUCRO, the Lloyd's Underwriting Claims and Recovery Office, processed no fewer than 43,000 claims on 11,500 excess of loss policies written on Piper Alpha. The total loss to the insurance industry was about $1.4 billion, but the total of claims—by insureds on their insurers,

insurers on their reinsurers, reinsurers on their retrocessionaires, and so on up the spiral—was more than $15 billion.

Meanwhile, the opacities of the spiral meant that some of the worst-afflicted syndicates continued to *look* profitable as their true economic condition collapsed. Claims went first to the lead underwriter, then to others on the slip, then from each of these insurers to their reinsurers, then from the reinsurers to *their* reinsurers, then back to other retrocessionaires, so that half a dozen *years* might elapse before the parcel came to rest in the hands of the residual loser. The Gooda Walker loss review committee noted, in its explanation of how so much money could have been lost, that after earlier catastrophes such as Hurricane Alicia in 1983, "payments moved so slowly that it was only in 1990 or 1991 that 'spiral' syndicates began to exhaust their 1983 protections. . . . [T]he slowness of claims settlement allowed the earning of investment income on the funds retained to pay claims. This meant that the financial impact of these claims was, to an extent, mitigated." Partially automated settlement came to Lloyd's in the late 1980s, with more rapid calls upon the reinsurers to reduce the burden on those they had reinsured, and "brought to light the shortcomings of the London spiral market."[12]

Nevertheless, the delays remained long enough to trap thousands of unsuspecting Names into syndicates that were already in truth, if not report, deeply insolvent. Devonshire 216, a nonmarine syndicate heavy into LMX, reported profits *after syndicate expenses* of 21 percent of gross premiums in 1985, 30 percent in 1986, 5 percent in 1987, and 22 percent in 1988 (when in fact its incurred liabilities to those for whom it had written reinsurance had already become a large multiple of its reported profit). The next year's syndicate reported a loss of 244 percent.[13] And things were really much worse than even these numbers indicate, because the syndicate doubled in capacity between 1988 and 1989 (after all, it reported itself as doing so awfully well). The total profit of the four earlier years was about $10 million, and the total loss in 1989 was about $85 million, with more to come as the account "deteriorated."

This certainly wasn't insurance. It might or might not have been trading. Or something worse.

•

The locus classicus of the LMX spiral was the group of syndicates administered by the Gooda Walker agencies. Tony Gooda was second-generation Lloyd's; the son of a popular underwriter, he clearly was not going to have his father's skills. With the single exception of a life insurance syndicate launched in 1987, all the syndicates controlled by The Gooda Walker Group were founded in W. G. Gooda's lifetime. Young Tony, still in his forties in the early 1980s, had been assigned at an early age to cultivate his real talent, which was to play the charming Name's agent who recruited on the golf course and on his boat. Derek Walker was an older man, whose career at Gooda went back to 1943. Though experienced, he was flashy; he had previously been Christopher Moran's partner in what Lloyd's regarded as bad behavior, but had been acquitted in court when prosecuted for fraud. He was also, as demonstrated in the Lloyd's loss review, thoroughly incompetent.

The Gooda Walker syndicates wrote essentially two kinds of vertical insurance policies: excess of loss (XL) on other reinsurers' excess of loss on specific risks, and "whole account" excess of loss for other syndicates, by which Gooda Walker would pick up the losses of that syndicate above a certain deductible. This was, of course, excess of loss with a vengeance, and should itself have been reinsured in a way that provided a cap on the Gooda Walker syndicate's total exposure. Such caps were not purchased, and in fact would have been virtually impossible to buy.

As the loss review committee noted bleakly in its comments on syndicate 298, "The underwriter failed to appreciate that the whole account reinsurance policies that he was accepting could all become total losses in the event of a moderate catastrophe entering the reinsurance spiral. He appreciated this effect on his XL on XL writings but not on his whole account writings. He did not realise that many reinsurers were purchasing whole accounts as an alternative to XL on XL, as it was cheaper, thus making the whole accounts written as volatile as the XL on XL business they were protecting. Accordingly, because he did not consider that exposure on these contracts would aggregate, he bought virtually no reinsurance to protect them."[14]

The 1988 year of this syndicate was closed with a loss of $100 million; as of December 1993, the 1989 year, which had been left open, showed a loss of $430 million, which meant that every Name who had accepted $15,000 worth of premium on this syndicate for this year showed a loss of $100,000 beyond the loss of the premium.

The progress of this syndicate in the 1980s was a remarkable demonstration of Tony Gooda's recruiting abilities. Except in 1986, the syndicate always ranked in the bottom half of Chatset's "league tables" for marine insurers, yet the stamp capacity rose from a tiny $3 million in 1983 to $60 million in 1989, when the wheels came off. As a members' agent, Gooda Walker always put its own Names onto its own syndicates, arguing that they were as a group highly diversified. "We adopt a conservative policy in our underwriting," the Gooda Walker 1987 prospectus proclaimed, "with our aim being a steady return from a wide spread of business."[15] There was risk, of course: Gooda would tell prospective Names that they should not be at Lloyd's unless they could write a check for $30,000 "without mortgaging the cat." His partner Derek Walker had a favorite example of what might trigger substantial losses: "San Francisco falling into the sea." Barring that, nothing too awful was likely to happen to the GW Names.[16]

Syndicate 290, in any event—the syndicate where Derek Walker himself was the active underwriter—showed profits in the top half of the nonmarine market from 1983 through 1988 (in the top 10 percent for four of the six years), growing in the process from a stamp capacity of $16 million to $105 million (which Walker greatly overwrote, accepting $150 million in premiums in 1989). The total profits from 1983 through 1988 were $70 million.

Gooda did not have to sell this one: The loss review report noted that "members' agents approached the managing agent to request capacity."[17] Then losses on the 1989 year of account, as reported by Chatset in 1994, came to $380 million. "We would estimate further deterioration of 200%," Chatset wrote, "but some in the market speak of 500%."[18] That would put the losses on this syndicate alone at more than $1 billion.

And something was afoot here rather more dangerous than mere misjudgment. In three of the six years 1983–88, including two of those when the syndicate finished in the Chatset top 10 percent, Walker in fact had a loss in his insurance underwriting, and gained his laurels through the use of what Lloyd's calls "time and distance" (T&D) policies. These are nothing more or less than ways to discount anticipated losses to their present value, but in the odd bookkeeping Lloyd's demands (in fairness, only after irrational input from the British Inland Revenue Service), the discount can be taken as a profit. Whether or not what Walker did here was fraudulent (the Serious Fraud Office of the Department of Trade and Industry, after announcing that the matter was under investigation, dropped its inquiry in 1994 without prejudice to reviving it), many believed the tricky accounting made the reported results misleading, not only to the poor Names, but to their agents.

It's an interesting device. What worries the income tax people about insurance companies is that they can "overreserve"—assert future losses greater than they really will be—for the purpose of reducing the income they report for tax purposes here and now. For the same reason, tax authorities in all countries also worry about banks taking too large a loan loss reserve. In the United States, insurance companies calculate their expected losses, and put aside what they expect will be, at prevailing interest rates, enough reserves to pay these losses as the claims emerge. The Lloyd's category is IBNR—incurred but not reported. Tax examiners in both countries then come around and say that for one reason or another the insurance company is reducing its taxable income too much by setting aside these reserves, and the matter is negotiated out between the government and the taxpayer.

Lloyd's, for reasons buried in the mathematical limitations of nineteenth-century insurers, has never permitted its syndicates to discount their anticipated losses. Insiders have a self-interest here, because money put into bonds or banks to earn interest to help pay these losses would go out of the Lloyd's market. Instead, Lloyd's has required insurers to purchase *insurance policies* that fulfill the same function as the bonds or bank deposits—that is, they yield interest on the money set aside as a reserve. The insurer estimates how much money he will need in each of the next, say, ten years, and then buys from another insurer, through a broker, a policy that will pay precisely that much in each of the years. Lloyd's brokers get a commission on the business, and if the policy is placed outside the Lloyd's market, well, the fellow who gets it probably will have some reciprocal business to throw Lloyd's way. Or, as in the case of Gooda Walker 290, the policy can be placed through the brokerage arm of C. E. Heath at Lloyd's into an insurance subsidiary in Bermuda owned by C. E. Heath.

Because Lloyd's does not permit the discounting of future liabilities, *the entirety of the payments to be made under the time and distance policy to the successors to the syndicate that is being closed must now be written onto the books as part of the reserves of the syndicate buying the policy.* Meanwhile, making the awful still worse, the next year this syndicate, accepting a reinsurance to close the previous year, finds itself with less real reserves (and thus less opportunity to purchase reinsurance, which normally has to be bought at the beginning of the calendar year) because the reserves presumably transferred to the new year include this artificial write-up of the value of the time and distance policies.

Nevertheless, the man from Inland Revenue comes knocking at the door and says, "Look here, gentlemen—that's too much reserves." So Lloyd's generously concedes the point, and permits the closing syndicates buying time and distance policies to take *as profit in this year* the difference between the price of the policy and the total payments over the years. Both the managing agent and the Name's agent take commissions on those profits, and what's left is paid out to the Names. As the details of how Lloyd's syndicates make their profits or losses are not revealed to anybody (including Names' agents, let alone Names) unless the syndicate goes so far under water that a loss review is commissioned (and even then the copies of the loss review are labeled "Private and Confidential"), even analysts as sophisticated as Chatset simply show the syndicate as highly profitable. For Gooda Walker 290, the numbers were:

> 1981: a loss of $1.1 million after counting investment income, a time and distance "benefit" of $4.6 million, and a profit commission to Gooda Walker of $700,000;
>
> 1983: a loss of $200,000 after counting investment income, a T&D "benefit" of $2 million, and a profit commission of $340,000;
>
> 1985: a loss of $6.4 million after counting investment income, a T&D "benefit" of $11.7 million, and a profit commission of $850,000;
>
> 1987: a loss of $750,000 after counting investment income, a T&D "benefit" of $8.6 million, and a profit commission of $1.3 million.

It should be noted that the basic accounting device is not necessarily misleading. There is no difference between deducting from profits only the discounted present value of future payments on claims and deducting the full total of those anticipated payments and then writing back to profits the apparent "gain" from the discounting. But in the first case, the bookkeeper is constrained by the actual IBNR losses, while in the second case, he can buy any amount of T&D policies he wishes, regardless of anticipated losses, to make his current year look as profitable as he wants to have it look. Anthony Willard, active underwriter on Gooda Walker 299, told the court in the trial of the Names' case against the agents that Derek Walker had asked him to write a time and distance policy for another Gooda Walker syndicate in trouble with Piper Alpha losses. He had refused to write it, and had told Walker that if he did write it, he would have to tell his auditors—to which, he said, Walker replied, "Surely, Tony, you do not have to tell your auditors everything, do you?"[19]

The injury here is to the Names backing the syndicates that now must take over the old-year liabilities through the reinsurance to close. Kenneth Randall's report to the agency running off the Gooda Walker syndicates criticized "a double outflow of funds from the syndicates—first, to purchase the time and distance policy and, second, as a profit distribution to Names. This resulted in a diminution in the reserves held by the Gooda Walker syndicates."[20] And it also increased the taxes the Names had to pay at the time, though the governments later refunded the money after the true losses had been revealed.

The total losses on Gooda Walker syndicates will at the least approach $2 billion. The officers and directors of Gooda Walker rewarded themselves well for losing so much money for their Names. Though most Names on any of the Gooda Walker syndicates were on most or all of them, and the losses on the losers just overwhelmed the gains on the winners in 1988, Gooda Walker agents nonetheless took profit commissions of $7 million out of the Names' pockets in 1988, on the argument that "the money is required to run the Agency effectively."

On November 23, 1988, at a board meeting of The Gooda Walker Group, underwriter Eddie Judd reported that his "gross loss" from the 1987 fall windstorm would be about $90 million, and he had only $33 million of reinsurance to cover it. The information was in the "market form" he had to prepare for Lloyd's in planning his year-end position. He thought it would be unwise to tell Names while they were in the process of deciding which syndicates they were going to back in 1989: "If this was sent out," he said, "it would scare people to death." So people who might have decided the Gooda Walker syndicates were risky continued to believe Anthony Gooda's protestations that "we won't make you a fortune, but we won't lose you one, either." And not only Gooda. On October 31, 1988, Mocatta Dashwood Members Agents Limited sent one of its Names a list of the syndicates it would back in the coming year: Feltrim 540 and 847, Gooda Walker 290, and Devonshire 216 and 833. "It is certainly a very conservative portfolio," the accompanying letter said, "and, so far as can possibly be foreseen, can do you no harm at all." The loss on these five syndicates for 1989 averaged $1.2 million per Name.

In 1988, Anthony Gooda took a little more than $500,000 out of The Gooda Walker Group, counting salaries, bonuses, and dividends; in 1989, when the disaster was apparent and inescapable, he took almost $800,000—and his family took another $1.1 million. Derek Walker took about $500,000 in 1988 and about $1 million in 1989, and then another $600,000 in 1990—including a $150,000 bonus: Hurricane Hugo and Piper Alpha had already happened, and the syndicate's exposure to them was already known to be catastrophic, but the bonus, after all, was for the 1987 results, and the losses on the fall windstorm of that year had not yet been taken onto the books.

The Gooda Walker syndicates drew mostly from a middle-class community of newcomers to Lloyd's (there weren't many professionals willing to risk their fortunes with either Gooda or Walker). They were among the fastest growing at Lloyd's—most of them were six times as large at Armageddon in 1988–90 as they had been seven years before. The Gooda Walker Names had neither personal resources to meet the enormous cash calls that began as early as 1988 nor accumulated reserves from previous profitable years. As Fernanda Herford pointed out in her letter to Peter Middleton quoted in Chapter 3, a very high fraction of the losses on the Gooda Walker syndicates will not, because they cannot, be paid by the Names.

In the end, the Gooda Walker Names were excused from paying a large fraction of the losses. On October 4, 1994, Mr. Justice

Phillips handed down an opinion in *Deeny* v. *Gooda Walker*. Mr. Justice Phillips is a big man with bushy eyebrows and lots of big white teeth when he wants to smile; he dominates a courtroom. English judges, who sit in civil cases without juries, express themselves more than American judges. Mr. Justice Phillips, for example, had been confronted in this case with a German witness, the CEO of Munich Re. "Mr. von Eicken," the judge noted, "was not an ideal expert witness. He showed a keen appreciation of his own abilities and a contempt for any challenge to his views. This attitude was not justified, for in his report Mr. von Eicken had, in places, made sweeping statements of underwriting principle which could not be justified." Nevertheless, the judge noted—and you can hear his teeth grinding with regret as you read the decision—"Mr. von Eicken is qualified to express an opinion as to the principles that should be followed when writing excess of loss business."[21]

But the English witnesses were in many ways worse. One Gooda Walker underwriter admitted that he had accepted the top levels of reinsurance on Piper Alpha, at a tiny premium, because of his belief that it was "unthinkable" that a North Sea oil platform could self-destruct. Another said that he had taken reinsurance for a 1 percent premium, although "this tended to be in order to oblige brokers as he considered this rate too low. When asked why it was too low his answer was that it was half the rate that he had been writing in previous years."[22] The year after the Piper Alpha debacle, this same underwriter paid out so much of his premium income for reinsurance that his Names were guaranteed to lose money, whatever happened out in the great world. "The fact that Mr. Willard's 1989 Names were placed in a position where they were bound to make a loss resulted," the judge decided, "from a lack of competence in the conduct of the underwriting business."[23]

The judge was brutal in his ruling against both the Names' agents and the Gooda Walker underwriting agencies. "The fact that a Name who joins Lloyd's deliberately agrees to expose him-

self to unlimited liability," he wrote, "does not mean that he an-
ticipates or accepts that when he joins a syndicate the active underwriter will deliberately expose him to the risk of such
liability."[24] Counsel engaged by the E&O underwriters who would
have to put up the money (Gooda Walker itself having been liquidated) argued that the plaintiffs were asking to be recompensed
because their agents had shown bad judgment. The judge was having none of it: "The Plaintiff's case," he wrote, "is not that errors
of judgment were made, but that judgment was not exercised at all
in that the underwriters never acquired the data on which that
judgment might have been based."[25]

With some two thousand plaintiffs (all sole traders, you know)
and a finding of damages that totaled roughly $750 million,
Deeny v. *Gooda Walker* stands as the largest case ever tried in an
English court. And one of the most important.

•

When the first spate of losses was announced, in 1991 for the 1988
year, the serious damage was essentially confined to the LMX
syndicates. Both the syndicates and the Names that backed them
were by and large newcomers to Lloyd's. Prior to the 1983 rule
change permitting syndicates to spend much more of their premium income on reinsurance, there could not have been so much
demand for vertical reinsurance. Prior to the immense recruiting
drive for new Names that was recommended by Cromer in 1970
but not pushed forward until the early 1980s, there would not
have been enough stamp capacity in the market to write so much
reinsurance. Gooda Walker was by no means alone in going for
the gold by accepting the parcel in hopes that losses would never
climb to that level.

The Devonshire agency—successor to the carnage of Alexander Howden and the Grobfather—concentrated on XL, waxed fat,
and then failed. The Feltrim agency was successor to Peter
Cameron-Webb's enterprise, taking over its post-1983 business
after Lloyd's itself had assumed liability for everything earlier

through the Lioncover device. Its well-liked underwriter Patrick Fagan apparently pulled Feltrim 540 up and out of a deep hole by writing excess of loss policies on high levels in the expectation that total losses would never get there. But the truth is that Lloyd's had given Fagan a totally inadequate premium on what was in effect the reinsurance to close on the risks surviving from 1983 itself. Having underestimated PCW's surviving obligations by a factor approaching one hundred, Lloyd's seized for itself $36 million of the $42 million in real reserves Cameron-Webb had inadvertently left within the grasp of British authorities. Endowed by its masters with only $6 million to buy reinsurance, Feltrim was always one of the worst risks in the market. But Fagan was popular with members' agents. From 1987, when Feltrim was first established, to 1989, the number of Names grew from 985 to 1,672.[26] On total premiums of $150 million received by Feltrim 1988–90, the losses are now calculated at more than a billion dollars. About $50 million of that loss, ominously, is in reinsurance policies Feltrim did buy, which the auditors now believe will not pay Feltrim's claims.

Adam Raphael reported on a reinsurance conference in London in May 1988, at which the two most significant papers were presented by two of the people who would presently be attacked by the asbestosis monster: John Emney, who had moved on from Merrett to Charter Re after getting Bowring out of the shit, and Richard Outhwaite. Emney, Raphael reported, "rehearsed the possibility of a catastrophe exhausting the protection of participants in the LMX spiral because they had reinsured each other." Outhwaite's paper was entitled "The Catastrophe Time Bomb," and he supplied some numbers: "The maximum insured value of a platform on the North Sea is around $2 billion. At least 60 per cent of that is insured in London and, looking through the list of marine companies and Lloyd's, I made an estimate of what each would maintain his retention was, should this platform be a total loss. On the most generous basis this would not exceed $100 million. There is no dispute that if there was such a total loss the London market would pay $1.2 billion net. Where will the other $1,100 million come from? It will come from the LMX market. . . . If this is true, which it clearly is, why is this not recognized?"[27] Outhwaite testified as a defense witness in *Deeny* v. *Gooda Walker*, and Mr. Justice Phillips quoted his speech back at him in his opinion.

Actually, it was possible to make money on excess of loss reinsurance at Lloyd's during the years that the LMX spiral syndicates lost their Names' patrimony. The Walker report noted that "although 87 syndicates were writing significant LMX business in 1988 or 1989—in one case 93% of that syndicate's stamp capacity—95% of the losses attributed to those syndicates for the 1988 account were encountered on 12 of those syndicates and 79% of the losses of the LMX syndicates for the 1989 account were attributable to 14 of them."[28] G. S. Christensen and Others 958, for example, a small syndicate with more than half its business in XL, showed a minuscule (0.18 percent) loss in its 1989 year of account, and respectable profits (3.91 percent and 7.4 percent) in its 1990 and 1991 accounts, when the larger LMX syndicates went down the tubes.[29] C. F. Palmer 314, with a fifth of its business in XL, showed a profit every year.[30] M. H. Cockell 570, also about a fifth in XL, never had a losing year—indeed, before 1990, when profits dropped to 4 percent of premium income, it never had a year with less than 5 percent profits to the Names, after payment of all expenses. Perhaps significantly, this syndicate's capacity grew at less than the rate of inflation from 1984 through 1990.[31] D. P. Mann 435, with a third of its business in property XL, described its activity as reinsuring insurance companies "against large losses from hurricanes, tornados, earthquakes, conflagration, floods, riots and other catastrophes. In other words, against all manner of unpredictable misfortunes that may threaten their profitability and solvency." Most commentary on Lloyd's in the 1980s and early 1990s points out the extraordinary burst of losses on just those risks through this period—but D. P. Mann's Names saw a profit of more than 5 percent in every one of those years.[32]

In total, perhaps 4,000 of what were then 32,000 Names were

hard hit when the LMX spiral fell apart in 1988–89. Lloyd's reaction to the devastation was predictable: Bad luck, fellows, pay up. But this was a *systemic* destroyer: The managing agents of the bad syndicates had followed a course of business that was inevitably at some point going to produce enormous losses for their Names. When Richard Outhwaite told the reinsurance conference in early 1988 that "there is an almost universal ostrich-like unwillingness to face facts" in connection with the LMX spiral, he was saying that the Council of Lloyd's had failed to exercise the regulatory responsibilities it had requested and Parliament had given it in the Lloyd's Act of 1982.

Lloyd's could argue that the decision to reinsure asbestos insurers was a judgment call beyond the authority of its regulators to intervene. But permitting the underwriters of LMX to hazard the fortunes of their Names in this way—*without giving the Names any inkling of the perils involved*—was too irresponsible to go without punishment. The upshot was that Lloyd's had to deny in open court that it owed even a duty of good faith and honesty (let alone a duty of care) to the Names who had undertaken unlimited liability in a Rota interview before they were allowed to pay their initiation fees.

Lloyd's has paid heavily, and will pay further, for its failure to police the LMX spiral, the underwriters who operated it, and the Names' agents who placed their Names on the bad syndicates. Because so high a fraction of the Names in these syndicates were newcomers to the market, few had reserves that could be charged before there were cash calls to pay losses—and many lacked personal resources apart from their Lloyd's deposits and reserves. Losses on corporate general liability for disease and debility, like asbestosis, would land on Lloyd's drip by drip for years, and there may be time to play let's-pretend about them. But losses from hurricanes and earthquakes, oil spills and explosions, would come due soon after the "event." Because claims in the age of the computer moved much more rapidly through the reinsurance chain than would have been true in earlier years, the syndicates had to find a lot of money fast to pay what they owed. Many Names couldn't—and with the passage of time, increasing numbers of Names *wouldn't*—put up the cash. Where syndicates were continuing in business, this year's premiums could be used to pay off previous years' losses—but when syndicates went into run-off and their managing agents liquidated, the failure of the Names to pay might mean that the claims would not be paid.

Thus, maintaining with every breath that all the Names at Lloyd's were sole traders, each for his own part and not for any other, the council in order to pay what were not only valid but also well-publicized claims would have to take steps to "mutualize" the losses. It was because cash might be needed quickly that Lloyd's in 1992 imposed a 6 percent tax on *all* premium income to beef up the Central Fund that pays claims when Names fail to pay their cash calls. Some syndicates got into very bad habits. In June 1993, C. H. Bohling 833/834, part of Devonshire, had a $36 million overdraft with the Lloyd's American Trust Fund at Citibank, plus loans of about $22 million from other syndicates managed by the same managing agent. These were remarkable numbers for a syndicate that never had more than $35 million or so of stamp capacity in any year. On the larger scene, to which we shall return in Chapter 10, what they mean is that Lloyd's American Trust Fund had as $36 million of its assets a promise to pay from a busted Lloyd's syndicate.[33]

As the lawsuit by the Gooda Walker Action Group came to trial in spring 1994, there was reason to believe Lloyd's was hoping the Names would win it. If the Names lost, Lloyd's would have to find at least a billion dollars to pay claims that lay on Gooda Walker Names who had nothing like enough money to pay such bills. If the Names won, however, the award to them would trigger contributions by the external errors and omissions insurers who had sold policies to Gooda Walker in the 1980s and perhaps by the accountants who had certified Gooda Walker's annual statements. Much of the E&O insurance had been placed at Lloyd's itself, which presumably was not helpful—except that these other syndicates had more Names with the resources to pay, which would spread the Gooda Walker losses more evenly around the market, and delay the moment of truth for Lloyd's as an institution. When the Gooda Walker Names *did* win, the first concern at Lloyd's was that somehow the payments to the plaintiffs should be given to Lloyd's itself, not to the winners of the case.

•

There was another form of reinsurance in the Lloyd's market, which probably imposed the most horrific losses of all. This was "personal stop-loss" (PSL) insurance, by which Names could in effect reinsure their own exposure, over a certain deductible and under a certain cap. Derek Walker was of course one of the relative handful of underwriters who took on large amounts of this business (most of the others wrote only a few such policies for their friends, who often enough wrote similar policies for them—the argument that Lloyd's insiders lose money just like the external Names fails to consider the extent to which insiders protected one another at the expense of one another's Names). With Robin Kingsley, the tennis-playing Name's agent who recruited athletes and Canadians, a nice, ruddy fellow who when I saw him was enjoying the last days of his residence in the lovely house in Richmond that Lloyd's was about to take away from him, Walker developed a theory that stop-loss insurance gave the Names who backed it a splendidly diversified portfolio of risks, because they were insuring Names on a diverse collection of syndicates. In fact, of course, they were inevitably victims of adverse selection, because the Names most likely to seek out stop-loss insurance were those who knew they were in risk-seeking syndicates.

These are little syndicates. Gooda Walker 387 had an annual stamp capacity of about $10 million at its height, but its 1989 year had lost almost $100 million by the end of 1993, and would probably wind up losing several times that amount. Among the Names on Gooda Walker 387 is former Lloyd's chairman Peter Miller, who told the Outhwaite 317 claimants that they shouldn't sue because Lloyd's would take care of everything. Mackinnon 134, the other specialist in PSL policies, never took in more than $1.5 million in premiums in a single year. From the point of view of the Name who accepted $15,000 or 1 percent of it, however, the losses are even more terrible, and the views of the underwriters are even more unprintable, than those to be found in larger syndicates. On 134, for example, the accumulated losses on the 1983 year, which has never closed (infected by Posgate's syndicates—the same names come around all the time), are already over $170,000 for each $15,000 accepted, with more to come.

Syndicate 134, moreover, had its own little spiral. Chatset explained: "Syndicate 184 commenced in 1977 when the Sasse Syndicate died. In 1979 application was made and granted to start a parallel Syndicate 134 in order that one Syndicate could write the other's stop-loss. In other words if a Name on 184 wanted to purchase stop-loss it was written by 134 and vice versa. This was supposed to spread the risk, but in practice it has created a spiral of its own between the two Syndicates. The reason for this is that once each Syndicate has exhausted its own reinsurance when a Name with a stop-loss policy written by the other makes a claim, the cost of that has nowhere to go but to the Names of that Syndicate. If those Names have stop-loss themselves it is immediately passed back to the Syndicate from which it came. Thus it can be assumed that the majority of policies written by the two Syndicates will be total losses."[34] Huge amounts of money are involved here. The 583 stop-loss policies Mackinnon 134 wrote for Names on Merrett 418 for 1985 may well incur losses of $200 million—and the same syndicate wrote another five hundred policies for Names on seven other syndicates still open from 1985, which may together impose losses almost as large.

Robin Kingsley's Lime Street members' agency was by far the largest source of Names to Gooda Walker 387, and a major supplier to Feltrim 540. Because Tony Gooda discouraged his Names from purchasing stop-loss insurance, the keep-it-in-the-family self-insuring between Gooda 387 and the other Gooda syndicates is pretty much restricted to the Kingsley Names, and Mackinnon 134 seems to have been unwilling, for a wonder, to write stop-loss for Gooda Walker Names. Still, it does seem likely that some scores of Feltrim Names will expect reimbursement for some part of their losses from themselves as Names on Gooda Walker 387. It is hard to think of any more convincing demonstration of the negligence of Lloyd's as a regulator than the fact that it permitted a situation to develop where Names were paying brokerage commissions and expenses in connection with stop-loss policies that involved their reinsuring themselves.

A wide variety of other syndicates, several dozen in all, wrote significant amounts of stop-loss business, and with most of the market now in a condition where the Names show losses on their membership, these policies are being called. Like the asbestos policies in the real world, PSL policies (and their twin, "estate protection" policies, which pay off the losses of deceased Names so their estates can be settled) remain in effect as long as the syndicates on which the Name has losses are open. The syndicates that wrote them and their successors who have accepted a reinsurance to close remain at risk forever. Chatset throws up its hands when asked to estimate the dimensions of the loss that can result from such policies, and the IBNR category is presented as zero or infinite, according to taste. Some of the money paid out on PSL will be refunded if the Names win their lawsuits, but the same syndicates that wrote stop-loss also wrote errors and omissions, and the money to repay the losses on the PSL policies will simply reappear as losses on the E&O policies.

In the end the specialist stop-loss syndicates simply will not be able to pay the claims. Regardless of cash calls, threats, writs, judgments, the Names on these syndicates simply don't have that kind of money. The great irony may be that the first policies on which Lloyd's may fail to pay "valid claims" are the stop-loss policies written to protect its own Names.

CHAPTER 8

THE COLONIES
TO THE RESCUE

Readers of American newspapers found Lloyd's of London on their front pages in summer 1994, when it was revealed that Stephen G. Breyer, President Clinton's nominee to replace Justice Harry Blackmun on the Supreme Court, was a Name at Lloyd's—and couldn't get out. The White House released an analysis of the situation by University of Pennsylvania law professor Geoffrey Hazard, who claimed "a close analogy between the kind of investment as a Name and an investment in a mutual fund."[1] This was a truly peculiar analysis, though it is of course correct that the Name at Lloyd's has no more control over the risks an underwriter insures than the owner of a share in a mutual fund has over the stocks or bonds the manager of the fund decides to buy. (In fact, it's worse: The purchaser of a share in a mutual fund at least knows the securities the fund owns, but the member of the Lloyd's syndicate that went down never knew the risks the underwriter had undertaken with his guarantee.) But the mutual fund purchaser is in no way a "sole trader"—not to mention the fact that the Lloyd's Name hazards not just the purchase price of a share but everything he owns.

Breyer was one of the earlier American members of Lloyd's. Married to an Englishwoman whose family controls Pearson's, publishers of *The Financial Times* and *The Economist,* among others, he had joined in 1977, while still a professor at Harvard Law School. Among the syndicates his wife backed was Merrett 418, which did well for her. At some point in the early 1980s, Mrs. Breyer dropped out of Lloyd's, but Breyer, by then the chief judge of the U.S. Court of Appeals for the First Circuit, maintained his membership, resigning only in 1988 (effective January 1, 1989). He made a lot less money as a judge than he had at Harvard, where the professors do very well as consultants to law firms, and he must have looked forward to the supplementary income he received from Lloyd's.

Some years he did well, some not. When his wife resigned, he wanted to pick up her Merrett 418 participation, but he couldn't. Donald Mott of Roderick Pratt Underwriting Agencies, then his Name's agent, wrote him in 1982 "that it could be counter-productive for Timothy to raise the question of a share for you with Stephen Merrett. I think it would be better to hold this in abeyance for the time being."[2] Then, in summer 1984, like 1,204 other Names who wanted to be inducted to the fellowship of Merrett 418 in 1985, Breyer got lucky: The Pratt agency had found him a 0.01799 percent share of the syndicate, which meant he would be accepting about $37,500 of premiums.

It seems fair to say that he paid attention to the numbers but not to the realities of what was happening at Lloyd's. In his testimony to the Senate and in his questionnaire responses to the lawyers handling the Merrett 418 Names' case against the underwriters and agents and accountants, Judge Breyer said that it was 1986 before he learned about the pollution and asbestos risks his syndicates were running. But his papers, submitted to the White House and then to the press, contained Stephen Merrett's letter to his Names in spring 1985, noting that "in common with many syndicates in the Lloyd's market, Syndicate 417 had been badly affected by the significant number of claims advices in respect of pollution and seepage and also asbestos-related items." Syndicate 417 had by then been paired with syndicate 418, so that the losses on one were automatically shared by the other.

One of the syndicates Judge Breyer was on in 1988 was Janson Green 932, which had to be left open the next year because of un-measurable asbestos, pollution, and directors and officers insurance. Another that Judge Breyer supported in 1986 (Sturge 498) was later described by Chatset as writing "a predominantly US liability account. . . . " The 1986 account still included coverage for officers and directors of S&Ls. But the judge got out before Sturge 498 fell apart, and the senators who questioned him, perhaps not being au courant with the actual risks undertaken by different Lloyd's syndicates, didn't ask him about it at his confirmation hearing.

The rundown of Judge Breyer's syndicates for 1987, sent to him in summer 1990 by his Name's agent, showed that about half of them had "long-tail" liabilities involving asbestos or pollution. By 1990, it was more or less moot because he had resigned, but, of course, it takes three years before a Name's potential liabilities are known even on syndicates that will close, let alone the two that as of summer 1990 had gone into run-off. Not to worry, of course, as Lloyd's told the story: Sedgwick noted that on Merrett 418, "the 1987 account produced a reasonable profit but this was not enough to cover the 25% cash call for Names involved on the 1985 Year of Account. Due to the remaining unsettled run-off disputes the 1985 account will remain open for another 12 months. However, we anticipate that the year will be closed at the end of this year. . . . "[3] But Judge Breyer told the lawyers for the Merrett Names' action group in 1992 that he "did not know there were 11 run-off policies (or the *specific* nature of the problem) until I heard from you."[4]

On the other hand, there is evidence that Judge Breyer really kept up with the profit-and-loss figures from his involvement with Lloyd's. Like some Names who did business with Lloyd's, he had moments of intense confusion because the numbers supplied to him did not add up. This experience becomes quite devastating when one document shows a resigned member that she still has some thousands of pounds in her letter of credit to Lloyd's while another informs her that money has been taken from the Central Fund to pay her losses, and she must immediately send a check for some thousands of pounds, plus interest.

In 1988, Judge Breyer wrote to his Name's agent asking a question that "grows out of my belief that 'capital appreciation' refers to the earnings that the syndicate makes by investing premiums. If so, I should think that, unless interest rates fall dramatically, the more premiums, the higher the investment earnings. Yet, in 1983 when my allocated premiums were £175,000, the capital appreciation was £10,000; in 1984 when my allocated premiums were £225,000, my capital appreciation was £9,000; but in 1985 when my allocated premiums were £250,000, my capital appreciation dropped to £4,700. Why, when I have approximately 65 percent more premiums invested in my name than in 1983, does that investment earn in total nearly 60 percent less?"[5]

Shortly thereafter, Judge Breyer transferred his representation to Sedgwick, where at least his statements made sense to him, with one column for the "underwriting results" for each syndicate (i.e., the premiums accepted minus the claims paid), another for "gross capital gain" (on the appreciation of the investments into which the premiums had been put), another for "gross investment income" (the interest on those investments). Alas, the results for the 1988 account were discouraging. His closed years showed an apparent profit from the syndicates of about $15,000 on premiums of about $500,000—and that $15,000 would, incidentally, be the number Lloyd's would report as his results as a Name. But then he had managing agent fees of $4,600 to deduct, and managing agent profit commissions of $2,300, a $2,200 contribution to the Central Fund, $4,000 "subscription" for the Lloyd's membership, $2,800 for Sedgwick's fee, $1,500 for the leftovers on the "winding-up fee" since Judge Breyer had resigned, plus $550 of profit commission for Sedgwick itself, leaving a net loss on the

Sedgwick account itself of about $3,000. Then there were two syndicates that hadn't closed, in which Judge Breyer's position was still being managed by the Oxford agency, and they showed a loss of about $24,000, leaving the judge $27,000 out of pocket for the 1988 year of account, considerably more than he'd ever made in any year as a Name, with worse to come.

Meanwhile, Sedgwick had put the judge's account through the Lloyd's solvency test, and reported those results to him, too, in an entirely different format. The "Members' Agent Report" on the solvency test ended with a pimpling of footnotes, and a final, rather discouraging "GENERAL" comment: "The Lloyd's Solvency Test is complex and not easy to explain. We hope that these notes are helpful, but if Names have any questions, they may put them in writing to T. R. Riddle at this Agency."[6] Shortly after receiving his solvency report, which said he was healthy, Judge Breyer asked Sedgwick to find him an unlimited run-off policy that would get him out of Lloyd's forever, and the answer came back from Seascope Special Risks, Limited, on September 17, 1990: $200,000, open until October 1. It looked like a lot of money to Judge Breyer, and he took the risk that the result might be even worse.

By late 1993, he was fully conscious of the handicaps his Lloyd's membership placed on his performance as a judge. As Professor Hazard put it at the end of his otherwise very supportive letter to the White House when the Senate Judiciary Committee was considering the Breyer nomination, "It could be regarded as imprudent for a judge to invest as a Lloyd's Name. . . . The business of insurance is complex, sometimes controversial, and widely the subject of public concern and suspicion. The insurance industry is highly regulated and insurance company liability often entails issues of public importance." All Judge Breyer's Sedgwick accounts were now closed, but Merrett 418, left over from his representation by Pratt (which had been sold to Oxford which had been sold to Sturge), still hung around Judge Breyer's neck as it does around mine. He wrote his agent at Sturge, "What are the prospects for my leaving Lloyd's. I resigned in 1987 [actually in 1988]. My reasons were related to my job, and the case disqualifications that membership required, not to any Lloyd's losses (for there, then, seemed to be none). Yet, apparently I am 'captured' for the rest of my life—and that, despite the small likelihood that losses will exceed my stop loss. Is anyone proposing to do anything about this kind of problem?"[7]

James K. Glassman of *The Washington Post* commented: "It's like the Cosa Nostra. *They* decide who leaves."[8] In November 1994, Lloyd's decided that Justice Breyer would indeed be permitted to leave. For a premium of about $110,000, a Lloyd's syndicate agreed to take all his losses beyond his existing stop-loss policy—and Lloyd's itself, in an extraordinary act of what Hiscox might call grace and favor, gave the Supreme Court justice a letter saying that if by any strange chance his reinsurer should go broke, the Lloyd's Central Fund would pick up any unpaid claims on his policies. His membership in Lloyd's was terminated, and his surviving deposit was returned (he had a surviving deposit, for he was liable under his stop-loss policy for only the first $40,000 of what Merrett had cost him).

•

Professor Breyer, when he joined Lloyd's, was arguably a sophisticated investor, experienced in the stock market, a professor of mostly commercial law at Harvard. Though the law that forbids both rich and poor to sleep under the bridges also protects both the rocket scientist and the schoolchild from the predations of the stock swindler, it's reasonable to say that the likes of Professor, later Judge, Breyer can be left to make their own decisions on what is a "suitable" investment for them. Therefore the Securities and Exchange Commission (SEC) has an exemption from the disclosure requirements of American financial law, permitting the sale of unregistered securities to "sophisticated investors" who have some preexisting and "substantive" relationship with the issuer. The exemption (under the commission's "Regulation D") has always been easier to win if the security in question is not marketable, so there is no danger that the sophisticated and informed investor who is the original purchaser can unload it onto the public market.

In 1970, Lord Cromer reported to the committee that then ran Lloyd's that their market faced a danger of insufficient capacity. Up to then, only male British subjects had been eligible to become Names at Lloyd's. Responding to Cromer's concerns, the committee voted to permit female membership at Lloyd's (which automatically meant also that women were permitted to work in the Room, previously, like the New York Stock Exchange until the late 1960s, a male preserve), to require lower standards of income and wealth before people could qualify as Names, and to accept foreigners. Alan Smallbone remembers that he was opposed, on the grounds that Americans lacked the sense of noblesse oblige, and if they began to lose money, they would sue in circumstances when the English would grit their teeth and pay up. It would obviously be harder to collect from people far away. But in those early years the recruitment of foreigners to Lloyd's focused on people who already had some reason to know about Lloyd's—insurance agents, employees of Citibank who were involved with the trust fund, spouses of Englishmen or -women, government people who had worked in or with England.

Lloyd's did not consider a Name's contract with his Name's agent to be a security, and still does not—though the "value at Lloyd's" proposal giving Names a preemptive right to continue on a syndicate and to sell that right will make membership at Lloyd's very much like a security under any definition. (Objecting to proposals within the SEC to require the registration of Lloyd's contracts in 1988, Lloyd's lawyers cited as the most important bar to considering them securities the fact that "Underwriting Agency Agreements . . . are in no way transferable or tradeable.")[9] Despite Lloyd's objections, however, the SEC does define the word "security" so broadly that it could cover Lloyd's contracts.

The SEC developed an interest in Lloyd's early in 1987, perhaps because of a complaint by a Name involved in one of the emerging scandal cases in London. If so, this would be an annoyance to Lloyd's, then gearing up for a major increase in the number and underwriting capacity of American Names, perhaps as part of a generalized expansion drive, perhaps because it was becoming essential to find new Names on whom old losses could be loaded. On April 24, Douglas Hawes and Sheila Marshall from Lloyd's leading American law firm—LeBoeuf, Lamb, Leiby and MacRae of New York and ten other cities—met in Washington with William Morley and Linda Quinn of the SEC's Division of Corporate Finance.

The fifteen-page letter LeBoeuf sent five months later maintained the argument that a Lloyd's contract is not a security, but suggests that with 2,700 "U.S. persons" already members of Lloyd's and another 2,300 anticipated in the next few years (this was not to happen, of course), there might be "a more formalistic compliance with the requirements of Regulation D."[10] Moreover, the law firm asked the SEC to decide that if there was a security involved, it was the Name's contract with his members' agent, not the subsequent acceptance of premium income from the syndicate and the managing agent who ran it, and certainly not the Name's acceptance as a member of Lloyd's: "The activities of the Corporation are best characterized as ministerial in nature: it provides the premises, administrative staff and support services to enable Members to conduct the business of insurance. . . ."[11]

So Lloyd's would instruct all Names' agents recruiting in America to make sure they obeyed Reg D, offering membership only to "Accredited Investors" in the context of an "offering memorandum" submitted to the SEC with the letter. "As a matter of internal control," LeBoeuf, Lamb wrote, "Lloyd's intends to permit the solicitation of U.S. persons only by those Members' Agents that have satisfied Lloyd's that they are prepared to follow the procedures worked out by this firm on behalf of Lloyd's and the SEC."[12]

The rules for Reg D meant that nobody could be offered a

membership in Lloyd's who had less than $200,000 a year in annual income, or less than $1 million in net worth, either in his own name or that of a spouse or parent or child residing at the same address. Lloyd's spokesmen have claimed that this net worth had to be exclusive of the Name's residence, but the "Applicant Questionnaire and Certificate" submitted with the LeBoeuf letter noted that " 'net worth' means total assets at fair market value, including home and property, less total liabilities." Still, the memorandum was fair enough in its description of what was going to happen to the Name if he was placed among the elect. "The Agency Agreement," it proclaimed, "grants the members' agent the sole control and management of the underwriting business of the Name and prohibits the Name from interfering with the exercise of such control and management."

Among the powers granted were "to borrow money from any source for the purpose of paying any liabilities, expenses or other obligations of the Name, if such payments are necessary for reasons arising in connection with such Name's underwriting business." In other words, the Name is not only on the hook if his agent wishes to draw down his reserves from the premium trust fund at Lloyd's, but must also repay (with interest) whatever loan the agent may arrange on his credit. And the agent may "delegate to other persons any of the powers granted to the Members' Agent by the Agency Agreement."[13] In this agreement, as none of us seems to have noticed, the agent does not agree to give his Name so much as the time of day, let alone efforts to advance the Name's interests and save him from harm. The obligations, as we were to learn, run one way.

The SEC apparently was not entirely convinced by the LeBoeuf argument, and another meeting was held in December 1987. Reg D, the commission pointed out, was designed to cover only a "limited" not a "general" offering of securities. Not to worry, said LeBoeuf: "Each person recommended to a Members' Agent is known to a current Member of Lloyd's."[14] Still, there were questions. How many candidates did Lloyd's turn down? LeBoeuf said that 30 percent of those who make initial contact with a members' agent do not pursue the matter, 30 percent of those who do pursue it never fill out the actual application forms, and 20 percent of those who do fill out the forms are rejected.[15] In a later letter, responding apparently to a doubting Thomas at the agency, LeBoeuf said that, well, in reality, very few of those who follow through on the application are turned down, but that was because the people at Lloyd's were such gentlemen, and made sure that no application that would be turned down ever got to that stage.

The SEC wanted to know about the money Names' agents paid to recruiters. "In the past," LeBoeuf replied, "in limited situations, certain persons may have been compensated small amounts of money for the introduction of persons to become Members of Lloyd's. These practices are not consistent with the normal and traditional manner of recruiting persons for Membership at Lloyd's. Lloyd's is prepared to adopt a formal rule which would prohibit the payment of sums of money to any third party for the introduction of Members."[16] But in fact the payment of commission for the recruitment of Names was a common practice.

In 1977, Charles E. Parnell, whose company was chaired by David Coleridge—also chairman of Sturge (the largest agency at Lloyd's) and a member of the Lloyd's Committee—offered a deal to the San Francisco office of E. F. Hutton. If Hutton could find Parnell ten American Names with an average of $300,000 of premium income limit each, Parnell would pay Hutton 20 percent of its annual underwriting salary attributable to these Names, plus 25 percent of the profit commission earned on their underwritings. These payments were to continue for as long as the Hutton clients remained Names. "No one in your office," the letter making the offer added cheerily, "will be required to spend any of their valuable time explaining the advantages or whatever in joining Lloyd's. We will undertake to do all this work and you will be required only to introduce us to prospective interested persons."

On March 23, 1981, in a letter marked "Strictly Confidential," Parnell listed twelve Names recruited by Hutton, and began paying quarterly installments of about $1,800 as Hutton's share of the underwriting salaries. In August 1984, when the first profit commissions came due, a letter from Sturge to Hutton announced that "on behalf of Charles Parnell Underwriting Agencies Limited, we enclose a cheque for £10,148.77 being the first payment of Introductory Commission due to your company, as agreed." This acceptance of commissions from an issuer should be disclosed to the customer under the Securities Exchange Act. It may also be a violation of state securities laws: On November 17, 1994, the Ohio state securities commissioner found that Sturge and two of its agents had violated two provisions of Ohio law when recruiting Names for Lloyd's, and ordered them to cease and desist.[17]

American law professor Andrew Grossman reported that he had a letter dated June 1991 from then SEC general counsel John Doty confirming that the commission had launched an "informal investigation" into Lloyd's recruitment of U.S. Names. If the SEC were to take an interest in their plight, some American Names might be able to claim as a defense against Lloyd's actions to seize their assets that their contracts with their Names' agents were void from the beginning because they were not in fact "accredited investors" and should not have been sold securities that could legally have been offered only to "accredited investors."

On March 28, 1995, SEC general counsel Simon M. Lorne wrote to the counsel for the American Names Association that "as a general matter, the Commission does not exempt individual entities or enterprises from the registration requirements to the Securities Act, and has not done so in the case of Lloyd's"—and also that "The application of the definition of accredited investor under Regulation D was not an issue in these discussions with Lloyd's, and neither the Commission nor the staff determined or opined that the Lloyd's Means Test meets the requirements of Regulation D."

There can be no doubt that the LeBoeuf, Lamb lawyers thought they were discussing the applicability of Reg D, and on February 10, 1992, SEC chairman Richard Breeden wrote to Representative

John D. Dingel that "The staff also concluded at that time, based on the representations of Lloyd's counsel, that an exemption from U.S. registration requirements would be available. Lloyd's counsel stated that Lloyd's would comply with Rule 506 of the Commission's Regulation D, which exempts offers and sales of securities made primarily to sophisticated or 'accredited' investors."

Another American investigation of Lloyd's was launched in 1991 by the Senate Permanent Subcommittee on Investigations then chaired by Senator Sam Nunn. Members of the committee staff went to London and interviewed various players in the game—then returned home, and could not talk about what they had learned until they completed the investigation, although the British scandal sheet *Private Eye* claimed that Prime Minister John Major asked President George Bush to intervene to stop these investigations when he visited Washington in early 1992. Sources in the committee, however, say that there was no political pressure, that Senator Nunn's interest was solely in how well protected American policy holders were, and that when the Blue Cross/Blue Shield scandal broke, they needed to turn their attention to that.

At best, the Lloyd's contract as amended in 1986 (and all ongoing American Names had to sign the amended contract) effectively deprived American Names of the protection of American law. Disputes under the contract would be "subject to arbitration in London, England in accordance with the statutory provisions for arbitration then in effect in England by a sole arbitrator appointed by the individual occupying the office of the Chairman or a Deputy Chairman of Lloyd's." Other disputes would be "generally subject to resolution under English procedural and substantive law governing judicial proceedings."[18] Dale Schreiber of the New York firm of Proskauer Rose, who sued Lloyd's syndicates for the largest group of bitter American Names,[19] said the English system is "stacked against the Names—in business matters it's very formal." (In fact, the Names have done well in the English courts once the action groups broke Lloyd's procedural logjam.)

Schreiber's case was dismissed on motion in the district court in New York, on the argument that the syndicates could not be sued because they had no juridical existence—they were a gathering of the Names themselves. On appeal, the circuit court affirmed the dismissal, on the argument that the Names had voluntarily signed a contract under which disputes were to be settled in England according to English law. The Supreme Court refused to hear the case, and it's dead. If Schreiber had been able to procure a letter like Lorne's, however, the outcome might have been different.

Every decided case brought by an American against Lloyd's or participants in Lloyd's has failed one way or another—except *Leslie* v. *Lloyd's* in federal court in Houston, where Magistrate Frances H. Stacey rejected Lloyd's motion to dismiss. Charles Robert Leslie was one of the earlier Lloyd's Names; he signed up in 1976 and became a member in 1977. His Name's agent was Sturge, and among the syndicates onto which Sturge had placed him was Outhwaite 317, which through its Fireman's Fund deal had accepted ruinous asbestosis losses under general liability contracts originally written by Sturge. Leslie's original contract did not include a choice-of-law or choice-of-forum provision, which was not added to any of Lloyd's contracts until 1982 at the earliest, and in Leslie's case, not until 1986, when he was asked to sign a new contract—four years after Sturge had unloaded its asbestos liabilities onto Outhwaite.

Magistrate Stacey was not impressed with the new clause. This, she wrote in 1991, "is a case where defendants have come to Texas, and will in all likelihood continue to do so, to solicit local investors to participate in foreign commercial operations. It would be unreasonable to allow such defendants to avoid local laws requiring accurate and complete representation of their product, as all others who sell investments locally are required to do, by simply including forum-selection clauses in form contracts."[20]

The "most significant relationship" test of which law should apply led not to London, as Lloyd's argued, but to the home hearth, because the claims "concern solicitation of a Texas plaintiff, in

Texas, by and for the benefit of defendants. . . . Texas has a direct interest in protecting its citizens against this type of alleged wrongdoing, whether perpetrated by fellow citizens or by foreigners. . . . We can conceive of no similar interest that England might have in this matter." And the information alleged by Leslie, if true, constituted common-law fraud. The district court affirmed the magistrate's ruling without opinion in September 1991. Lloyd's announced an intention to request reconsideration, but never did anything about it. In 1994, Leslie briefly won an injunction against the drawdown of his letter of credit at Lloyd's, but the judge decided not to make the injunction permanent, on the grounds that Lloyd's remained solvent and could make Leslie whole if his litany of factual charges (repeated in the decision) could be proved in a Texas court. Leslie's case against Lloyd's was then scheduled for trial in 1995.

An editorial in Lloyd's publication *One Lime Street* cried foul: "In Houston, Texas, a District Court judge seemingly accepts as fact submissions alleging fraud by Lloyd's—although at no time was Lloyd's invited to make its own submissions to the court, to present evidence on its own behalf or to cross-examine those making the submissions. Hardly fair."[21] But, of course, Lloyd's, in this as in all other cases, has sought to proceed by winning procedural motions, not by presenting evidence or questioning the evidence of its antagonists.

One major case, still in the complaint stage, sues an American rather than an English defendant—Alexander and Alexander, for its administration of the affairs of Alexander Howden and its failure to defend the interests of the Names whose agency relationship it acquired with that purchase. On July 17, 1987, at the heyday of the emerging spiral crisis and the asbestosis menace, John Bogardus, chairman of A&A, addressed a meeting of the American Names represented by Alexander Howden and Beck, which had become a wholly owned subsidiary of his company. "I, for one," he said, "am convinced that Lloyd's is totally attentive to the needs of Names. . . . Can Lloyd's serve both Names and policyholders without conflict of interest? Yes, it can. The number of working members of Lloyd's who are also Names should give you comfort on that score. Having spent last weekend with an external Member of Lloyd's Council, and a Name, I am even more impressed as to the attention that Names' interests are receiving. . . . We are committed to providing each of you with the highest quality, efficient service and sound guidance."[22]

Meanwhile, AH&B was putting its Names into the very worst of the spiral syndicates—Gooda Walker, Feltrim, Devonshire—in the year preceding December 1988, when the agency was sold. The sales price was, of course, determined in large part by the number of Names AH&B could deliver to its purchaser—which was, incidentally, London Wall, the agency that was just then beginning to take care of Andrew Wade, whose fate was described in Chapter 3.

Among Alexander and Alexander alumni was Carlos Miro, one of its most successful brokers in the 1970s, a con man who later went to prison for frauds associated with Transit Casualty of Los Angeles and Anglo-American of London, whose connections with Lloyd's went back to 1979. "My first noteworthy recollection of this London market initiation," he told the Subcommittee on Oversight and Investigations of the House Commerce and Energy Committee, "was how expert Lloyd's brokers were at churning the same dollar of premium and 'raking off' a commission as the 'retail' or direct broker, then again by reinsuring the policy-issuing insurance company, and yet again by arranging the reinsurer's own reinsurance premium. . . . " Asked if he thought the Lloyd's brokers "were essentially conning the underwriters," Miro said, "They would refer to it as clever broking, but yes, in a word, yes."

Miro became a Name in 1983, when he was already in trouble with American insurance commissioners, and in his ventures after that date identified himself to his victims as "an underwriting member of Lloyd's," which was true enough. At his interview, he recalled, he asked his questioner "how do you confirm whether somebody does have these means or not? He was taken aback and answered, "Well, we presume you're a gentleman or we wouldn't have asked you to join." Asked by the committee whether Lloyd's had ever checked up on him subsequently, Miro replied, "Oh, no, not at all . . . the primary concern was assuring a letter of credit was posted and renewed." In 1990, after the public exposure of his fraudulent activities in insurance markets, his Name's agent told Mr. Miro it would be "prudent" for him to resign, which he did, saving himself a good deal of money. Nevertheless, he said, he lost $60,000 at Lloyd's, over and above his stop-loss policy.[23]

●

Richard Rosenblatt is the founder and now elected president of the American Names Association (ANA). He began it with two impromptu meetings of curious Names at the ALM conference in Boston in June 1993. About thirty of us attracted by a hand-painted sign listened to Jackie Levin and Donald Kerr describe the Canadian Names Association. Dick is a former Marine aviator and public relations executive who comes from a family of artists and who designed for himself one of the most beautiful houses I know. He doesn't look like a Marine poster today, but he has accomplished his mission of uniting American Names in less than twelve months. The years have added pounds and subtracted hair; added a fringe of red circles, a partially bald pate. But the fighting spirit is certainly undiminished. He is indefatigable; he and his devoted wife Lois (also a Name) work eighteen hours a day. The letters from Sturge to Hutton, noted above, came to light as a result of his work. He talks incessantly to all callers and is worth hearing at any length. I was glad to accept his invitation to telephone collect. His obvious sincerity and genuine outrage make his speeches effective, despite their rambling style.

Membership in the American Names Association costs $1,500. Rosenblatt runs his organization very democratically. Openness allows everyone to voice his opinion and results in a loyal following. He's liked as well as respected. A couple of men whose motives I thought were highly suspect exploited the easy access of ANA, but they quickly lost influence and left the scene.

Rosenblatt was one of the earliest American Names, having joined in 1971. He was stimulated to his actions first by his own losses, of course, and then by the example of the Canadian Names, sixty-seven of whom had started their own association in 1991, and hired the Canadian lawyer Alan Lenczner to prepare a defense for them that might enable them to keep their homes from the predations of Lloyd's. It was Lenczner who developed the fraud defense on which Rosenblatt's ANA rested its hopes in the beginning. During the last year, groups from ANA have initiated complaints before federal courts and federal and state regulatory agencies.

"It is our belief," Rosenblatt wrote in the second number of his newsletter, in October 1993, "that we were defrauded at the moment we entered Lloyd's. When we walked into the rota committee they did not say 'Do you understand that you have unlimited liability, and that there are unquantifiable asbestosis and pollution losses which we are concealing, and there are good syndicates on which U.S. Names cannot invest, and members agents who will not handle American Names, and no disclosure, and no duty of care, and limited E&O, and the possibility of open years where you cannot ever get out, and no regulation in spite of a Regulation Department, and no limit on the salaries, commissions and expenses which can be charged against your account, and the possibility of increasing levies for the central fund, the obligation to live with any bylaws created in the future, and the immunity of Lloyd's by Act of Parliament, and the inability to sue Lloyd's in the United States, and the non-applicability of almost any U.S. laws which prevent outrageous behavior.' "[24]

A Name has a contract with his Name's or Member's agent, who has an agreement with the managing agencies where he places his Names on syndicates each year. Managing Agents report results of Names' accounts on syndicates under their control to the relevant Names' agents, who in turn notify their Names of a cash call, generally in late spring. This statement gives the amount due to be paid to the Name's agent within a few weeks in order to avoid interest payments above English bank rates.

The bill can be paid in three ways. The Name of course can use assets unrelated to his Lloyd's affairs. He can use monies in his Special and Personal Reserves if they are adequate. If he ignores the request, his Name's agent applies to the Central Fund of the Society, which is then drawn down and payment sent to cover the deficiency. The Central Fund is earmarked for the payment, plus interest in the member's name. Next the Corporation of Lloyd's invokes powers under the Name's letter of credit or bank guarantee to collect from the bank and repays the Central Fund. Immediately thereafter the bank withdraws whatever it has transferred to the Corporation of Lloyd's from the Name's collateral deposit for this letter of credit. If real estate forms the collateral behind a guarantee, the bank pays Lloyd's and informs the Name what he must pay the bank or face foreclosure on his property. A reduced deposit that supports a letter of credit must be replenished to its original amount or underwriting will be reduced or terminated the following year.

Most Names' agents require their Names to build a special reserve from part of their profits. These reserve accounts earn interest, tax benefits, and are readily available to pay cash calls, an advantage to everyone. Personal Reserves, under the same terms as Special Reserves, are especially helpful to Names who wish to accumulate wealth in England while living in countries with currency restrictions.

One of the reasons the first Lloyd's losses did not generate an immense outcry is that many of the losers were losing money they had considered part of their assets, but supposed to be available in case of losses to protect other assets. Once these reserves are gone the Name begins to feel the pressure.

Lenczner, studying the situation for the Canadian Names, found it vulnerable. A fairly recent Canadian case—*Angelica Whitewear* v. *Bank of Nova Scotia* in 1987—had held that if there had been fraud in the initial transaction, and the banks had been notified of the fraud by the person on whose behalf the letter of credit had been issued, banks were obliged to refuse the demand for payment by the beneficiary of the letter of credit. Starting in 1992, the Canadian Names began notifying their banks that they should refuse to pay Lloyd's on the bank guarantees, because the initial transaction had been fraudulent.

Four Canadian banks did refuse to pay Lloyd's, which took them to court in London, where the judge ruled that the Canadian precedent was indeed valid—but that the banks themselves would have to allege and prove the fraud before they could refuse the Lloyd's demand. The banks chose not to do that, paid out the money—but now must satisfy Canadian courts that they have the right to sell the assets which the Canadian Names had pledged to back their bank guarantees, assets that in most cases were their homes, Lloyd's having recruited in Canada among a middle-class community. Meanwhile, some of the banks are out of pocket for the money they have paid Lloyd's under the bank guarantee: In effect, they have a mortgage on the Canadian Names' homes, which pays them no interest, and on which they may not be able to foreclose. The banks won the first round in the trial court, but the case at this writing is on appeal, and the Names still have their homes but interest is mounting daily.

One of the first recommendations Rosenblatt's ANA made to American Names was that they send a form letter developed for Rosenblatt to inform their banks that they did not wish them to pay Lloyd's cash calls from their letters of credit. If such a letter has been sent, and the banks have paid Lloyd's anyway (which to date they have done), the Name may even be able to recover from the banks the assets they sold to pay Lloyd's on the letter of credit, if the courts ruled that these losses were in fact the result of fraud.

It should be noted that soon after this defense became popular, the Names' agents urged a number of new players to become involved in the game under new rules. Merrill Lynch has been the most active of them, enlisting several hundred American Names in 1994 to open Merrill Lynch Cash Management Accounts that can be used to back letters of credit Merrill's European bank would deposit with Lloyd's. Unlike the conventional letter of credit arrangements, however, which left the bank with the responsibility of paying out to Lloyd's and thus a vulnerability to Names' insistence that they would not pay, the Merrill arrangements with Lloyd's turned over control of the Name's money to Lloyd's from the first day, so that the Name's agent can automatically take cash from a member's Merrill letter-of-credit account as though it were a direct deposit. Merrill charges less than the banks for its letters of credit, which seems scarcely relevant in the larger analysis of the contract the Name must sign.

If there is not enough money in the reserve and the letter of credit, and the Name does not pay by the date Lloyd's specified in its demand for payment, Lloyd's "earmarks" a part of its Central Fund to pay what the agent says the Name owes. The Name then gets a new bill demanding payment to restore the money to the Central Fund, plus interest. Until late 1994, Lloyd's could then "issue a writ," which sounds awful but is really just a way to start a court action. If the Name did not take action to oppose the writ, the courts would read the Name's contract with his Name's agent, and give Lloyd's a judgment, which Lloyd's could then act to enforce, seizing bank accounts and property to the full value of Lloyd's claim. Since November 1994, the Lloyd's Central Fund has been barred from issuing such writs by a lawsuit we shall examine in Chapter 10, and has ordered the Names' agents to issue the writs themselves.

Claiming in court that a Name's agent or a managing agent or Lloyd's itself was negligent in representing the Name's interests in the insurance business has not been a defense against the Lloyd's writ: Some of the Gooda Walker Names who won the first major case for damages against Lloyd's syndicates were served with writs while the case was pending, and had to pay, even though it was generally believed that they would win. Lloyd's actually tried to prohibit suits by people who had not yet paid, but the courts have ruled that the separation of the two matters cuts both ways: The Name can't defend against a Lloyd's writ by alleging negligence, and Lloyd's can't defend against a Name's suit by alleging nonpayment.

Until spring 1994, the only valid defense against the writ was the allegation of fraud, which is what the American Names Association claimed, both in cooperation with the Canadians in the *Mason* case in Britain and in an American suit. In 1994, in the case of a dentist with an annual income of about $50,000 whose wealth was almost entirely his half of his family's home, who wound up losing $750,000 through his agent's choice of highly speculative syndicates, a British court ruled that the Name's agent had in effect breached *its* contract with him by putting him on unsuitable syndicates. Lloyd's therefore could not claim under the contract, either for already known or for possible future losses. We shall look at the possible effects of that case, too, in Chapter 10.

Even after Lloyd's has won a British judgment, of course, it can be enforced only against assets within the reach of a British court. Americans who have assets in Britain can expect to see them seized if court judgments are obtained. But assets in the United States cannot be seized unless Lloyd's applies to an American court to execute the judgment of the British court. And to date, though Lloyd's has issued writs against a number of nonpaying American Names (including 17 of the 110 Names who brought the suit the Proskauer law firm took to the Supreme Court and lost), and by no means all the American Names against whom the writs have been issued have paid, Lloyd's has not yet followed through with an attempt to get an American court to execute an English judgment.

In the cases that have been decided in the United States, the suits have been brought by Names against Lloyd's or its agents, and the courts have referred them back for trial (or arbitration under the Lloyd's contract) in Britain. As Andrew Grossman has pointed out, Lloyd's has won these cases, with the single exception of the Houston case, on procedural defenses. In one Chicago case where a Name sought the protection of the bankruptcy court,

Lloyd's filed motions and took depositions from witnesses but never actually filed a proof of claim against the bankrupt, thereby protecting itself against potential counterclaim. This case was settled, apparently inexpensively for the Name, who was able to withdraw his bankruptcy petition.[25]

Professor Grossman believed that Lloyd's would not in fact sue in American courts to get execution of British judgments: "Lloyd's has strenuously fought the issue of jurisdiction and one would not expect it to abandon that claim by appearing voluntarily in a foreign court even as plaintiff but rather to seek enforcement of the forum selection clause in the General Undertaking and, failing that, to abandon its claim against the Name. *Otherwise Lloyd's would risk a finding of fraud that could call into question the legitimacy of the Lloyd's American Trust Fund and subject it to attack.*"[26] Peter Middleton has grumpily declared that suing American Names might not be worth the legal costs to Lloyd's, and that statement may mask legal opinion in Britain that echoes Grossman's as well as other considerations. *May.* It's a strong enough reed to let some insomniac American Names fall asleep again, especially those who have given up on seeing any of their deposit ever come back to them, but they may have a rude awakening. On July 24, 1995, Lloyd's announced that agents would be issuing writs against a dozen American Names before September 20.

●

Every Name has had his own moment of awakening to the enormity of what has happened. For my friend Carl Aronson, an early American Name who had an insurance brokerage, it was the discovery that one of his syndicates—Devonshire—had been purchasing reinsurance from the North Koreans: "I think that may have made American Names subject to prosecution under the Trading with the Enemy Act." For James Deely, the former Citibank trust officer, it was his discovery that the man who had recruited him, presumably as a favor to him, had not only been paid a commission for doing so, but was continuing to collect a commission every year.

For me, it was when young Mr. David Shepherd calmly said of Merrett 418 (1985), "That syndicate will never close." At that time I had read in Sedgwick's annual report to me as my agent that Mr. Merrett expected to close 418 [1985] by this December 31 (at a very moderate loss), and wondered how in the world I got into this mess. (When Justice Breyer closed out his Lloyd's involvement, Sheila Marshall of Lloyd's law firm LeBoeuf, Lamb told the press it had been a grand gesture on his part, for Merrett 418 [1985] would very soon be closed in a way that would have cost him nothing.) For more sophisticated people, like San Francisco's Bill Stevenson, who owned a bank, it was something as simple as a lunch in the Captain's Room, and the realization that all those Lloyd's insiders were living so high on the hog on money that would otherwise have been flowing to the external Names.

"The one thing Lloyd's might not have counted on," Memphis stockbroker Henri Wedell told *Newsweek* in 1993, posing for a picture holding two double-bore shotguns, "is that Americans are prepared to fight."[27] At the Association of Lloyd's Members meeting in Dallas in autumn 1994, Graeme King, then in charge of collecting the money for Lloyd's, said sourly that he had reason to believe that some of the three hundred Names in attendance were people who had declared bankruptcy. He noted that it cost a lot of money to come to Dallas and stay at the huge, luxurious Anatole Hotel with its three football field–sized lobbies in giant atriums. In Britain, people who were bankrupt didn't have that kind of money. At one point, the meeting broke up into groups at tables, where people interested in a given topic could meet with someone from the Council or underwriters at Lloyd's.

The 1994 ALM meeting in Dallas was much different from the meeting fifteen months earlier in Boston. The earlier meeting had drawn seven hundred Names and it had been electric, people asking the speakers and one another what was really happening, what do you hear? what do you think? In Dallas, the much smaller group, about three hundred attendees, was mostly placid. These were all people who had joined action groups and were suing in England, and many of them had joined ANA, which had a little ten-dollar cash lunch on Saturday, invaded by Name's agent John Stace, who screamed at Rosenblatt. (It was the only rudeness I ever saw from a working Name.) What anger was expressed came from the substantial fraction of the three hundred who were "trading on," hoping to recoup their losses out of the future of glorious profits David Rowland as usual projected in his keynote speech to the group. (The chairman of the meeting, a diffident accountant named William McIntyre, somewhat stole the thunder of Rowland's remarks by telling the group that he wasn't trading on, himself.) Those who were not paying, they shouted, wanted to destroy Lloyd's, and they shouldn't be allowed to do it.

In 1994, Lloyd's offered to help American Names package a bankruptcy, and made an arrangement with Ralph Bunje, a San Francisco accountant who is a damaged Name, to help them with their planning. What was on offer, however, was only the most devastating form of American bankruptcy, Chapter 7, which requires the bankrupt to liquidate all his assets before he can gain protection from creditors. And the arrangement was that the Name would bare his entire situation to Bunje himself, who would then negotiate with Lloyd's the terms of the settlement. Bunje was being paid by Lloyd's as well as by the Name for handling these cases. He is a very precise man, Bunje; as he speaks, he moves his hands from one place on the table to another, apparently putting things in their right box. In Dallas in September 1994, he said he already had five or six American Names consulting with him about how Lloyd's could help them go bankrupt.

Different American Names have been fighting back in different ways. There are rumors that a number have moved to Florida, where the bankruptcy laws permit people to keep more of what they own when they settle with their creditors; a number of others have tried to "distance themselves" from their assets, to use the splendid English phrase, so that Lloyd's cannot reach them.

Others are still, like Lloyd's itself, in a state of denial, pretending that somehow Lloyd's will never reach *them*. And then there are the eager optimists, who believe that Lloyd's has solved its problems, the insurance cycle is turning favorably for the insurers, and new Names will dance on the graves of the old ones. John Robson, the elegant Name's agent, veteran of the Merrett agencies who could charm the paint off the walls, came to Texas in late 1993 and recruited five people to take more than a million dollars each in premium income in 1994, just in time for the Northridge earthquake that gave the insurance industry the worst first quarter in its history. In summer 1994, I met a man who had been a lawyer with the great firm of Davis Polk and an investment banker at Goldman Sachs—and had been recruited to Lloyd's by my agent, Sedgwick, in 1990. He was trading on: He had losses to recoup, he said. . . .

On July 18th, 1995, *The Financial Times* reported that the SEC had "forced" Lloyd's to stop accepting American Names "after a dispute over how membership of Lloyd's should be regulated in North America." With the decision to adopt "Value at Lloyd's" and auction places and syndicates, Lloyd's membership had become "more like owning company shares—and should be subject to more effective regulation in the U.S." But "under a compromise agreed with the SEC, existing members will not be affected."[28] William Lamb of LeBoeuf Lamb, still Lloyd's leading American counsel, said that except for its major premise—the fact that the Council of Lloyd's had voted not to accept new American or Canadian Names—this story was "entirely inaccurate," but of course he could not discuss any advise he had given his client. SEC spokesmen said that the contract between the Commission and Lloyd's had been initiated by LeBoeuf Lamb, and there had been no agreement of any kind: Lloyd's had moved on its own.

Lamb said he could not understand why there should be any interest in whether or not the SEC considered a Lloyd's membership a security, because Lloyd's had satisfied the requirements for a Reg D exemption: The is-it or isn't-it question was therefore "moot."

If the change in the Lloyd's regulations for syndicate membership had triggered contacts between LeBoeuf and the SEC, however, the question wasn't moot. In fact, Lloyd's membership criteria did not always satisfy Reg D criteria, though the SEC in the Ronald Reagan years had apparently decided to leave Lloyd's alone and *assume* satisfaction of Rule 506 of Reg D in every case.

Both LeBoeuf and the SEC were very tender when probed on these points in summer 1995. On December 23, 1994, Chairman Arthur Levitt had written Senator Christopher Dodd that his staff "monitors the various cases that have been brought by Lloyd's Names" and "is also reviewing . . . materials submitted recently by counsel for Lloyd's Names." As noted, the Ohio Securities Commission had barred Sturge from recruiting Names in Ohio. Money-losing Names argue that the SEC in the 1980s *did* fail to extend the protection of American securities laws to thousands of American citizens, and as Lloyd's weakens, the pressure on the SEC from these Names must become more effective.

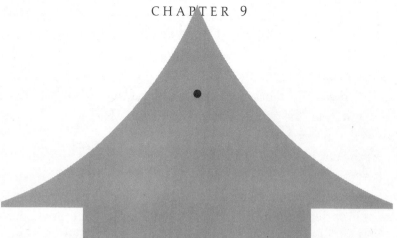

CHAPTER 9

PANIC ON LIME STREET

Starting in 1987, the world experienced a succession of natural and man-made catastrophes unparalleled in the history of the insurance industry. The word "catastrophe," it should be noted, is a term of art, meaning an insured event that costs the insurers more than $100 million. These events are listed at Lloyd's as "Cat 87J" (the windstorms of October 16–17, 1987) and "Cat 88D" (the explosion on the oil platform Piper Alpha), "Cat 89F" (Hurricane Hugo in Martinique, Dominica, Guadeloupe, The Bahamas, and the Carolinas), "Cat 89W" (the San Francisco earthquake), "Cat 89G" (the *Exxon Valdez* grounding), "Cat 90A" (the winter storm "Daria" in Europe on January 25–26, 1990, which may have been the most expensive of all to the reinsurers of its insurers).

These struck at a time when risk had been concentrated on a handful of LMX syndicates rather than spread through the market, when overcapacity in the industry had driven insurance rates on ships and airplanes, Lloyd's basic business, to startlingly unprofitable levels—and when the enormity of the "latent liability" risks for asbestos and pollution, unwittingly incurred but perhaps wittingly passed on by syndicates long closed, had risen inescapably to public as well as professional attention. In 1991, Lloyd's had to announce that the 1988 year of account had produced the market's first overall loss for its Names since the 1960s—$750 million. "We had thought Lloyd's might come apart," says an American insurance executive sympathetically, "but not that the triggering event would be earthquakes and winds and everything together."

At the end of 1991, Chatset made an estimate that losses on the 1989 year of account would be double those of 1988, with worse to come for 1990, and Lloyd's chairman David Coleridge turned on its proprietors John Rew and Charles Sturge. Their predictions of a $4.5 billion loss over three years were, he said, "without foundation." He commissioned Paul Archard, chairman of the Lloyd's Underwriting Agents Association, to make a survey of his membership. Archard returned with a report, loudly trumpeted by Lloyd's, that despite Cat 90A and the remaining losses from the 1989 disasters and the Chinese water torture of the "long-tail" attrition, Lloyd's losses on 1990 would be less than $600 million, and the market would be profitable in the 1991 year of account.

In autumn 1991, my agent, Sedgwick, had reported to its Names that "the 1990 underwriting year seems to us to be likely to produce a disappointing result, perhaps break-even."[1] It goes without saying that these Pollyanna reports (all written nine months and more after the end of the year that was being evaluated, when presumably a high fraction of the losses should have been known) were preposterously wrong: Losses for the 1990 year of account all by itself would be between $3.5 and $4.5 billion, depending on your estimate for "doublecounting," and losses in the 1991 year of account would be only marginally less.

Richard Outhwaite said he was leaving his 1982 year open because he rather expected that his proceedings to void some of the run-off contracts he had written would give the Names on Outhwaite 317 a better return than he could show in his first estimates; their losses, *after* recoveries of about $175 million on their lawsuit, now approach a quarter of a billion dollars.

Stephen Merrett circularized his Names in 1990 with illustrative figures showing that people who had been on Merrett 418 since 1983 still showed a profit after expenses; since 1984, a very small loss; and since 1985 (which had been left open), only a moderate loss. Meanwhile, he wrote, he had heroically renegotiated and "capped" (established a maximum loss on) four of his asbestosis reinsurance contracts, voided three others, and had the deductibles under the policies raised in another three, saving his Names, he reported, $150 million. Enough of them shared his confidence that his stamp capacity for 1990 was more than $300 million, half again as much as it had been in 1985. With 1990 also unable to close, those who had been on Merrett 418 in every year from 1983 through 1990 could show in 1994 losses six times as great as their profits on all the good years put together, with much more to come. But when Merrett stuck his neck out in 1990, he may well have believed what he said.

When almost a thousand of the 1,600 Outhwaite 317 Names met in 1988 for their first exploration of the possibilities of suing somebody, Peter Miller, former chairman of Lloyd's, was a Name on the Outhwaite syndicates. He went to the meeting and sat in the audience. After the initial presentation was made, he rose to assure all those present that they shouldn't think of lawsuits, Lloyd's was being run in a proper way, and if there were any problems, the Council would take care of them. Nevertheless, the Outhwaite Names under the leadership of Etonian accountant Peter Nutting raised more than $3 million to pay lawyers' fees (including a deposit for the legal fees of the Names' agents and Outhwaite, because in England the plaintiff must pay the defendant's lawyers if his suit fails). David Coleridge, still chairman of Sturge and about to become chairman of Lloyd's, proclaimed: The Outhwaite suit was really helpful to Lloyd's, he said, because after these Names lost, all the other possible suits against Lloyd's agencies by their Names would "drop into the sink."[2]

Throughout, the message from Lloyd's was Hang on, trade through, profits are around the corner and will pay off the losses, which are much less bad than our enemies say. To the insured and reinsured, the message was simpler: Lloyd's never has failed and never will fail to pay a valid claim, and whatever the size or nature of the insured losses you have suffered, the wealth of the English countryside will be mobilized to pay you.

In 1995, it should be noted that these messages proved false. Richard Lapper of *The Financial Times* has suggested that the case for dishonesty at Lloyd's rests on what he calls "the Murray Lawrence conspiracy hypothesis," the argument that Lawrence as vice-chairman of Lloyd's and the members of the Asbestos Working Group that reported to him knew for sure by 1980 that billions of dollars in losses lay ahead, that they kept their information secret from the existing Names and lured thousands of new Names to their ruin to help pay the losses.

One of the senior auditors of the market has told me that he believes that this hypothesis is the simple truth. Roger Bradley, a former underwriter, tells me that he was present at a dinner at one of the best restaurants in New York in 1979, when Tom Hopkinson of Citibank, reporting on the condition of the Lloyd's American Trust Fund of which the bank was custodian, told members of the investment committee that asbestosis was going to bankrupt a large part of the casualty insurance industry, and that Lloyd's should multiply its capital base to manage the losses.

Lloyd's must raise its "capital" separately every year—that is, Names must agree with their agents by August 31 that they are willing to accept premiums and thus supply backing to Lloyd's syndicates next year. They can then back out before the new year begins. Eddie Judd of Gooda Walker was surely not alone when he told his board in November 1988 that if Names knew the numbers he was passing on to Lloyd's central office, measuring the losses the syndicate had suffered that year, they would turn and flee. The Gooda Walker Names who stayed for 1989 were then trapped in LMX syndicates that had taken ludicrously inadequate premiums for reinsurance to close previous years (in part because of the abuse of time and distance policies taken to fake profits for those years), and were subject to the same atrocious underwriting practices that had devastated the 1988 account.

Even as his awareness of asbestosis liabilities soared in the early 1980s, Stephen Merrett enhanced the apparent profitability of 418 by *reducing* the premium each year paid its successor for reinsurance to close. In 1982, that premium was $17 million; by 1984, it was down to $10 million, reducing the reserves that would be available to pay the unquantifiable losses of the 1985 year of account.[3] An arbitration panel at Lloyd's, which included Merrett's fellow underwriter Frank Barber, found that Merrett's handling of his reinsurance liabilities was "foolhardy to say the least of it and bordered on conduct which could be described as grossly negligent."[4] In general, Chatset observed, "underwriters assessing the liabilities of an open year [the dying year is of course still open until its liabilities are reinsured into the next year] will only put in an allowance for IBNR that they feel they can pass on to their Names at that time. In other words, they prefer to pass losses on to Names as a steady drip rather than one big hit."[5]

Everyone at Lloyd's has an overwhelming self-interest in making the results of any year look as good as possible. In a rather touching letter to *One Lime Street*, Lloyd's house organ, Peter Nutting, who chaired the 1982 Outhwaite Action Group and negotiated the settlement that concluded that case, wrote in 1993 that "the case was settled in our favour after 49 days in court, before either side had an opportunity of introducing evidence about the state of knowledge of asbestos at the relevant time. . . . [T]he defendants had put together a formidable amount of evidence supported by a number of distinguished experts to demonstrate that many of those involved in asbestos litigation in the US, as late as 1982, were of the view that asbestos-related claims were likely to be entirely quantifiable and controllable."[6]

Nutting, a deeply conservative, roly-poly, English Santa Claus figure wearing a pink shirt tight over his belly, always wanted change rather than confrontation at Lloyd's and was never happy in the role of revolutionary destroyer. He never says anything bad about anybody else at Lloyd's; he smiles all the time and seems quite happy with himself and with the world. Moreover, the Outhwaite 317 case is not dead. Under British law, the Outhwaite Names who had *not* sued got nothing in the settlement. In his annual report for 1992, after the settlement, Outhwaite wrote, "If anyone had suggested to me a few years ago that Names who were loyal to the Lloyd's ethic, who stood by the advice of their agents and the Lloyd's authorities, would be worse off financially than members who sued all and sundry, I would not have believed it. Apparently, the Council of Lloyd's believes this to be none of their business. I would have thought that the equitable treatment of Names on a syndicate was fundamental to the business."[7] Five hundred of these Names are now seeking revenge, and reimbursement. In spring 1995, the House of Lords ruled that they were not barred from suing by the statute of limitations, because the information they would have needed to prosecute their case had not been available earlier.

Still, Nutting's abandonment of his victorious cause is a remarkable gesture, especially considering that the *arguments* if not the evidence on the world's understanding of asbestosis liabilities in 1982 were extensively presented by counsel in the opening statements. In forty-nine days, of course, much evidence had been introduced in the trial before David Coleridge in early 1992 summoned Nutting to meet with Stephen Merrett (who was the lead underwriter for Outhwaite's E&O insurance) in the chairman's office to get this thing settled. The evidence had demonstrated that it didn't matter what outside opinion on asbestosis liabilities might have been in 1981–82, because Outhwaite had not learned of it. He had never read the four reports on the subject from U.S. attorneys that Lloyd's had circulated to all its underwriters. Worse yet, Heinz Ulrick von Eicken, previously executive manager in London for Munich Re, testified on the stand that he had been shocked by the "sloppy and incompetent" manner in which Outhwaite kept his books. (Speaking on the BBC television show *Panorama*, von Eicken said, "Lloyd's is completely inept, and that's why they don't make money. *We make money."*)

Names who felt themselves cheated would surely be less likely to pay: The shortfall on the cash calls to Gooda Walker alone was something more than half a billion dollars. Worse: Insureds and insurance companies purchasing reinsurance might be less likely to come to Lloyd's with their business—and more likely to demand concessions on rates if they did deign to come—if the Lloyd's syndicates could no longer guarantee their grip if necessary on the ultimate cuff links of their Names. Thus David Rowland and David Coleridge before him and Murray Lawrence before Coleridge would all break into their soothing portrayals of a great future with blunt insistence that so far as past losses were concerned, *"The Names will pay."*

Lloyd's itself—its glamorous buildings in London and Chatham, its Adam Room and Captain's Room—is owned by the Society, its Names. The Lloyd's Act of 1982 totally insulates the Council from suit by those the Society regulates, an obviously necessary restriction (the New York Stock Exchange has a similar exemption) if the people who make the regulatory decisions and discipline those who break the regulations are to be safe from the vengeance of the regulated. External Names, of course, are and must be entirely passive, placing their bets only through their members' agency. Except for the annual assessment of their "solvency"—their financial ability to continue underwriting the risks on their syndicates—they are not in any way "regulated" by Lloyd's. It is by no means clear that Parliament really wished these external Names to be defenseless against Lloyd's, but that's what the courts have ruled.

The people with the best case against Lloyd's agents might well be Oakeley Vaughan Names, because Sir Peter Green as chairman of Lloyd's had commissioned no fewer than three reports on alleged misbehavior by the St. George clan that operated the syndicate, and each of them had found or intuited quite a lot of misbehavior even though they had very limited access to documents. Lloyd's had not informed its Names of the findings against the Oakeley Vaughan agency. If the Names had known what insiders at Lloyd's knew about the improper practices at Oakeley Vaughan, they would not have been willing to renew their membership in these syndicates. One of the investigations, for example, had turned up the fact that the syndicates' auditor had been keeping two sets of books.

By not revealing to those whose fortunes were at stake in the syndicates the incriminating information about what its own investigators had found in this racetrack-oriented insurance operation, Lloyd's shared responsibility with the St. George family in recruiting and holding Names for Oakeley Vaughan. And in this instance, the Lloyd's Act was not an automatic shield, for the incidents that had caused the worst losses had occurred before its passage. Nevertheless, the House of Lords ruled that Lloyd's could not be sued by its Names even for actions taken before the parliamentary grant of immunity, because Lloyd's owed its Names no obligations whatever—not even the obligation to be truthful in its communications with them.

But the members' agents *do* owe their Names a duty of care, and can be sued for failing to exercise it—the thing is now settled law, decided by the House of Lords. And the managing agents and their underwriters, though they have no direct relationship with their Names, can be sued for negligent underwriting. There is more money being asked in these suits than syndicates at Lloyd's can command. Time and again, as the suits have neared a court date, lawyers defending Lloyd's syndicates and underwriters have interposed procedural objections and this prevented the introduction of evidence onto the public record. Where initial opinions have been hostile, lawyers have appealed and appealed again, and asked leave to reappeal on some collateral issue, avoiding trials—and driving up the expenses of the plaintiffs, for under British law contingent fees are illegal, and the clock runs for British lawyers at rates comparable to those charged by American lawyers, three, four, sometimes five hundred dollars an hour. Such motions are entirely legal and are commonly used by advocates the world over. Despite procedural delays, cases were won by the persistent action groups.

In the Oakeley Vaughan case, the Names threw in the towel in February 1994, though many of them are not able to pay. Where victory looked impossible, settlements were reached. (Efforts would then be made to keep these settlements within Lloyd's: The Outhwaite winners, for example, were informed that their settlement would be paid only to their Lloyd's account, which was frozen because they were still on at least one [Outhwaite 317] open syndicate. Some who fought back got their cash, but most didn't.) In the *Aragorn* case, where evidence indicated that an underwriter was drunk when he signed a slip that lost his Names tens of millions of dollars, the syndicate kept the worst of the story out of the press by paying pretty much what the plaintiffs asked.

Gooda Walker was too much money to settle. The last appeals on technicalities were lost in the House of Lords in March 1994. The procedural phase of these legal actions is now finished, the evidence is coming onto the record and into the newspapers, and Lloyd's stands naked before the world. Lloyd's has to make a lot of what looks like news to keep the world's attention off the revelations of its recent past. So it hired the public relations firm of Hill and Knowlton, veteran spin doctors, to keep the ball rolling. When Hill and Knowlton did not make Lloyd's look good enough, Rowland hired Burston and Marsteller.

●

David Coleridge had another year to serve as chairman after the fiasco of the 1991 Annual General Meeting. He used it to hunker down, keep uttering optimistic platitudes, and consult with others in the City of London about what should be done. There was a thought that Lloyd's could raise a substantial loan to help Names through the valley of the shadow—or, at least, to pay off policyholders while the debt collectors pursued the Names. S. G. Warburg, the most eminent of the London securities houses, examined the situation and told Rowland they would not even lend money to Lloyd's. Finally, in the most important act of his chairmanship, Coleridge in 1992 persuaded the Council to impose a levy on all the Names, about $800 million to be paid in three years as a tax on gross premium income, to make sure the money was in the Central Fund to pay policyholders when Names failed to meet the cash calls. Though nobody likes to mention it, the obvious fact is that Lloyd's might have collapsed by 1994 without the funds from the levy, which permitted the syndicates to pay claims though their Names were heading for the hills.

Meanwhile, Coleridge and his predecessor Murray Lawrence, acting together, had approached David Rowland, who had made an unceasing racket about the need to change Lloyd's while he was on the Council, to chair a task force on where Lloyd's was headed, "to look beyond the immediate future and identify the framework within which the Society should, ideally, be trading 5–7 years hence."[8] There were twelve members of the task force, among them Bertie Hiscox and Stephen Merrett.

The task force report, published in early 1992, has gained a somewhat greater reputation than it deserves. Rowland himself has called it a "monumental achievement." Its basic assumption was that the expansion of underwriting capacity would generate current profits at a high enough level to enable the Names to pay out past losses. Even in theory, this involved a very optimistic assessment of future profits and an implausible confidence about the containment of past losses. If all happened as hoped, growing premium income on new years would be available to pay the losses on old years, which might detract from the security of the policies written in the new years. Lloyd's in 1990 had added a bylaw discouraging managing agents from leaving a year of a syndicate open, because syndicates left in run-off had to be funded from their own reserves and could not tap into the premium income of later years. When the Merrett Underwriting management agency was forced out of business in 1994 because the Names' agents refused to continue supporting a disliked as well as unsuccessful underwriter, a spokesman for Lloyd's said off the record that it cost the market $400 million in cash flow—i.e., $400 million would have to be found elsewhere to fund the claims on older Merrett policies because no stream of current premium income would be available for the purpose.

The availability of future premiums to pay past losses was indeed the admitted reason why growth was indispensable: "[T]he market has to be able to grow," the task force argued, "if it is to trade through the overhang of old years claims arising from asbestos and potential pollution problems. A contracting base could place the entire burden of all old years claims on a diminishing pool of capital providers for whom there would be an increasing incentive to leave."[9] Like all chain letters, this gimmick could not be sustained, and Lloyd's eventually had to shift its hopes to what is now called Equitas.

With some contradiction, the task force also urged that Lloyd's revoke the bylaw against open years, on the grounds that "allowing syndicates to remain open . . . isolates the problem. It allows new capital to join without risk of 'contamination'; it allows trading Names to see the profitability of their current underwriting unclouded by prior year deteriorations, thus increasing the incentive to remain a Name; it should revitalize the Personal Stop Loss market, as quotes for 1992 and onwards would not have to allow for old years problems." The task force even thought there was a case to be made for leaving open *all* the syndicates in the 1989 year of account, which in effect would allow Lloyd's to jettison *all* its existing Names and start all over again with new Names. And it was this idea, of course, that finally carried the day, with the proposal that all years before 1993 would go into one gigantic run-off syndicate.

There was still a heavy element of denial in the Rowland task force report. In spring 1991, as part of the campaign to stop managing agents from leaving years open, Lloyd's had created CentreWrite, a co-op agency under Lloyd's own administration to write reinsurance to close for syndicates that could not get such services in the market. Not surprisingly, CentreWrite did virtually no business. Lloyd's experience in running off busted insurance syndicates was highly discouraging, whether it was done by proxy, when the Council appointed new underwriters to run off syndicates orphaned by the bankruptcy of their managing agents, or directly, as in Lioncover, Lloyd's very own run-off syndicate to handle the unexpected but ever-growing losses left behind by Peter Cameron-Webb. When CentreWrite did give estimates for the costs of reinsuring a syndicate that could not buy reinsurance elsewhere, they were typically far beyond the resources of the Names that would have to pay the premium. "CentreWrite," Rowland's task force noted, "has not yet looked at syndicates with asbestos and pollution problems, given the difficulties of quoting, and thus will have little immediate impact on the syndicates with the largest number of Names involved."[10]

By midyear 1991, more than half the Names at Lloyd's— 17,500, the task force reported—found themselves with open years. This meant they couldn't quit, which in turn meant that new Names were much harder to recruit. The task force thought that CentreWrite could be turned around to concentrate on getting individual Names off the hook rather than closing the open years of busted syndicates. "At present," the report concluded, "only a syndicate level RITC, written into another syndicate, provides the Name with a legally effective mechanism for leaving the Society. CentreWrite itself cannot effect closure for an individual Name with sufficient finality to wind up all his affairs at Lloyd's. More work must be done to develop a mechanism allowing individual Names to leave effectively. CentreWrite can then adopt this mechanism in its new individual exit policy. *The Council should work with CentreWrite to develop an effective mechanism to release individual Names, and close entire syndicates, through a policy underwritten by CentreWrite; this should be treated as an urgent matter.*"[11]

But this seems hopeless: Either the premiums would be so high nobody would pay them, or Lloyd's as a whole would have to run risks that Names whose syndicates were still functioning more or less properly would never be willing to accept. The truth is that despite its acknowledgment that "the market has changed dramatically while we have been working," and that "there will be very serious losses in the 1989 year of account and serious losses in the 1990 account,"[12] the task force was still looking for a good fairy.

Nowhere in the document was there a discussion of segregating out the old years by any means other than leaving the syndicates open—and nowhere was there an acknowledgment that the losses on the 1989 and 1990 years of account would be different in *kind* from the losses of 1988. In 1988, the losses had been the result of red ink from past years drowning a 5 percent profit on the current year. The losses on 1989, 1990, and 1991 would be the result of *both* inherited inadequacies in reinsurance to close *and* dreadful results from current underwriting. Chatset divided the reported $4.5 billion loss on 1990 into three categories: $825 million on deterioration of old years, $900 million on inadequate reserving for 1989, and $2.7 billion of losses on the "pure year" 1990.[13]

Rowland as head of the task force assumed that the Names would stand and deliver when called upon to pay the losses in the market. "Mutualization" of the losses from the old years—the construction of a system by which the market as a whole would rescue the most afflicted of the losers—was rejected out of hand, because those Names who had minor or no losses (which still meant slightly more than half the market) would never sit still for it. The Central Fund, committed to the payment of policyholders, could not be abused for that purpose. And even if Lloyd's wanted to do so, of course—as would be demonstrated in 1994—there wasn't enough money in the fund to make a deal attractive to the burned Names. There was also, as the Council occasionally points out to an unsympathetic press, a political problem within Lloyd's: "Why should I pay," says Lady Rona Delves Broughton, who purportedly represents the interests of the external Names on the Council, "for those people who refuse to pay while lying on their yachts trailing their fingers in the Mediterranean Sea."

Three of the trial balloons floated in the task force report would later be asked to do some heavy lifting. One was diversification of Names' risks, through the creation of Members' Agents Pooling Arrangements, or MAPAs. It had become an article of faith that diversification lessened the riskiness of a Lloyd's investment, though it is by no means easy to see why this should be true. In the stock market, losses on any investment are limited to the investment itself (and it's a very rare stock that goes to zero), while the potential gains are unlimited. Thus diversification, increasing the chance of catching on to a rising star, offers advantages over efforts to pick winners. Even here, one should emphasize, despite the Nobel Prize in economics won by the gurus of diversification, the case is far from proved. Some of the most admired investors, men like Warren Buffett and Peter Lynch, have always stressed the value of investing in businesses you know something about.

At Lloyd's, however, the winnings are limited by the premium income of the syndicate (and every insurer has to pay off on *some* of his policies), while the losses can be infinite. A large dartboard portfolio of Lloyd's syndicates in 1988–91 would probably have produced losses greater than the average losses of Names who had been involved with the Lloyd's market for a decade or more and knew their way around the place. Nevertheless, Lloyd's would later encourage the formation of MAPAs by permitting Names to accept four dollars of premium income for every dollar of their deposit at Lloyd's if they let their member's agent put them into his MAPA, as against only three dollars if they wished to back individual "bespoke" syndicates. Another nice aspect of this increase in capacity, from market insiders' point of view, is that it generated a much appreciated increase in agents' commissions and fees, which are based on capacity.

The task force also faced up to the likelihood that individual Names would not put up the additional funds necessary to expand the capacity of the Lloyd's market in the 1990s. Under those circumstances, Rowland and his committee urged the admission of "corporate capital"—i.e., investors rather than Names, who would be gathered into a company with limited liability, which would then back syndicates at Lloyd's. Quite apart from the Lloyd's Act, which clearly envisaged Names with unlimited liability, there was a tightrope to be walked here, which Rowland and his collaborators basically failed to see.

The task force proposal for corporate membership left the corporations on an equal footing with the sole-trading Names, except that Lloyd's could establish higher minimum solvency ratios for corporate members—and had to pledge that they would never be assessed for the losses of earlier years. But this was clearly inadequate. If corporate investors could not lose more than their deposit, they also could not be permitted to leverage that deposit to as much premium income as was permitted to sole traders. Thus, in the end, the MAPA Name was permitted to accept premium income totaling four times his deposit, and the ordinary Name could accept premium income totaling three times his deposit, but the corporate investor would have to be limited to twice his deposit. In 1994, one notes in passing, very rich gamblers were allowed to accept premium income *five* times their deposit, if the deposit was at least $300,000 and they could show additional liquid assets of at least $750,000 easily accessible by Lloyd's if necessary.

At the same time, the corporate investor would have to be totally insulated from past losses, or no corporation would join. Because the Central Fund—that is, all Lloyd's Names—would be liable to policyholders if the losses on a corporate member's syndicates exceeded its deposit, corporations would have to make a higher annual contribution to the Central Fund than was demanded of Names. This aspect of changing the nature of the membership, entirely ignored in the task force report, led Lloyd's to promulgate an extraordinary and ultimately fatal rule that forbade 1993's syndicates to purchase reinsurance to close from 1994's syndicates (which would be backed in part by corporate capital) for any liabilities growing out of pre-1985 insurance policies.

With these refinements, worked out over eighteen months, the task force suggestion was put before the membership in 1993, and passed.

The third of the task force's suggestions was for the establishment of a Name's *right* to membership in a syndicate once he was accepted by the managing agent. While syndicates would continue to dissolve themselves every year and re-form for the next year, each Name would be entitled to the same proportionate share of next year's syndicate that he had accepted for last year's syndicate. That right to membership, by definition a right to a proportionate share in the syndicate's assets and future profits, would be marketable, like a share of stock (which also can be seen as simply a share in a corporation's assets and future profits). Because the purchaser of a syndicate participation would acquire not only the joys of a share of future profits but also the sorrows of an obligation to pay off losses from inadequate RITCs, the instrument itself would be tricky, almost certainly requiring a "novation," a new contract between the managing agency and the new Name.

Theoretically, this program of "Value at Lloyd's," which was partially adopted in early 1994 following a separate study by a "Value Group" headed by Bertie Hiscox, offers a neat solution to a number of the market's difficulties. The central problem of the Lloyd's system has been that reserves against the bad years must be built by the Names themselves because the syndicates are dissolved and re-formed every year, distributing the most recent year's profits in the process. And Names, like other human beings, tend to spend their year's income, leaving them at best angry and at worst desperate if their syndicates later come to them to meet losses. If membership on a syndicate became a marketable right, Names would have less reason to demand the full payment of each year's profits, because the future gain in investment income predicted by larger reserves in the syndicate would show up as an increase in the value of their "shares." Conversely, the attractiveness of the syndicate that reported higher profits by paying too little for its reinsurance to close would be diminished because the market for its shares would fall.

The allocation of capital across the market to different syndicates would presumably be improved by the creation of a market for participations. The best syndicates would be recognized not by Chatset league tables, which did not account for risk, but by the price Names could command for their shares in that syndicate. Syndicates would be discouraged from undue expansion because it would drive down the price of the shares. (The Value Group report decided not to trust the market to police expansion, and instead urged that any syndicate wishing to expand its capacity by more than 15 percent in one year be compelled to get a vote of its Names before doing so. This was not likely to be much of a barrier, because the existing Names would retain the same proportional share of the syndicate whatever its size. Expansion of the capacity of a syndicate, like a rights issue in a corporate stock, would give the old Names new shares that cost them nothing but could be sold to others for cash.)

Among the improvements at Lloyd's that could be gained by establishing a marketable right to a syndicate participation was one not mentioned in the task force report but rather bitterly stressed by the Value Group two years later: the fact that it would compel managing agents to play fair with their Names. "At present," the Value Group wrote, "managing agents are free to negotiate different fees and commissions with each syndicate member. . . . A system of value could be distorted if managing agents continued to be able to negotiate differential fees and commissions. Accordingly, as soon as practicable, managing agents will be required to charge the same rate of management fee and profit commission for all members . . . of a particular syndicate."[14]

But the major reason to proceed was the same every time somebody looked at the proposal. Names who were stuck with losing syndicates and had cash calls might be able to realize enough from the "value" of their place on successful syndicates to keep them solvent. As the task force put it, rather eloquently, in 1992, "The opportunity to crystallise the value of future profits offers a way to *raise funds from the incoming capital providers to help offset the cost of meeting old years liability.*"[15] There was a disadvantage to this, too, of course, in that smart, strong Names with lots of assets would have an incentive to subsidize the sale of their bad syndicates to weak, dumb Names who might default on their obligations and thus "mutualize" losses because the Central Fund would have to pay.

The major reason to oppose the "value" scheme also remained in place: Making people pay for the chance to back syndicates would increase the volatility of returns to Names (and corporate members), who would gain both by the profits of the syndicate and the increase in the value of the shares in good years—and lose their investment in the shares as well as God knows how much money in the syndicate in bad years. In other words, it would increase the leverage of the capital supply to Lloyd's, which was in deep trouble because there was already too much leverage in the market. From the point of view of corporate capital, moreover, each dollar spent to buy a place on a syndicate diminished the amount of premium the corporate member could accept for the same capitalization.

There was another reason why "value" was a bad idea, touched on by the task force but ignored by the Value Group, perhaps because Hiscox had visions of sugarplum fairies bringing goodies to managing agents like himself. "A market," Rowland's committee wrote, "can only function with good information. The difficulty at Lloyd's is that such information can be elusive. . . ."[16] Names have learned the hard way that some managing agents did not give them adequate information about what policies they had backed, what reinsurance had been written for them, what expenses they have paid for the syndicate. A review of about forty syndicate reports turns up only three (Wren Syndicates Management Limited, B. F. Caudle, and Frank Barber) that tell the Names the investments that have been made with the premium income. All they recieved from agents were incomplete analyses (some of these merely "illustrative"), and the underwriter's opinions about the state of the world, which may or may not be amusing. Since 1992, the syndicates have had to tell their Names the salaries paid to the people who work for the syndicate—but they don't have to tell about the perks.

David Rowland in introducing the Value Group's report noted nervously the need "to insure that a fair and reasonable balance is struck between the interests of Names and the interests of managing and members' agents. . . . [W]e must recognize the contribution made by managing agents." This principle was illustrated by the hypothetical case of a syndicate that had to replace members who had died or resigned or cut back on their capacity. "Until a workable system for realising value has been developed," Rowland wrote, "the Council has determined that managing agents should be entitled to retain their existing discretion"[17]—i.e., if there's money to be made by the sale of replacement slots, the managing agent not the Name should be making the money.

But the big money for the agents would come from their ability to sell for their own account the participations placed by the Members' Agents Pooling Arrangements. Hiscox himself, as chairman of the Value Group, informed his Names that they would not be permitted to sell their MAPA participations, and if they dropped out for any reason, Hiscox would inherit the "value" of their right to be on Lloyd's syndicates. Lloyd's continues to pay a price for the unfortunate decision in 1970 to permit the agencies to incorporate: Hiscox has stockholders as well as Names to worry about, and he cannot be expected to give away his stockholders' interests to please the management of Lloyd's. In fall 1994, he sold a controlling interest in his agencies to the Trident operation formed by banker J. P. Morgan and insurance broker Marsh and McLennan, Americans both, and they surely would not be likely to give away anything of value to them to keep David Rowland happy.

In spite of all the objections cited, auctions began the first week in August 1995. Mr. Hiscox made it happen.

●

The centerpiece of the task force proposals for reform was the assertion of primacy for Lloyd's as a society, and an insistence that the members of the Society yield a great deal of new authority to the center, especially the new salaried chairman (who would be Rowland himself) and a CEO. By the end of 1992, these individuals were in place—Rowland as chairman and Middleton as CEO—and by April 1993 they had presented the Names with a business plan to which they gave the perfect Lloyd's title *Planning for Profit.* To gain that profit (targeted at no less than 10 percent per year on capacity, which meant 33 percent per year on a Name's deposit), Rowland and Middleton wrote, "we will adopt a more directive management approach. We will move from an environment of consensus-based decision making by committees to one where the central management team will take decisions."[18]

The time had passed when David Coleridge as chairman could say his job was "to keep the coffee house." Costs of doing business at Lloyd's had been rising at a rate of 20 percent per year through the 1980s; somebody would have to put a stop to that. The age of electronic processing had not just dawned but neared its zenith, and Lloyd's agents still had their records on slips or in account books (or, at best, on IBM cards). Speaking of his experiences at Lloyd's, the American con man Carlos Miro had told a U.S. House committee that he had been "trotted out to confuse the Lloyd's underwriters with a complicated high-tech sales presentation that was totally alien to the quill-and-scroll types in London."[19] Neither policies nor claims reports were standardized. The Names' agencies were full of somebody's children who had neither education nor training. Agents were ripping off their Names by taking their vacations as expenses to be paid by the Names, charging profit commission on gross returns before the deduction of costs, imposing exorbitant fees. The central office itself was wastefully run, with 2,200 employees in 1992, when only 1,600 were really needed to do the job. The chairman's Rolls-Royces and most of his Waiters would go, as would the bottle of champagne on a silver salver at five o'clock every afternoon.

Peter Middleton received a large bonus in 1994 for his success in cutting costs and introducing procedures in 1993. But the prin-

ciple of centralization is by no means universally accepted, even
by the optimists. "The future," wrote M. H. Cockell, whose syndicates 269 and 570 made money every year through the crisis, "will
be much more a franchise operation, not a free enterprise, individual business exercise. The rules under which the franchise will be
allowed to operate will be much more tightly drawn than anything anyone would have contemplated as acceptable in the past.
A few Market operators of recent past years have brought this
fundamental change in the Market of each for himself, by their totally irresponsible and incompetent underwriting. Sadly something dramatic had to be done, and with great courage it has
been."[20]

H. J. Jago, whose large syndicate 205 was even more profitable,
was even more irritated. "Names at Lloyd's have suffered appallingly, not least from the ignorance and stupidity of some of
their appointed underwriters," he wrote. "Market forces have subsequently caused a revolution, . . . leaving a core that has, in the
main, survived profitably. . . . Lloyd's now depends utterly and
completely on these few making the successful market of the future. They should be encouraged and sustained, not subject to the
ideology of central control. . . . Consideration might also be given
to our underwriters, whose time is taken up with budgets, sched-
ules and quarterly statistics, little of which has value and for which
there are no qualified interpreters. We could be in danger of losing
our best. After what we all have suffered, it would be a pity."[21]

And it is not quite so clear as the Lloyd's proclamations insist
that in fact the modernization of the marketplace has produced
only improvements. At one underwriting agency office I visited,
the active underwriter showed me the big books of account in
which he still kept all his records, because the printout from the
central office was inaccurate—he filed all his records on the right
forms, but too often they came back garbled. A rather sinister announcement from Lloyd's in summer 1994 revealed that the
shedding of personnel from the bloated headquarters had ceased,
because it turned out more people were needed to process all the

additional information the reforms were generating.

P. J. Oxford of G. S. Christensen and Others wrote his Names in spring 1994 that "it is almost a full time job trying to interpret and understand the implications to our business of the new regulations, byelaws and best practices/guidelines which are pouring from the 'center.' . . . " Oxford did not think much of either of the two acclaimed electronic improvements, electronic trading support (EPS), which hooks all boxes into a central computer, or electronic agreement for outwards reinsurance (LORS), both of which were pushed on the market through the imposition of deadlines. "Not wishing to get bogged down in technical detail," Oxford wrote, "neither system assists our day to day trading, both are very slow and cumbersome to use, EPS makes it uneconomic to underwrite small risk business (the very business that has given our Syndicate the stability and broad spread of account since commencing in 1980). Both systems would have benefits to the Syndicate, if introduced after a successful trial period, but both have been hastily implemented and obviously designed by people who have little experience of transacting business in any insurance market, let alone the Lloyd's environment."[22] Brian Smith, one of the old-timers who has computerized, says he always relies on his own printout, not on Lloyd's records, when asked to pay a claim.

These days computerized record-keeping is essential to insurance trading, especially for "long-tail" policies where the details must be available for eighty years. The initial glitches had to be overcome at Lloyd's. It took time because the computer experts who installed the system knew little about insurance and the technology was foreign to the personnel using it in the market. The use of data processing machinery to process transactions in financial markets has not been something London does very well. The London Stock Exchange had to scrap four years of work when its computerized clearance-and-settlement software failed its trials. The Bank of England took over—thus far, ineffectually.

●

The crucial change in the fifteen months between the task force report and the new business plan was the revelation to Lloyd's leadership that the conventional way of running the institution would not give Lloyd's enough money to pay off the claims on the policies its central signing office had stamped on behalf of its syndicates. Halfway through the period, the Council imposed its $800 million levy to beef up the Central Fund, which presumably would take care of claimants under reinsurance policies that would not in fact be backed by the Names. But the latent liability "APH" policies (for asbestos, pollution, and health hazard) could not be reinsured in the usual Lloyd's way, in part because nobody knew (or knows to this day) how bad the damage would be—and also because no responsible estimate of its size leaves it manageable by the Names who are "on" such syndicates. And so long as there was any considerable belief in the market that survivors at Lloyd's were going to wind up paying the bills of these "long-tail" syndicates, recruiting new individual or corporate Names was going to be like pulling teeth.

The tactic developed to insulate future members from past losses was extremely clever—not the least of its clevernesses being the fact that it involved the creation of a whole new complicated institution, and thus a delay of at least three years while the music could keep playing. The principle of the new institution would be the management of claims under Lloyd's policies written in and before 1985. The year was chosen because it was then that Lloyd's syndicates changed virtually all their policies in the area of asbestos and environmental damage by corporations to cover only "claims made" during the course of the policy. Policies written in the years before 1985 had used the word "occurrence," and the U.S. courts had ruled them continuously and permanently vulnerable to claims by anyone who had suffered contact with the dangerous substance while making or consuming a product involving that substance. Policies written since 1985 would close off at the end of the period insured, because no more claims could be made, and they would stay closed.

This was noted at the time, incidentally, by a group of nineteen state attorneys general in the United States, who brought an antitrust action against Lloyd's to prevent Lloyd's as reinsurer from denying coverage to American insurers who did not follow Lloyd's prescriptions. Ralph Nader's Center for Responsive Law wrote a report: "In the mid-1980s, Lloyd's and other reinsurers used their coercive market power to prohibit primary insurers from using standard commercial policies—known as 'occurrence forms'—containing provisions which these companies found objectionable. Insurers abandoned certain lines and threatened to boycott others unless new, anti-consumer policy forms—known as 'claims made' forms—were used. As a result, U.S. businesses and public bodies experienced 'severe restrictions in the availability and affordability of insurance coverage.' "[23]

The Nader lawyers began their jeremiad with the words: "If the American people were told that a major sector of the U.S. economy—the property/casualty insurance industry—is controlled by an unknown foreign entity, accountable to no federal or state agency and subject to virtually no U.S. regulatory laws, they would have reason to fear for their ability to obtain child care, engage in business, receive health and other professional care and engage in many daily activities taken for granted each day. . . . Lloyd's of London, the most powerful insurer in the world, today exerts significant economic control over the property/casualty insurance industry—one of the most powerful and critically important industries in the United States. . . . [T]he American public . . . may not realize . . . that, today, Lloyd's is using its economic power to drive a nationwide, insurance industry–initiated campaign to change our civil liability laws—laws that have protected U.S. citizens for over 200 years."[24]

By 1993, this war had long been won by the insurers, because it was obvious that the maintenance of the civil liability laws as the courts had begun interpreting them would bankrupt the insurance industry in the United States as well as England. So there was an immediate, vital difference between the pre-1985 policies and the post-1985 policies, providing an objective reason for separating their treatment at Lloyd's.

The instrument that would take care of pre-1985 claims was projected as a limited-liability insurance company that would write a reinsurance to close for *all* the Lloyd's syndicates in run-off because of their inability to quantify their future liabilities. This company would be owned by Lloyd's itself. It was given the name NewCo (since renamed Equitas, in response to a contest mounted by Peter Middleton, who gave a bottle of champagne to the winner). It would gather up the reserves Lloyd's syndicates held against these "long-tail" claims, supplement that sum with an assessment against the Names in these syndicates (*not* the market as a whole: still each for his own part and not for any other), and centralize the process of accepting or fighting the claims. The result would be to "ring-fence" the "old years," allowing the market to go on about its business with new corporate and individual Names who would never have to trouble their pretty heads about what had happened in the 1980s.

Speaking only a few months after the announcement that this was the way Lloyd's would go, deputy chairman Richard Keeling explained the logic. Lloyd's reserves were dedicated to the payment of insurance (and reinsurance) claims. Most of these claims were to be paid quite soon, and thus the money had to be invested in short-term very liquid instruments, which don't yield much of a return. And what return might be available from very safe investments was further vitiated by the desire of the Names, the beneficial owners of these reserves, to have their earnings tax exempt as much as possible.

The claims NewCo would have to pay, by contrast, would arrive at Lloyd's over a period of many years. Thus reserves allocated to NewCo could be invested in longer-lasting notes and bonds, and perhaps even some equities, which would boost the average yield on the syndicates' investment portfolio. And given the extremity of the crisis, it was silly to pay attention to tax considerations when looking at the need for reserves. The shift in investment policy would be symbolized by a shift in manager of those trust funds that were transferred to NewCo, in the United States from Citibank to J. P. Morgan. Keeling thought it reasonable that Morgan could earn something over 1 percent a year more than Citibank had earned with the trust funds.

On the other side of the equation, Keeling stressed that "a twenty-year-old insurance claim is not an insurance claim, it's a *deal.*" The term of art in the insurance business is "commutation"—which means, in practical terms, paying $20 million today on a $40 million claim that goes back to the 1950s. Such commutations might be more welcome than you might think to American insurance companies, which are subject to state regulations that require adjustments on the balance sheet if a reinsurer fails to pay a claim on him within ninety days. Simply by not paying a claim, the reinsurer can force his policyholder to write down for regulatory purposes the credit he has taken on his books for this reinsurance. Once 20 percent of a claim is overdue, in most states, the whole of the asserted value of the reinsurance contract must be written off the books entirely. The stockholders in the insurance company taking these haircuts never hear about it, because the insurance commissioners do not require publication of such bad news, but the company's first and most important public is its regulator. Incidentally, many experts believe applying such a rule to Lloyd's as a whole would leave the Lloyd's market obviously insolvent.

Faced with the need to take a hit to regulatory capital without any cash to show for it, an insurance company fighting with its reinsurer may be happy to settle. Where the syndicate seeking commutation is the direct insurer, however, the commutation may be more difficult, because accountants will allow the company that claims under the insurance policy to continue to carry the claim under the policy at face value so long as the matter is being litigated. And much of Lloyd's asbestos exposure is direct with the asbestos producers and fabricators, not on a reinsurance chassis.

Still, NewCo would have fear going for it in the negotiations. If you feel your insurer or reinsurer will not be there in a few years, you may be quite willing to take a little less now rather than run what looks like a real risk of getting nothing tomorrow. Lloyd's cannot make that threat without suffering loss of reputation and business; NewCo will have neither, and can play hardball. Moreover, and the numbers here run into tens of millions of dollars per year, NewCo will clearly be much less expensive to run than four hundred run-off syndicates, each with its own officials with their own expense accounts. These expenses are indeed remarkable. In its presentation to a select committee of Parliament in spring 1995, the Names Defense Association reported that as of the end of 1993, managers of run-off syndicates had taken $120 million from their reserves for *future* general and administrative expenses.

Despite much publicity to the contrary, Equitas, as it is now called, cannot in fact relieve the Names of their obligations; if Equitas fails, the insured can still come after the Names on the policies. But the same thing is true of any reinsurance to close: The insureds are not consulted in the matter, and retain their rights if the reinsurer does not live up to his obligations and the claims go unpaid. In practice, despite the "sole trader" rules, Lloyd's has found ways to stand behind busted syndicates and pay the claims under their policies, even when the reinsurance arrangements have failed (viz., the Peter Cameron-Webb episode).

When the policies move to Equitas, Lloyd's will be out of the picture. Equitas can fail to pay on a policy, and Lloyd's will still be able to boast that it has always paid every valid claim. David Coleridge, chairman when the task force report was written and the business plan was commissioned, said that "it doesn't matter if NewCo doesn't pay, because every year it will be further away from Lloyd's. When it sinks, it sinks. NewCo," he added, "will be distanced from Lloyd's," using the term Names use when they talk about concealing assets from the Lloyd's debt collectors.

Keeling vigorously denied that NewCo was a way to delay and conceal default. "If this were merely an exercise in moving the goalposts," he said, "I would not have any part of it." Lloyd's has assigned major figures in the market to the gaggle of committees that are working to get some handle on the liabilities the run-off syndicates really must carry, and the reserves they really have available for the purpose. To manage this effort and bring credibility to the NewCo proposal, Lloyd's hired a distinguished actuary, Heidi Hutter, a large, muscular, pleasant, no-nonsense American lady in severe suits, not yet forty, who came to Lloyd's from Swiss Re on a three-year contract for $1.5 million whether she could get NewCo up and running or not.

Hutter had a staff of 30 people within Lloyd's central office, plus no fewer than 550 co-opted from the agencies or hired from other insurance operations as part-time consultants. Because the bookkeeping has been so amateurish at so many of the syndicates, the task of calculating what they really owe involves consultations with brokers and others even before one undertakes the quasimystical exercise of calculating the claims incurred but not recognized. But the calculation of their real reserves involves even more exegesis, because these reserves are a mess of claims on reinsurers and time and distance policies valued at the total to be collected on them rather than at their present value. One reasonably authoritative estimate says that the money Morgan is to manage for NewCo may be as little as 60 percent of what is carried on the books of the open syndicates.

"A recent survey which we undertook for a major American client into policies which they had purchased through the 60's, 70's and 80's," Ken Randall wrote in the November 1993 Chatset rundown of the open years, "showed that more than 60% of potential recoveries due from London market reinsurers was in respect of policies purchased from companies which are now either insolvent or in run-off. One of the market's greatest fears is the potential for the collapse of a truly major reinsurer."[25]

In 1994, Lloyd's (especially Keeling) made much of the theory that liabilities had been overestimated at Lloyd's by failure to eliminate "double counting"—i.e., the estimators had counted both the losses of a syndicate and the losses by other syndicates with respect to the personal stop-loss insurance they had written for the benefit of Names on the loser. In September 1994, the Association of Lloyd's Members went a step further, charging that Lloyd's was making things look worse than they were—and preventing many Names from continuing to underwrite by denying their solvency—by saddling the Names on the syndicates that had written errors and omissions policies with the losses anticipated under those policies from the lawsuits wending their way through the courts, while refusing to credit the Names who had brought the suits with their potential recoveries.[26] But, of course, there has been similar double counting of reserves, as syndicates claim assets in the form of reinsurance while the reinsurers claim assets to back the reinsurance policy. As was demonstrated when the claims came in, the LMX spiral syndicates were a great source of artificial reserves.

What blights the prospects for Equitas, however, is not any of these objective analyses, but the changing political situation at Lloyd's. The disasters of the 1980s were caused in large part by the brokers, who were denied ownership of managing agents at the same time that their power over the market was escalating. New insurance companies were growing all over the world, and outside Lloyd's in London; the brokers could take the good business wherever they pleased, and could cut deals that compelled underwriters to bear dangerous risks to get the more desirable business. While they owned the managing agents, the brokers were inhibited from passing on junk insurance or reinsurance: It would be like giving poison to your children. Once these ties were cut, they were free to maximize their commissions at the expense of the Names, and they did.

In the 1990s at Lloyd's, the power has passed back to the underwriters, because they can jump ship, and they will if they feel it's no longer advantageous for them to be in the glamorous surroundings of Lime Street. They have been much more recalcitrant about the new centralized administration than commentators have realized. To get them to accept the new electronic record-keeping on policies, for example, Lloyd's has had to pay for the equipment to be used at the underwriter's box, which was not originally part of its budget. Ms. Hutter's data questionnaires were answered tardily and incompletely. ("We understand the timing of the questionnaires was not convenient for managing agents," she said in a speech to the Insurance Institute of London early in 1994. ". . . Future data requests will be organized as best as possible to avoid peak work periods.")[27] Perhaps the most striking example of Lloyd's inability to control the underwriters came when the council tried to limit managing agents' fees to 0.5 percent of capacity in 1994 and 0.4 percent of capacity in 1995. In early 1994, it was revealed that several successful agents had told the new Lloyd's management to stuff their limitation rules, and the management had backed down, declaring that the rules were merely guidelines.

When the time comes to launch NewCo, the managing agents will have to provide the cash from their reserves. But the managing agents feel strongly that while the liabilities on the policies belong to the Names, the reserves belong to the syndicates. They have the example of the Feltrim agency, which gave up the Peter Cameron-Webb reserves to Lioncover and then died horribly on the LMX spiral. For the syndicates in run-off, of course, the reserves would simply be transferred to NewCo—and topped off with the proceeds of the cash calls on Names Ms. Hutter and her fellow actuaries consider necessary to cover the losses projected for those syndicates. But a crucial part of the losses NewCo is to cover grow from policies that have been reinsured year after year into syndicates that are still very much alive.

Starting in December 1993, the managing agents were not permitted to reinsure those risks into the next years of their syndicates, to protect corporate capital and new Names from any responsibilities for the disasters of the 1980s. Before NewCo can be launched, Hutter and her colleagues will have to reach agreement with the managing agents on how much of their reserves—

which they count on to provide the income that makes profits for their Names—will have to be handed over to relieve them of their latent liabilities or not-yet-recognized reinsurance obligations. The best of the agents will have bargaining power to give up little if any of their reserves beyond the specific reinsurance contracts.

"It is imperative," M. H. Cockell wrote in his report for 1993, "that Lloyd's make sure that the NewCo reserves are fair as between syndicates. To allow those who may not be fully reserved, not to bring their 1985 and all prior up to the level of the best, would mean that the whole concept could start out on a flawed basis. The open syndicates' Names will probably be asked for cash calls involving substantial amounts of money if a proper level of fairness is to be achieved, but, to give NewCo a real chance, that will be the price of the ring fence."[28] And the syndicates have a strong lever available to help them move Lloyd's around: The Names are counting on stop-loss insurance to cover much of their losses, and the question of whether assessments to launch NewCo are in fact claims under personal stop-loss policies is very much in the air. In October 1993, the stop-loss underwriters "reserved their rights in respect of PSL coverage for premiums paid to NewCo."[29]

NewCo may reach fruition, anyway, under its new name Equitas—it is hard to imagine a minister of the Department of Trade and Industry who would have the courage to deny certification to so politically important a project. The task of satisfying the insurance commissioners in the United States may be more difficult. The Lloyd's publicity about Equitas stresses that it will succeed by "commuting" the policies it reinsures, and the world may not allow Lloyd's to continue claiming that it pays all valid claims in full while bragging that it plans to escape paying old claims in full by putting a new name on the insurer. And then of course there will be the "orphan syndicates" of 1986–92, with their losses on those years of account far beyond the capacity of the Names to pay. From early on, spokesmen for Lloyd's indicated a wistful desire to reinsure these liabilities, too, into NewCo. Richard Keeling stepped down from responsibility for NewCo at the end of 1994. In May 1995, Rowland announced plans to take *everything* before 1992 into Equitas, thereby severing what he called "old" and "new" Lloyd's. The term "ring fence" went out of fashion; the new term was "firebreak."[30] The only similarity between the old Lloyd's and the new Lloyd's would be that the insiders would continue to profit hugely by the operation of the market.

Announcing the "global results" in 1994, Lloyd's proclaimed the return to profitability for the market in the "pure year" of 1992. That year's underwriting, it was said, earned a profit of $130 million (after eliminating a "double count" for losses incurred by the stop-loss insurers and malpractice insurers, which presumably will be paid to Names on syndicates showing their own losses). But after the deduction of expenses and contributions to the Central Fund, the *Names* still showed a loss on the pure year of $530 million, with—of course—more to come. New or old, Lloyd's measures profitability without reference to the actual gains or losses of the Names.

It has dawned on the leaders of the action groups that a large proportion of the losses assessed against their Names were not in fact losses on insurance policies but outrageous commissions and expense accounts paid to brokers and agents. Even those who feel continuing obligation to the policyholders see no reason why they should be bankrupted because Lloyd's insiders have lived and continue to live very high on the hog. Rowland's and Middleton's popularity will diminish as the realization grows that they are working not to pay off the policyholders and certainly not in the interest of the Names but to protect the fortunes and promote the income of the Lloyd's brokers and agents and underwriters.

Lloyd's has become a slow payer of claims ("They never pay," says Eugene Anderson, the lawyer who won the *Keene* case that dug the pit into which Lloyd's fell, "until you sue"), and the Names have become slow payers of cash calls, and Peter is lending to pay Paul. And, of course, the world of Lloyd's is full of lawyers and lawsuits, which are just as expensive in Britain as they are in

America. "They wear down a lot of claimants," Anderson says.

In mid-1994, I discussed the prospects for NewCo with Roger Pascal, executive director of the Association of Lloyd's Members, which represents essentially the interests of those who are trading on and therefore sympathize with management. He argued that NewCo not only would be able to pay off the claims but would in fact make money (perhaps by using its reserves to back Lloyd's syndicates!), and would pay dividends to the Names who would own it in proportion to the reserves they had contributed. Gaily, he pledged that he would give me a bottle of champagne on the day I received my first payback from NewCo.

I thought about this offer later. It sounds like betting one's convictions, but in fact it's the opposite. A bet would have been my promising *him* a bottle of champagne if NewCo paid off for me as my cheerful gesture of admitting I'd been wrong and he'd been right, while *he* promised *me* a bottle of champagne to help me nurse my wounds if NewCo failed and it turned out I was right and he was wrong. And he wasn't right, so he was totally safe, he'd never have to part with his champagne. There echoed in my mind the warning I had been given thirty years before by Alain, Baron de La Cam.

●

CHAPTER 10

THE STRUGGLES

The Annual General Meeting of Lloyd's in June 1993, his first as chairman, was a horrible experience for David Rowland. He had to announce by far the largest losses Lloyd's had ever experienced ($4.5 billion in one year), and he had to stand on the stage of the Royal Albert Hall and listen to dozens of the members of his Society denounce the Corporation of Lloyd's for negligence in its regulation of the market and chicanery in its dealings with the Names. One Name, John Podmore, uttered a truly Shakespearean warning: "If you do not temper the winds of the shorn lamb, then otherwise those who have been fleeced will have their revenge, this I assure you, either here or in the hereafter."[1] Because Lloyd's itself was immune from suit under the 1982 act, Rowland could be much more forthcoming verbally about the failings of his predecessors than corporate chieftains who might have to worry about stockholder lawsuits. But he had to assure Lloyd's the resources to pay the claims, and he had to tell the Names that however badly they had been treated by their agents, they would have to pay up on the losses those agents had incurred.

Closing down Lloyd's, Rowland warned, was not a possible answer. It "would be," he said, "a disaster of almost unimaginable proportions. We are governed by the Lloyd's Act; in it there are no provisions for cessation of trade. Winding up the Society would provide no magic solution, names would remain liable come what may for all insurance contracts underwritten by them, steps would be taken to freeze our assets and the cost of organising a 'run off' of our liabilities would be enormous. No new income would be generated from new business and the names concerned would be left to pay for administration and claims with every lawyer in the world, from the USA or elsewhere, chasing them. And who will pay for this? The membership. . . . It would mean greater suffering, much greater suffering, for the membership of this Society."[2]

At some point in this stage of the game, however, it seemed to have occurred to Rowland and Peter Middleton that Lloyd's had moved into a new area of peril. Standard & Poor's, the ratings agency, was looking at Lloyd's and its policies, and by June probably had indicated to management what it published in July, that Lloyd's "does not appear to offer the highest level of security." David Bruce, Lloyd's recently appointed finance director, who had joined with enthusiastic endorsements of the new management only two months earlier, was beginning to indicate the concerns about Lloyd's prospects that would lead him to resign abruptly in August "to pursue other interests" after only four months on the job. Bruce made no statement at the time, and has said nothing since, to explain his abrupt departure.[3]

Dangers had emerged at the heart of the enterprise. Feeling that they had not been treated fairly, an ever-increasing number of Names were looking for ways not to pay what Lloyd's said they owed. It was already obvious that some Names couldn't pay, and that the Central Fund, which David Coleridge had augmented in 1992 with a levy on premium income to be paid over three years by all Names, would have to be tapped heavily to make up the shortfall.

Now something approaching half the membership was either

suing or threatening to sue their agents or the syndicates. The position that Names had to pay first and sue later was beginning to erode. The suits themselves were terrible publicity. If they were lost—and it had begun to dawn on the new leadership that they might be lost—many more Names would probably come to believe they could get away without paying their Lloyd's bills. Showering writs on the membership would be even worse publicity, and would endanger policyholders' beliefs that their Lloyd's policies would pay if needed. Warburg's had already warned Lloyd's that it would be difficult to raise a loan to tide the insurance market over any substantial and prolonged shortfall of cash to pay the policyholders.

Obviously, Names who were continuing to underwrite would have to continue paying on past losses to remain in the game, but Names who dropped out would have much less incentive to do so. The first line of attack, then, was to paint the rosiest possible picture of future "profits" at Lloyd's. In 1993, this presentation was not completely credible. It was already clear that the 1991 year of account would show a considerable loss (even after deductions for "double counting," it ran about twice what Rowland was predicting in 1993), and it was hard to be too optimistic about the 1992 year of account, which included Hurricane Andrew, a devastation of south Florida that ranks as the largest single cause of insured loss in the history of the casualty insurance industry.

Two steps, then, had to be taken. First, the assurance of 1993 "profits" had to be hyped. Lloyd's would announce that managing agents would be encouraged to credit Names with 5 percent of their 1993 premiums even before the year ended, to help them continue to underwrite in 1994. (There wasn't any *cash* in this, you understand: just a credit to your account that you couldn't take out of Lloyd's.) And committees would be appointed to explore the possibilities of a once-and-for-all "settlement" between Lloyd's and all the Names in the action groups who were suing their agents. One committee, headed by the distinguished former judge Sir Michael Kerr, would look at the relative strength of the cases that had been brought, and determine the likelihood that each would prevail in the British courts. The other, headed by Sir Jeremy Morse, former chairman of Lloyd's Bank and officer of the Bank of England (and a member of the Council of Lloyd's), would look at the resources available to Lloyd's to help the burned Names, and would establish the "quantum" that could be awarded each of the action groups.

The brilliance of both the advance profit allocation and the settlement proposal was that neither of them would deplete Lloyd's resources. The money would not be paid to the Names but credited to their accounts. By summer 1993 the majority of the market—including virtually all the people who were suing—had losses to be paid. Though a number of people had been bankrupted, Lloyd's had called only a fraction of these losses, and the calls for the 1990 year were just beginning. The profit allocation and any settlements would be used to meet the cash calls, not withdrawn from the system. For many, that would enable them to continue underwriting, which would encourage those who had debts over and above the new credits to keep paying what Lloyd's said they owed.

The easy analogy is to a bunch of gamblers who have been playing a roulette wheel in Las Vegas, and having compared notes go to a lawyer and ask him to sue on the grounds that the casino has been running a crooked wheel. The casino, pained, says it has not been running a crooked wheel, it runs an honest wheel, these fellows are just sore losers, if the matter ever came to trial the casino would win hands down, but to avoid bad publicity it's prepared to offer a settlement: It will give the plaintiffs markers so they can return to the casino and continue to play the wheel.

Rowland obviously could not appoint representatives of the action groups to the Kerr committee, where they would have to sit in judgment on the validity of one another's claims, but he did invite several of them, headed by Christopher Stockwell of the Lloyd's Names Associations' Working Party, to be part of the Morse committee. All the action groups bestirred themselves mightily to make their presentations to Justice Kerr in the summer of 1993—at great expense, too: There were those who felt the whole project was a scheme to denude the action groups of resources and diminish their capacity to carry on their lawsuits. Delegates from LNAWP met often with Sir Jeremy.

The Kerr committee took a rather restrictive view of the statute of limitations as it applied to suits against Lloyd's entities, but did find a number of "strong" and "medium" cases against both Names' agents and managing agents. The Morse committee then published a grand estimate it had received from Lloyd's (it was not given access to anyone's records) of the malpractice (errors and omissions, or E&O) insurance carried by the agents in the 1980s— most of it within but some of it external to the Lloyd's market (about $450 million, Morse said). Adding the contributions that could be made by the Names' agents themselves (because they were being sued for large amounts of money, about $75 million), plus an ex gratia payment Lloyd's could make from its Central Fund to get out from under the lawsuits ($825 million, most of the fund), the committee came up with a total of about $1.35 billion. That would be the end of it.

People with "strong" cases in the Kerr analysis would be offered more, people with "weak" cases would be offered less. All losses above and beyond the number in Rowland's offering letter would have to be paid in full. There could be no cap on future liabilities of the Names. As part of the settlement, Names would have to acknowledge that they owed whatever Lloyd's might in the future claim from them, and give up to Lloyd's any claims they might have on earnings from the existing reserves in their syndicates, on external insurers of Lloyd's agents, and on the syndicates' accountants who had approved what had turned out to be seriously deficient reinsurances to close.

The money from the Lloyd's Central Fund, interestingly, would be channeled *through* the E&O insurers, relieving them of much of their potential obligation for negligence by their insureds, which would be a great relief to those who had backed the syndicates that wrote the E&O policies. One Lloyd's antagonist worked the numbers, and came out with savings of $700,000 for Rowland, $1.3 million for Nutting (who had urged Names to accept the deal, and publicly regretted his own victory in Outhwaite 317), $1.4 million for Stephen Merrett, then on the Council, and $950,000 for Lady Rona Delves Broughton, whose column in *One Lime Street* warned Names that if they didn't accept the offer, they'd have nothing but lawsuits to show for their pains.

The key question for the leaders of the action groups represented on the Morse committee was the amount of E&O coverage the agents had from the years before these policies were canceled. Lloyd's refused to let the representatives of the Names see the real number, which the action groups thought was much higher than the $450 million Morse had allocated. In fact it was much higher, and Lloyd's knew it: A study had been commissioned of the E&O cover available to the agents involved in the spiral, and the number was $1.4 billion. Stockwell and his colleagues suspected that they had deliberately been given a lowball number by Morse acting under instruction from the Council, and also felt that Middleton had promised the people on the "long-tail" syndicates a cap on their future losses, and had broken his promise.

As noted in the first chapter, I had a drink with Chris Stockwell of the Lloyd's Names Associations' Working Party at the Reform Club right after the last meeting of the Morse committee, in November 1993, when he was crestfallen and angry. The offer had been cleverly constructed, he said, to give the claimants who were victims of the spiral a good percentage of what they had asked— up to 42 percent in the case of the Gooda Walker Names—but they would probably feel it wasn't enough, and the Names on the "long-tail" syndicates, who were mostly offered less than a third of their already recognized losses and nothing against their future losses, would feel cheated.

The only time Judge Breyer lost his cool in his correspondence on Lloyd's matters was when he was asked to react to the settlement he was offered in return for accepting any and all future

losses on Merrett 418 (1985). He wrote his agent at Sturge to inquire about how his existing stop-loss insurance would work, and
was told he would have to pay out losses and claim his reimbursement later (usually about six months later) from his stop-loss insurer. He then asked whether the money under the settlement if
he accepted it would go to him or to the stop-loss insurer, and was
told that the settlement funds "would have the effect of reducing"
his loss position, and therefore would be added to the deductible
on his losses before the stop-loss insurance kicked in.

"My total losses to date," Judge Breyer wrote to the corre-
sponding secretary of the 418 Action Group, "are close to 25,000
pounds. When they reach 25,000 pounds, my stop loss policy will
begin to reimburse me (up to 125,000 pounds). If I accept the settlement (say, of 10,000 pounds), my stop loss policy will not begin
to reimburse me, as the stop loss insurers will consider that I have
lost only 15,000 pounds, not 25,000 pounds. That means that, if I
were to accept the settlement, I would simply have to pay out the
10,000 pounds for losses over the next year or so, instead of having my stop loss policy pay for them. I would have gained nothing; only my stop loss insurer would have gained. . . . Why would
any person accept a settlement under such circumstances (unless
he does not understand them)?"[4]

Meanwhile, Judge Breyer's agent at Sturge wrote coolly that
she believed the number in the settlement offer he had been sent
was wrong, and Lloyd's would be sending a new estimate of what
the Morse committee had allocated to Merrett 418. So it did:
About a month after the original offers under the settlement had
been mailed to Names, a new envelope appeared in the mailbox
adding about 5 percent to the original figure because there had
been calculation errors in the first analysis. For some, this indication of continuing incompetence at Lloyd's was the last straw.

The Association of Lloyd's Members solidified its reputation as
Lloyd's ally by endorsing the settlement offer as an act of gen-
erosity by Lloyd's and the best the Names could hope for. Charles
Sturge of Chatset denounced the offer to Names on the "long-

tail" syndicates as entirely inadequate, but urged the Names on the spiral syndicates to accept, on the grounds that even if they won their suits, there probably wouldn't be much more in the kitty than they were being offered. It is not clear where his guidance would have left the deal, which Lloyd's had made contingent on acceptance by 70 percent of the stamp capacity in the syndicates that were suing, for in the end all but one of the action groups voted to turn it down. The only exception was Merrett 421, a syndicate with too few Names to support a full-scale legal attack.

Chris Stockwell had told Morse, then Rowland and Middleton, that the settlement offer would fail, but they continued to claim a silent majority until the votes were counted in February 1994. I thought Rowland might be right, because so many Englishmen still stand in awe of traditional authority. And he wasn't entirely wrong: The offer *was* accepted by a little more than half the Names to whom it was made, but turned down by more than 60 percent of the stamp capacity. Rowland and Middleton angrily washed their hands of settlement, said they would pursue the Names for their money by all legal means, and they would help the agents defend the lawsuits in every way they could, and there would never again be an offer from Lloyd's to its Names: The future Lloyd's would rise from their ashes, with some help from corporate capital.

So the case of the Names against Gooda Walker, advertised as the largest lawsuit in English history, more than three thousand plaintiffs and a claim for more than $1.3 billion, came to trial in April 1994. I went to the Royal Courts of Justice to hear the opening arguments in the case. Only the British could maintain dignity with two pigtails at the back of the wig bouncing up and down off their shoulders. Because they didn't have to waste time bringing the subject matter down to the comprehension level of the jury, they were free to ask their learned friends all sorts of very technical and boring questions. Jeffrey Vas, the barrister representing the Names, was young and relatively inexperienced, and you could see he was nervous. But as he got into the meat of the case,

he lost his inhibitions, and his examinations of the former Gooda
Walker underwriters were devastating.

•

The period 1993–95 was necessarily a holding action for Lloyd's, a
scramble to collect enough money from the Names and from the
new premiums accepted by the ongoing syndicates to pay the
claims. The claims were incessant, piling up from past reinsurance
of insurers of natural disasters, transportation and industrial accidents, professional malpractice, and some part of the latent liabilities unluckily insured in prior years. Presumably the bad fortune
of 1988–92 would in itself raise rates in the insurance cycle to
make the Lloyd's market profitable again—especially after the
new management cut costs and Darwinian selection weeded out
the most incompetent underwriters. But syndicates that kept accepting reinsurance to close from previous syndicates saddled with
"long-tail" risks would never gain the full benefits of the better
rates, and the pileup of open syndicates would give Lloyd's still
more losing years taking the market as a whole, even after the
"pure year" results turned profitable. Even the optimistic report
for 1992, showing a tiny profit on the pure year before members'
expenses, showed a $1.2 billion loss when the policies reinsured
from previous years were counted.

Ongoing Names and new corporate capital thus had to be assured that the losses from the old years would be taken off their
shoulders. NewCo had to be *assumed*. For the years 1994 and
1995, the rule would be that nobody could reinsure risks from
1985 or before—some part of all syndicates with such risks would
have to remain in run-off for a year or two. Thereafter, all these
old risks would be absorbed in the new insurance company Lloyd's
would spin off for that purpose, equipping it with enough reserves
to pay off these "long-tail" liabilities as they came due in the years
ahead.

As a matter of analysis, NewCo's problem was that it was unlikely to work. Richard Keeling, in charge of the project, cheerfully

admitted that providing sufficient reserves to *guarantee* that NewCo would pay the claims that might be brought under pre-1986 Lloyd's policies required a number that "would knock your socks off." Thus assumptions would have to be made in four areas: the amounts NewCo would have to pay out; the reserves the syndicates would transfer to NewCo; the amounts Names would pay NewCo to be reinsured out of their future obligations under old Lloyd's policies; and the earnings NewCo could anticipate from the investment of its resources.

All these would be judgment calls, made more difficult by the poor record-keeping procedures of most of the syndicates that had got in trouble and the difficulty of reconstructing the records of the managing agencies that had already gone broke. Only the brokers had complete information about which syndicates backed which policies, and the reserves came in a great variety of forms, a mishmash of real investments in bonds that could be marked to market, reinsurance contracts (which might be with shaky insurers, inside or outside Lloyd's), time and distance policies that were being carried like lottery winnings at the total of their payout over the years rather than their actual discounted current value, and loans to other Lloyd's syndicates that might well be unable to pay them back.

In the end, the reserves claimed for NewCo would be in considerable part guesswork. Obviously, Names would have to pay into these reserves to get the monkey of annual cash calls off their backs, and for many of them it would be simply impossible even if they wished to do so to make the contribution in a single lump up front. Perhaps, project director Heidi Hutter suggested, they could pay on an installment plan over a period of years (with interest, of course).

Only one of the estimates Ms. Hutter was to make could be entirely validated before NewCo opened for business: the amount of their reserves the managing agents with ongoing syndicates that carried "long-tail" liabilities would be willing to turn over to NewCo as a reinsurance of those liabilities. In this negotiation, the managing agents would hold all the cards, for they could move their business out of Lloyd's if Hutter was too demanding. Still, the sums of money involved were not so large that a shortfall in this category would doom the enterprise, though a sense that the insiders were getting away with something might damage the willingness of Names to make their contribution to the pot.

One does not criticize the integrity of the people working on this project by noting that the Council who pay their salaries expect their judgment calls to let NewCo be born. If it becomes necessary to assume that claims under old Lloyd's policies will be "commuted" (i.e., claimants will agree to take less than the face value of their policies says they should receive), NewCo will assume commutations. Values for doubtful reinsurance policies will be optimistically calculated, it will be assumed that loans to other syndicates are going to be repaid with interest by the Names on those syndicates, interest rates will be assumed to increase the present value of the time and distance policies, and different interest rates will be assumed to give encouraging estimates of the earnings NewCo should expect from its reserves.

A few months after his private admission that a real guarantee of NewCo would require a number that would knock your socks off, Richard Keeling suggested in a public speech that Lloyd's might have *overreserved* for its "long-tail" losses, a suggestion that was dropped quickly when outside observers noted that since 1985 the syndicates with such losses found themselves compelled to demand an increase in these reserves virtually every year. Since 1992, moreover, Lloyd's has recommended to managing agents a policy of calling cash from Names only when the money is needed for policyholders, not to build reserves, which argues strongly that the market is under- rather than overreserved.

Meanwhile, as *The Economist* has unkindly pointed out, Lloyd's has hired as assistants in the NewCo project several veterans of the Department of Trade and Industry office that will have to pass on the adequacy of NewCo's financing and risks before licensing it as an insurance company. These worthies, *The Economist* sug-

gests, "can help nudge their former colleagues towards a more understanding view."[5] Middleton gave me a very blunt statement of
his view of the NewCo solvency scenario: "We'll choose a figure,
and the DTI and the U.S. Commissioners will have to prove us
wrong."

Though Lloyd's in fact has become an engine by which the
wealth of the English counties is transferred to American law
firms, the myth at the British government is still that this part of
the insurance industry makes a significant contribution to the nation's balance of payments by its "invisible" earnings. All the political pressures will be for the chartering of NewCo, or Equitas, as
the name will be. And, of course, the decision is safe for years to
come—however inadequate the Equitas reserves might eventually prove to be, the nature of "long-tail" liabilities guarantees
that push will not come to shove until long after those who approved its creation have moved on to other jobs.

If NewCo could have solved its dilemma, then, Lloyd's might
have been home free. Unfortunately, the "long-tail" liabilities are
only part, and not the largest part, of what the Lloyd's syndicates
owe. The spirals began to go in 1988, and from 1989 through 1992,
the "pure year" of new policies took severe losses. Under policies
written in 1986 and later, Lloyd's Names have losses that run
more than $6 billion, many of them not yet the subject of cash
calls because they are being fought in the courts, or are still winding their way up the chain of reinsurance. And many believe
Lloyd's simply does not have the cash to pay these bills.

Hence the decision in May 1995 to fold *everything* into Equitas—and hence also the two-steps-forward, one-step-back tactics
Lloyd's employed with its Names throughout 1994. One month
there would be a shower of cash calls, earmarkings from the Central Fund when the cash calls go unanswered, and then writs to
compel Names to repay the Central Fund for money expended on
their account. Rowland or Middleton or the Council through its
spokesmen at the public relations firm of Hill and Knowlton
would proclaim an end to Mr. Nice Guy, a decision to go after

Names with professional bill collectors, a statement of respect for and sympathy with all the other, good Names who had paid their legitimate debts and now were livid about the deadbeats who wouldn't bear their share of the burden.

In fall 1994, Lloyd's appointed professional debt collectors to handle its relations with resigned Names—"the Rottweilers," as Christopher Stockwell called them—but charged them to negotiate rather than simply impose Lloyd's demands. Graeme King, who had been at the tables in Dallas to discourage people who wanted to talk about suing, resigned, and bankruptcy lawyer Philip Holden, a sinister-looking young man with slicked black hair (Stockwell's original Rottweiler) was installed at the head of a new Financial Recoveries Department. Names who dealt with Holden and his assistants thought their job was to nose out the total assets of the debtors with whom they made contact, to make sure Lloyd's got absolutely everything that was there.

At the meeting of North American Names in Dallas in September 1994, Ralph Bunje, who had been hired to tell Names he represented their interests and would see them through their Lloyd's negotiations, told a group of Canadians that they should not look for salvation to the lawsuits by the action groups, because Lloyd's council was about to pass a bylaw expropriating for its premium trust fund any moneys that might be paid out to Names in connection with court awards. They needed a new bylaw, as Bunje did not explain, because in the case of *Napier* v. *Kershaw* in 1993 (approved by the Court of Appeal as *The Society of Lloyd's* v. *Morris*), the courts had ruled that recoveries in lawsuits by Names against Lloyd's agents had to be paid to the Names directly, not to their Lloyd's account, if they requested it.

As most of the plaintiffs in the lawsuits involving the spirals had already paid Lloyd's and were seeking reimbursement for the losses imposed on them by their negligent agents, seizure of the proceeds by Lloyd's under a new bylaw would be seen as a final outrage, especially by the Canadians to whom Bunje was speaking. But it was true: In October the council proposed what Bunje had described, and announced that a month later it would submit its amended premium trust deed to the government, where the minister of Trade and Industry, wearing his other hat as president of the Board of Trade, would have to approve it before Lloyd's could enforce it.

"Many Names will use their recoveries [in the lawsuits]," the Lloyd's proposal explained, "to satisfy their outstanding underwriting liabilities. Others may not and in these circumstances Lloyd's only remedy will be to seek recovery of amounts owed through the Courts. In the case of Names living abroad the proceedings will have to be commenced in Courts in the appropriate foreign jurisdiction. This will be an extremely costly and time consuming exercise for the Society to have to undertake."[6]

Then, a few weeks after their belligerent pronouncements, Rowland or Middleton or the Council would reverse course, proclaim sympathy with the Names, and announce a willingness to consider what each Name could afford to pay. Each time the cycle went round, the tactics were less productive. At its peak in July 1994, the total of unpaid cash calls approached $3.5 billion, more than double the amount in the Central Fund, and in October Lloyd's was still almost $2 billion light, and borrowing wherever it could find willing lenders. To gain the Department of Trade and Industry certificate of solvency to write insurance in 1995, Lloyd's had to pledge the new building (valued at about $600 million, which is more than it's worth in today's property market) as part of its reserves.

All Lloyd's had left by fall 1994 was aggressive statements of optimism—1993 had been "very profitable," 1994 looked good (despite the Los Angeles earthquake, the USAir and American Eagle crashes, the sinking of the Baltic car ferry, the Italian floods), and 1995 was extremely promising, though in point of fact rates were deteriorating. There was an almost desperate need among many of the badly wounded but surviving Names to accept such claims: "Trade through" and Lloyd's will make you whole. As John Rew put it, "People believe the money they've lost is still connected to them by an invisible thread. All you have to do is find the right mantra, and it will all come back."

The loss of the Gooda Walker case left Lloyd's in several different limbos. Of the four thousand Names on the Gooda Walker syndicates, about nine hundred did not sue. Some doubtless were too broke to join in engaging a firm of solicitors to prosecute the case, others were probably working Names, whose participation in the lawsuits was vigorously opposed by the Council. Among the weapons Lloyd's could wield was that the judges in these cases permitted counsel for Lloyd's defendants to choose whichever of the Names in the suit they wished as subjects for special "discovery" to determine whether or not they had known what they had signed on for. Lady Rona Delves Broughton had been a member of the Gooda Walker Action Group, and the agents had singled her out to be one of the named plaintiffs subject to discovery. Lady Broughton's money derives from marriages and love affairs, and as a member of the Council of Lloyd's she might have some difficulty asserting ignorance as to what was going on, so she withdrew from the action group. After the case was won, she told friends about the recoveries she would receive when the judge assessed the final award, but the fact was—as nobody wanted to tell her—that having withdrawn from the suit, she was no longer entitled to a recovery.

British law does not know "class action" lawsuits, in which individuals can petition to be added to the class after the case is won, and Lady Delves Broughton, like the nine hundred who never sued, will have to continue paying the claims on her Gooda Walker participations. But even an English court bound by rules rather than equity might find it hard to enforce Lloyd's future writs against Names whose losses had been described in another court as the result of underwriting that was "unintended, unplanned and unjustified by any proper analysis of risk."[7]

In early 1995, the Council adopted a number of amendments to the premium trust deed that determines how a member's premium income may be invested. The most advertised of them was one that would have required winners of lawsuits against Lloyd's agents and underwriters to deposit their winnings at Lloyd's so long as any of the syndicates they had backed were still open. But the most far-reaching was a group of amendments that made it easier for managing agents to borrow from premium trust funds, explained to Names as intended to "improve short term liquidity and could lead to savings in borrowing costs."[8]

With the publication of the New York State Insurance Department report on Lloyd's in late May 1995, it developed that Lloyd's had *always* been borrowing from the premium trust funds of Names who had money for the benefit of policyholders whose Names didn't have money—and had indeed structured its operation in such a way that such borrowings were unavoidable. "[E]ach Name's assets in LATF [Lloyd's American Trust Fund] is for the purpose of meeting that Name's liabilities and not liabilities of other Names," the department reported glumly. But "an LATF allocation by Name is not maintained by the Trustee or centrally by Lloyd's."

It should be noted that two weeks after the publication of this document revealing that Citibank did not have and would not have a record of which Name owned what, Lloyd's submitted an affidavit on this subject as part of its reply in a lawsuit in a New Jersey court. The affidavit was by Andrew Alexander Duguid, secretary of the Council of Lloyd's. He swore under oath that American policyholders were protected by a provision in the trust deed that "an American business policyholder who obtains a final judgment against any name in respect of the Name's liability under a policy of American business may deposit an authenticated copy of that judgment with the United States Trustee, Citibank N.A., which is required to pay that judgment out of the assets of the LATF of the responsible Name."[9]

"[I]n instances where a claim is required to be paid from LATF and there are insufficient funds in a particular group account," the New York report continued, "Lloyd's instructs Citibank to draw down on a pool of funds held in certain other group accounts, regardless of whether or not these group accounts are under the control of the same Managing Agent and despite the fact that a Name's funds that are drawn on may have no liability for the claim, in order to ensure that the claim is settled. In effect, Lloyd's borrows one Name's assets to pay for another Name's liabilities.

"As LATF Deed did not provide for the use of one Name's assets to pay another Name's liabilities, Lloyd's was asked to produce documentation to support this practice. Lloyd's advised that it was its United States counsel's opinion that such practice is permitted so long as it is prudent and that it will amend the LATF Deeds to provide the Trustee with the requisite powers. In view of the fact that certain Names are unable or unwilling to fund their Lloyd's liabilities, it is questionable as to whether or not it is prudent to make such loans."[10]

In fact, all the evidence is that before Lloyd's as a whole became squeezed for cash, borrowing from the LATF was *not* permitted. When C. H. Bohling 833/834 reported such borrowings in a report for 1992, Lloyd's management made a scandal of the matter and circularized the membership to tell everyone that LATF was not to be treated as a source for loans, and that the market had to be out of all such liabilities by the end of 1993. Certainly no Name knew that his resources were being made available for such purposes. And, as the department points out, the quality of the assets in the LATF becomes highly suspect if the fund's reported $5.7 billion in short-term investments includes loans to busted syndicates. Moreover, all Lloyd's accounting is suspect if in addition to the published "earmarkings" from the Central Fund to cover the debts of Names who can't or won't pay, there are additional unreported borrowings from the assets of Names held in trust in New York. And that appears to be the case.

●

The most remarkable and unlikely—and perhaps the most damaging—of the cases against Lloyd's was the brainchild of John

Flynn, an Irish Name, who decided that the Lloyd's system could be challenged under European Community law. With breathtaking fidelity to the letter and the spirit of the law, the Writs Response Group that grew out of Flynn's initial suggestion argued that the Central Fund gave Lloyd's syndicates an unfair advantage over other European insurance companies, an advantage made even more unfair by the practice of giving syndicates full credit in their reserves for reinsurance or T&D policies purchased at Lloyd's but only partial credit for such policies purchased elsewhere. Because of the Central Fund and its access to Names' total resources, Lloyd's syndicates could offer greater assurance of payment than could be offered by companies that had to rely entirely on their own assets, thus violating Section 14 of Article 85 of the European Community Treaty.

If the Central Fund is illegal under European law, then it cannot bring suit to collect from Names the payments made on their behalf when the syndicates of which they are members notify Lloyd's that they have not met a cash call. This being the mechanism by which the losses under policies are transformed into claims against Names, the entire Lloyd's process must shudder to a halt. Brought in the name of John Stewart Clementson, the case was developed by Richard Slowe of S. J. Berwin, a gifted young lawyer with Byronic good looks who is a barrister as well as a solicitor, and it was argued by Jeremy Lever, Q.C., who is not only a barrister but also a fellow of All Souls College at Oxford, England's tip-top club of meritocratic geniuses.

In December 1993, Justice Saville ruled against the Names, who appealed. I went to the hearings, together with a number of young law students (you could tell they were law students because they all wore black suits—a tradition of the British courts is that the judges "cannot hear" anyone who is not wearing all black). The judges, chaired by Sir Thomas Bingham, the Master of the Rolls, wore the most formal of British legal wigs, with white horsehair curls going down their shoulders. The appeal was heard in one of the wood-paneled modernized courtrooms at the Royal Courts of

Justice, pale birchwood walls and ceiling lights encased in plastic, without so much as some stone statuary to distract the visitor. On the first day it was so boring I'd rather have been at the dentist.

But then I became caught up in the case. If I were a Brit, I would be proud of such a judicial system. Both sides had entered long submissions, and the three judges had obviously read them and other material they had decided would be relevant. Their questions explored every aspect of the subject. After each question, Lever would pause briefly, and then answer in complete detail, with case citations. Every so often his solicitor would offer him a bundle of papers to check the references, but he wouldn't look at it, he had everything in his head.

On November 10, 1994, the Court of Appeal overruled Justice Saville and held that the matter was indeed something that could be decided only by the courts of the European Union. The case as presented was too strong. Over and over again, Justice Bingham used phrases like "I do not feel able to reject Mr. Clementson's argument . . . as plainly wrong in law." Both he and Justice L. Hoffman, who entered a concurring opinion, considered it possible that Lloyd's could have gained exemption from the provision of the European Community Treaty if it had applied for one. "The doubts which exist about the compatibility of various Lloyd's by-laws and directions with European competition law," Justice Hoffman wrote, "seem to me to stem from the ambiguous nature of Lloyd's in the insurance world. For some purposes it presents itself as a single institution seeking to preserve or increase its market share against outsiders and for other purposes it acts as an association of individual insurers, each competing with each other as well as with outside insurers. Rules which are entirely acceptable on the first hypothesis may well be anti-competitive on the second. Lloyd's could have resolved this identity crisis by notifying its rules to the Commission, as it repeatedly said it would do. But for reasons which have never been explained, it decided not to."[11]

The result of the case was that until the European courts ruled in Brussels, which would take at least two years, Lloyd's was barred from issuing writs to seize the property of Names who had not paid their calls. *One Lime Street*, with the cheery optimism that had come upon it after the American public relations firm of Hill and Knowlton took over Lloyd's representation, noted that the decision "only affects Lloyd's ability to obtain court judgments among members for their debts. . . . Lloyd's ability to draw down members' funds at Lloyd's and make cash calls is unimpaired."[12]

Less than a month later, on December 7, 1994, the Lloyd's Council decided not to seek approval from the Department of Trade and Industry for the proposed bylaw that would commandeer the Names' winnings on the Gooda Walker case for the Lloyd's Central Fund. The proposal, Rowland said, was still on the table, but would not be pursued at that time. The truth seemed to be that his letter to Names announcing what the Council was going to do about the Gooda Walker verdict had provoked a storm of angry responses, including a threat of litigation from the action groups. For just about the first time since they formed their working party, all the chairmen of all the action groups agreed to a united action, hiring counsel to enjoin Lloyd's from seizing the proceeds of court actions against its various agents.

In public statements, Lloyd's simply brushed aside the Court of Appeal ruling in the *Clementson* case: "Lloyd's is confident of overturning this judgment," *The Economist* reported.[13] Once that nuisance was removed, the issuance of writs would be legal again— but for the time being, obviously, writs were out. Then Lloyd's decided an appeal could *not* be won, and asked for expedited hearings on whether the Central Fund was indeed illegal under the European treaty. A little later, Rowland found he really needed the money from the writs the Central Fund could no longer issue, and instructed the Names' agents to issue their own writs against Names who hadn't paid, on pain of losing their affiliation with Lloyd's if they refused. These people are, of course, agents for *Names*, not for Lloyd's, receiving their income from their clients— but an order is an order, and the letters went out. A quarter of a century earlier, Lord Cromer had observed with amazement the absence at Lloyd's of any sense of fiduciary obligation to the members, any understanding of what the word "agent" meant.

Despite Rowland's insistence in February that Lloyd's had made its last and best offer to the Names, he had already indicated in his talk to the American Names in Dallas in the spring that he was looking for a way to resume negotiations. Now he announced that efforts to find a settlement should be resumed. Michael Deeny of the Gooda Walker Action Group suggested that putting another billion dollars in the pot might boost a settlement offer over the top. But where would the billion dollars come from? In December 1994, the Central Fund was already overcommitted by about $300 million, and Hutter could scarcely sacrifice any Equitas reserves for this purpose. And, as Rowland already knew though the rest of the world did not, the New York State Department of Insurance was about to demand another $500 million deposit to the Lloyd's American Trust Fund if its syndicates were to continue writing reinsurance in America.

So Lloyd's could not do without the credits from the Gooda Walker award, and did demand from Michael Heseltine, the minister for trade and industry, approval of a Lloyd's charter change that would seize for the Central Fund any lawsuit winnings by Names who still had open years at Lloyd's. Heseltine granted the change—but only with the proviso that the money would have to be held in escrow pending approval by the English courts of the changes to the Premium Trust Deeds, which left Lloyd's hungrier for funds. The Lloyd's Names Litigation Committee promptly brought suit. Some observers cast doubt on how much Lloyd's could hope to recover, even if the new bylaw was ruled acceptable. Many of the Gooda Walker Names had been on Gooda Walker syndicates alone, so that Lloyd's would have no color of justice in taking their money. It would not be easy to argue that Lloyd's was entitled to money from the Gooda Walker Names because they still owed on contracts the court had already ruled were so negligently drawn that they should receive a refund on previous losses.

CHAPTER 11

THE ENDGAMES

Among the casualties of the Lloyd's episode is some of the traditional Anglo-American amity. Americans believe firmly that the British had kept Lloyd's for themselves while it was a good thing, and opened it up for foreign membership only after the losses of the 1960s had demonstrated the dangers of unlimited liability. When those dangers had become disastrous—after the U.S. courts opened the door to unlimited awards on the other side of the general liability insurance contract, and the U.S. Congress created retroactive liability for industrial polluters—Names' agents crossed the ocean to recruit and lure the innocent to take losses. These losses were proportionately much greater for them than for the established members, because they were placed into dangerous and incompetently managed syndicates and denied access to those syndicates that would continue to be profitable through the years of heavy losses for the market as a whole. Awakening to their peril, the American Names were comforted with incomplete information by their agents, inaccurate projections by Lloyd's itself, and misleading stories in the respectable British press, most of which swallowed the Lloyd's line year after year. When, like red-blooded Americans, they went to their lawyers to sue, they found that they could be refused the protection of their country's laws because they had signed a contract agreeing to resolve their disputes with Lloyd's under British law.

British Names feel just as strongly that they have been victimized by an American legal system that is run essentially for the benefit of the lawyers, who bring far-fetched lawsuits because under the contingent fee system one winning case pays for a lot of losers. More than half the money insurers have paid out to asbestosis victims has gone into the pockets of the lawyers, and there's been a lot of money to the lawyers of plaintiffs who are not really asbestosis victims but worked with asbestos years ago and now claim it's made them sick. The pollution cases are even worse in terms of the fraction of reward that goes to the lawyers (on both sides) rather than to the cleanup. And the malpractice cases are perhaps the worst of all, with lawyers advertising on public transportation and on the back covers of the telephone books to alert people to the idea that they can sue their doctor if the operation doesn't restore them to perfect health.

The Pan Am Lockerbie case illustrates the reason for British resentment. The American courts have ruled that Pan Am's baggage handling practices in Germany were sufficiently negligent that the airline is liable to the families of passengers killed by the terrorist bomb. The airline itself is long bankrupt, but its insurance policies survive. Lloyd's share is apparently something like $400 million, and the size of the first awards in the case ($19 million to the wife and children of a businessman who died in the crash) argue that the entire amount will be needed. Most of that is supposed to come from syndicates that took the last pieces on the spiral. Those syndicates are dead, their Names are tapped out— and those Names that have anything left will have the Gooda Walker and Feltrim decisions to hold them harmless. So the entire burden will fall on the Central Fund, which doesn't have the money.

Because lawyers can put their hands in what the courts consider the deep pockets of insurers, Englishmen and Englishwomen have had to sell their homes, pull their children from the boarding schools to which the family has sent its young for generations, descend to a genteel poverty from which there may be no escape. Meanwhile, rubbing salt into the wounds, an increasing number of Americans who could pay won't pay, and Lloyd's may not be able to do anything about it. Sometimes at meetings in England I speak very softly, hoping people won't notice my American accent.

The truth beneath the surface may be that the blame for the destruction of Lloyd's does rest on Americans—not so much the lawyers as the giant insurance brokers. Lloyd's was organized on a basis of trust between the insurance brokers and the underwriters, that the former would never conceal from the latter any unusual elements of danger in a risk being carried to the box, and the latter would all but unquestioningly accept the former's evaluation of the strength of a client's claim. Forbidding foreigners to own Lloyd's brokers, which the Committee that ran Lloyd's before the 1982 act did, was part of the background of this trust. Forbidding underwriters to become corporations and sell stock in themselves to the public was another part—if the Names had unlimited liability, it was unseemly for the managing agents to be listed companies, especially as they did not put their own capital at risk behind their policies and thus did not need much capital.

When the advertising agencies went public in the United States in the 1970s, a veteran of Procter & Gamble told a reporter that "the purpose of taking an advertising agency public is to make old advertising men rich." The purpose of taking Lloyd's managing agents public was to make Lloyd's underwriters rich. The curmudgeonly Alan Smallbone, who began writing letters to the editor in the 1970s about the disasters that would befall Lloyd's because the managing agents had incorporated, was right as rain.

Once the managing agents had become publicly owned companies, the apparent guarantor of trust became the ownership of the larger underwriters by the brokerage firms themselves. A run-of-the-mill Lloyd's underwriter, who signed slips on risks other people led, could be comforted by the thought that a broker was un-likely to do harm to his own underwriter. But when the great American brokers came into the picture in the late 1970s, they brought with them more of the buyer-beware attitudes that have always characterized large enterprises.

A lawsuit approaching trial in the American courts in 1995 al-leges that Alexander and Alexander concealed important informa-tion from Names underwriting through its Alexander Howden subsidiary to conceal the extent of its losses on its purchase of the Alexander Howden operation at Lloyd's. Individuals, and small organizations dominated by their leaders, may have a conscience. Large corporations often do not. In response to a general feeling of chicanery, brokerage and underwriting operations at Lloyd's were separated by Chinese walls, and then, not unreasonably, by legis-lation.

Lloyd's thereupon made a Faustian bargain with the giant American brokers—Marsh and McLennan, Alexander and Alexander, Johnson and Higgins, Frank B. Hall. These are compa-nies with brokerage revenues measured in the billions of dollars every year, and for the most part they can place their clients' busi-ness where they choose. With their help, Lloyd's expanded rapidly. More than two-thirds of the threefold increase in Lloyd's business in the 1980s was American, brought to the market by the world-wide American brokers. An ever-increasing proportion of this business would be reinsurance, much of it vertical excess of loss insurance that generated new premiums each time—with com-missions for the brokers higher than those paid elsewhere.

The most advertised exploiter of LMX commissions was En-glish—Bill Brown of Walsham Brothers (who broked a large frac-tion of the Gooda Walker spiral policies)—but much of the profit of American brokers came from this source. Explaining why his company was planning to back Stephen Merrett's return to the in-surance business, a broker said, "We need him. They used to do forty-five percent of our business in London with him. All the other underwriters at Lloyd's simply hold each other's hands.

Stephen was the last real risk-taker at Lloyd's. He generated an immense amount of reinsurance business."

As Lloyd's declined, the commission to the brokers necessarily increased. The young CEO of a midsized American insurance company, who does business at Lloyd's and would not like to be quoted, says that when he dies he wishes to be reincarnated as a Lloyd's broker. One analyst has estimated the brokerage paid by Lloyd's in the four years 1988–91 at almost $11 billion—roughly the mirror image of the Names' losses. The rise in premiums on catastrophe reinsurance from 1989 to 1993 approached 300 percent, and brokerage commissions, stuck at 15 percent, rose proportionately. AXA, the French insurance company, moved its American catastrophe business from London to Paris in early 1993 to take advantage of lower commission rates on the Continent. Soliciting 1994 business, a number of Lloyd's underwriters decided they could not continue to pay such commissions. One Lloyd's broker, R. K. Carvill, set up a separate North American catastrophe division that would charge only 7.5 percent: "We have recognized," a spokesman said, "that if London is to survive, we must deliver the best product to our customers in the most efficient manner." Richard Keeling suggested that 15 percent would continue to be acceptable on premiums under $2 million, but over that brokers should be satisfied with commissions calculated according to a sliding scale.[1] But few other underwriters felt strong enough to make such demands.

"Of course, brokers and agents desire the ongoing health of the Society," Rowland told the annual meeting in 1993. "Their livelihood *in part* depends upon it. Brokers particularly have choices. We are not the only insurance market in the world. There are many others. There are many others who are eager competitors for our brokers' business. We have to temper our demands on our interface with our clients so that we get the best deal once again for you, the members. . . . If we introduce terms and conditions in terms of our relationship which prevents that happening, however desirable they may seem on paper, we will not be serving you."[2]

By 1993, especially after Standard & Poor's refusal to rate the security of the policies, Lloyd's had to buy business one way or another, by paying the brokers higher commissions or charging the customers lower premiums.

●

Indeed, the situation in the United States may be more grim than anyone realizes. Lloyd's operates in America mostly as a reinsurer, under the terms of fifty separate state laws. In all but two of these states, it has always been an "unauthorized" insurer. In New York, for example, its policy must "bear across its face, in not less than ten point bold red type, the following legend: THIS INSURANCE POLICY IS WRITTEN BY AN INSURER NOT LICENSED BY THE STATE OF NEW YORK, NOT SUBJECT TO ITS SUPERVISION, AND NOT PROTECTED, IN THE EVENT OF THE INSOLVENCY OF THE INSURER, BY THE NEW YORK STATE SECURITY FUNDS."[3] Brokers are held responsible for knowing that at the unauthorized insurers with which they place policies, "management is trustworthy and competent."[4] The laws in nearly all these states require unauthorized reinsurers to maintain in the United States trust funds sufficient to pay off their estimated American liabilities, plus $100 million. The trust fund, New York law says, must be "for the exclusive protection of all direct policyholders and beneficiaries of direct policies covering property or risks located within the United States where the insurer does business on an unauthorized basis."[5] In May 1995, New York told Lloyd's to put up an additional $500 million—by the end of the month—if it wished to continue writing insurance policies for businesses or other insurance companies in that state.

The terms of the Lloyd's American Trust Deed (LAT) were first made a matter of public knowledge in late 1993, as part of a Traveler's Insurance lawsuit against a group of Lloyd's syndicates. The trustee under the trust (Citicorp) has no liability to anybody for following the instructions of a Lloyd's Names' agent. The money in the trust is available not only to pay poli-

cyholders, but also to pay "any salary, commission, or other remuneration payable to the Agent or any other person, or any
proper expenses of the Agent or any other person, in connection
with the conduct or winding up of the American business"—or,
indeed, any other "expenses whatsoever from time to time incurred in connection with any underwriting business of the
Name, whether the American business or not."[6] Names are not
to be consulted about the expenditure of money from what is
supposed to be *their* trust fund, which they thought until recently was held in their names individually though the assets
were commingled. Only the Names' agents can speak to the
trustee. Robert Hall, senior vice president of American Re-
Insurance of Princeton, thought his readers might "find it alarming that all these operating expenses are drawing on assets intended to collateralize obligations" to policyholders.[7] It is even
more alarming that Names' assets can be drained, under Lloyd's
expansive reading of the trust deed, to pay the expenses of the
agents of other Names.

Lloyd's response to the insurance department findings was first,
to amend the Lloyd's American Trust deeds written since 1986,
which the Council had the power to attempt to amend, subject to
approval by the Minister of Trade and Industry, and to request
Names with deeds dating back before 1986 to agree to amendments that would legitimize the alteration. The letter from the
Name's agent requesting this change said that the agent would
take care of it, and that while the matter was important, "no action
is required" by the Name. When I wrote Sedgwick, my Name's
agent, not to sign away my rights, they wrote back that my objec-
tion would be noted. . . . Lloyd's next response was to comment
that, after all, once Equitas was in being, all the assets were going
to be mingled anyway, so why this fuss right now? If there's no
way to tell which of the assets in the fund belong to which Names,
all Names, solvent and badly burned, may become suspicious of
their required contribution to join Equitas. Already complaints
and rumblings of yet another lawsuit are heard among action

groups. Suspicion may spread to policyholders and regulators.

Moreover, it turns out that the assets of the trust fund do not really, as the National Association of Insurance Commissioners' Model Act requires, cover all the anticipated liabilities under the policies the Names have backed. Instead, the required assets of the fund are calculated net of reinsurance recoveries, most of which are in syndicates at Lloyd's. Measuring Lloyd's American liabilities by the formula DTI claims to use in England, the insurance department found a shortfall of $7.8 *billion* in Lloyd's American accounts. ("In response to a request for the United States dollar component of the reserves used for the solvency test," the department reported, explaining why its actuaries had to do their own analyses, "Lloyd's advised that no such listing existed.")[8]

Money can be and is normally taken out of the trust fund to buy reinsurance—indeed, profits are paid to Names out of the trust fund as the residue of premium income and earnings on it after the purchase of a reinsurance to close. G. Larry Engel, of the San Francisco law firm of Brobeck, Pleger & Harrison, notes "the nightmare of one cynical policyholder where Names arrange to strip the LATF on the eve of their U.K. insolvency by paying a reinsurer a 'reinsurance premium.' "[9] Indeed, even if straightforward borrowing were prohibited, syndicates wishing to lend money to other syndicates could easily do so through the trust fund channel by purchasing reinsurance for their Names from the syndicate they wish to help. It was perhaps for that reason that the New York State Insurance Department required Lloyd's to post another $500 million to the U.S. trust fund, pronto, if it wished to continue writing policies covering New York risks.

NewCo, Engel notes, will make the situation of the American policyholder even more dubious. If NewCo goes under, Engel's "cynical policyholder" would expect the "transfer of U.S. trust funds to the NewCo provisional liquidator's insolvency estate in the U.K. . . . especially assuming that the Lloyd's American Trust deposits of Names were transferred to NewCo as reinsurance to close premiums."[10]

From the same symposium that presented the Hall and Engel views comes a general comment by Allan Gee, partner of the accounting firm of Ernst & Young in the Cayman Islands. "The present flavor of the month for solvency concerns," he notes, "Lloyd's of London, was founded in a coffeehouse in London. Under the present climate in the United States, London at that period of time would have been classed as an offshore jurisdiction with no insurance laws or regulations! Perhaps that is still the situation with respect to Lloyd's of London."[11]

●

After an evening meeting with Peter Middleton on January 24, 1995, Chris Stockwell informed the members of the Lloyd's Names Associations' Working Party that Middleton was agreeing to "every request that is being made and thereby has produced considerable scepticism about whether he either:
  a. Understands what he is agreeing to
  b. Has any intention of honouring any of the agreements
  c. Understands the implications of what he is agreeing."[12]

Lloyd's in 1995 would offer caps to liabilities, hopes to individuals that by paying an amount determined by actuaries at Equitas, they could get out now, promises to those persuaded that if the institution could be kept alive they would get it all back, and more. Lloyd's very badly needed the cash it could get by making settlements with any Name who would settle. In the market, American brokers tell me, Lloyd's syndicates have been writing catastrophe risks at prices well below those other insurers charge because they need income from premiums. "Cash-flow insurance," an insurance company CEO in North Carolina called it.

Meanwhile, in perhaps the most shameful of all the proceedings conducted behind the Lloyd's cloak, several of the prominent Names' agents were liquidating, stripping the assets of their agencies reputed to be on their way out. Stockwell set up an Agents Watch group and reported in his newsletter on agency after agency: Dawes and Henderson, Ltd., and Osborne Bell, Ltd. ("an investigation into a breach of Section 151 of the Companies Act is underway. . . . The companies passed solvency at Lloyd's on the basis of audited figures which included loans now worthless"). Stancombe and Kennington Agencies ("an investigation is underway by the liquidator . . . the payment of $400,000 dividend"). G. S. Christensen and Others Underwriting Agencies, Ltd. ("being investigated by the liquidator . . . a substantial sum of money has been removed"). London Wall (Andrew Wade's agents): ("payment of large dividends [$1.5 million in 1990 and $600,000 in 1991] when potential claims would render the company insolvent"). K. C. Webb, Wendover, Gardiner Mountain, the list went on and on. "There is no doubt," Stockwell wrote, "that agencies are clearing out their funds and taking what would be compensation for the Names."[13]

In the last week of April 1995, a rash of stories appeared in the London newspapers the *Telegraph* and the *Independent* to the effect that Lloyd's would be going down for the third time in the fall. Rowland in response admitted that the results to be reported for 1992 were going to be ghastly, but kept a stiff upper lip: Profits were lovely for the "pure years" 1993 and 1994 and would be for 1995. Maybe so, but maybe not. The first quarter of 1994 was the worst quarter in the history of catastrophe insurance. Jay Brown of Talegen comments that the profits Lloyd's has claimed for 1993 and 1994 "don't match with the book of their business that we see here. The only way they can be making such profits is if they aren't reserving properly for their long-tail liabilities."

Anyway, Rowland added, the British government stood foursquare behind Lloyd's and would certify its solvency for 1995. In early May a bureaucrat in the Department of Trade and Industry supplied Lord Alexander of Tunis, victim of the Oakeley Vaughan debacle, with the reasoning that permitted DTI to issue such certificates in the face of the evidence. Lloyd's Names, R. H. Hobbs of the insurance division explained, merely *thought* that they were sole traders. Under Part II of the Insurance Companies

Act of 1982 (which "are not applied to members of Lloyd's so long as the section 83 [usual solvency] requirements are met"), all the assets of all members of Lloyd's could be seized by the Secretary of State "to be placed in trust to the extent of their domestic liabilities. . . . Section 40 provides that no assets held by a trustee in compliance with a requirement imposed under the section shall be released except with the consent of the Secretary of State."[14] To the extent that the assets in the Lloyd's American Trust Fund are the property of the Names, which is what Lloyd's has always said they are, the New York State Department of Insurance may have a more difficult time than it knows, for by the terms of the Hobbs letter the long arm of the British government could reach into New York and remove the assets pledged to back American policies for the purpose of paying off British policies.

If the DTI has known all along that mutualization of losses is required by the Insurance Act of 1982 (to which has now been added the European Insurance Directive of 1973, just to make the cheese more binding), the British government was clearly allowing a deception when it permitted Lloyd's to continue offering contracts that told Names they were underwriting "each for his own part and not for any other."

Meanwhile, Lloyd's and its assigns retained their old habits. What damaged Lloyd's more than any other single cause was the immense increase in the cost of operating the market that accompanied the eruption of the American brokers in London. In early 1995, a respected member of the Society asked the Council to consider allowing underwriters to take business from brokers not on Lloyd's accredited list and to deal directly with policyholders, not using any broker at all, in hopes of cutting down on brokerage charges. The answer was "No," without explanation. The market continues to rely on the services of Lloyd's brokers regardless of the expense.

American policyholders may have a new deep pocket to plumb if Lloyd's reneges on reinsurance—the responsibility of the brokers to their clients for assuring that "management is trustworthy and competent" at the reinsuring company. Finding against Gooda Walker, Justice Phillips wrote, "Suppose a profession collectively adopts extremely lax standards in some aspect of its work. The court does not regard itself as bound by those standards and will not acquit practitioners of negligence simply because they complied with those standards."[15] Given the opinions of the British judges, the American brokers might find it hard to defend themselves against charges that they, too, were negligent.

●

Somewhere some econometrician and scholar of the insurance market must have done serious analysis of what a Lloyd's collapse would mean, but no one has come forth as yet. In Britain, Names often say that the reinsurance Lloyd's provides is so important to the solvency of American insurance companies that the American government will certainly ride to the rescue when needed. In the United States, apparently sophisticated Names will sigh and say, Well, bad as it looks, you have to remember that the British government simply cannot afford to have Lloyd's go under, and at the last minute Parliament or the queen will bail everybody out. I hope they are both right; I fear they are both wrong.

Certainly, the effort to unload the losses onto Equitas must tarnish the brand name of Lloyd's. Business comes to Lloyd's from brokers, who will be hard put to explain to the policyholders they originally led to Lloyd's why they should continue to give their business to a market that has organized a default at one remove on policies written as recently as three years ago. One benefit Lloyd's could hope to achieve from extending forward the mandate of Equitas was yet another year's delay, with the fees and commissions and perquisites for the insiders implied by a year's delay. But that might be the end of it. The real losses from the operation of the Lloyd's insurance market (and, in fairness, the U.S. courts) may have to be divided up among many losers: the Names, the policyholders, the insiders at Lloyd's, and governments if the operation of the market fails. Leaving that division to the courts of the two countries may be inefficient, unjust, and unwise, but perhaps the only solution for so many conflicting interests.

Companies will still need the insurance that has been written in the Lloyd's market, and will have no reason not to get it from the insurers with whom they are accustomed to doing business. If a syndicate defaulted on its policies, the value of the Lloyd's anchor stamp on other policies would be much diminished, but a proprietor's name on a Lloyd's syndicate that has performed well through the crisis would hold its value. Each for his own part and not for any other.

Though the effort to entice American money to the new world of corporate limited liability at Lloyd's did not succeed in the United States, some very sophisticated American investors have come on the scene to purchase Lloyd's managing agents. In autumn 1994, the Trident Fund, a partnership of J. P. Morgan and Marsh and McLennan, purchased a quarter of Hiscox's agency for $23.2 million, most of which was then made available as backing for the acceptance of premiums on the Hiscox syndicates for 1995. Investment Partners (led by Chase Manhattan Bank, the Robert Bass interests from Texas, and a subsidiary of American-owned Zurich Insurance) has joined with the Harvard University endowment fund to buy a quarter of Charman Group, perhaps the most consistently successful managing agent at Lloyd's, specializing in offshore oil rigs, ships, and aircraft. The price here was $137 million, and again the money was made available to back the policies. Robert Spass, managing partner of Investment Partners, explaining why his group had not accepted Lloyd's invitation to become corporate Names, said, "We were uncomfortable with an investment in which we would not have control of the people."[16] An appealing explanation of the Trident and Chase/Bass/Harvard investment is that they have acquired control of small insurance companies cheaply and could separate them from Lloyd's if need be.

The syndicates can easily fly the Lloyd's coop, to become independent companies backed by shareholders. Names, who had profited for years from fine management, doubtless would be happy to continue support in the changed form. Other Names and outside investors might be very interested in participating. I would.

Garwynn, an independent service company, currently investigates and pays claims for Brian Smith's tabled syndicate 45 and a few others. Garwynn could expand or become a model for a similar service to syndicates wishing to leave Lloyd's.

Many of the stronger Lloyd's syndicates *are* overreserved—indeed, they are profitable not because they consistently insure people who don't make claims (or because they refuse to pay claims) but because their earnings on their reserves overwhelm their losses on a careful insurance business. "In casualty reinsurance," says Frank ("the Bank") Barber, now retired, who underwrote from 1928 to 1986 with only one losing year (1956), "you have to be *very* pessimistic." Being pessimistic means not only attention to the risks insured, but also accumulation of reserves beyond the obvious needs. Malcolm Cox, trained by Barber to become his leading underwriter, says that Barber gave him the most important gift an underwriter can have: the courage to say No. Brian Smith says he reserves three times his assessment of his risk on every policy he writes. These reserves are indeed the property of the Names. Having closed their open years, managing agents leaving Lloyd's could call the reserves capital, describe their Names' continuing guarantees of the policies as "additional capital on call," and qualify to do an insurance business anywhere in the world.

The Names on these successful, mostly smaller, syndicates really do have "value at Lloyd's." They are part of a tightly knit group of business associates from many years who have historically had access to the best Lloyd's can offer. These Names are unlikely to sell their places on their favorite syndicates. Council leaders must rely upon persuasion only to influence Names' agents (as distinct from losing Names). In December 1993, an all-out effort by Peter Middleton and David Rowland, who each canceled all his other appointments for successive weeks, proved insufficient to persuade the Names' agents, many of whom are owned by brokers, to continue providing support for Stephen Merrett—even though J. P. Morgan had in effect promised to give Merrett matching funds for every pound of stamp capacity the Names provided. Rumors abound that Sturges Managing Agency is the one in biggest trouble in 1995, in spite of a small investment by Morgan through Trident. Losses at Sturges are now estimated at more than $1.5 billion.

In 1992, 12 percent of all the reinsurance bought by American insurers was placed in the Lloyd's market. That proportion was already down from 20 percent in the late 1970s, and may have dropped to 6 percent in 1994–95. The end of the spiral produced a considerable reduction in Lloyd's capacity and appetite for reinsurance business, without major systemic effects: Rates were up in 1993, but fell back the next year despite the very costly loss experiences of 1994. There is no shortage of capacity in the reinsurance industry. For the past half-dozen years, J. P. Morgan and Marsh and McLennan have littered Bermuda with reinsurance companies, launching new ones when they get capital by selling a previous venture to the public. A joint venture of these two with Traveler's Insurance, the Americans' first effort to keep Stephen Merrett in business, was not consumated early in 1994. Sandy Weill's Primerica bought Traveler's and pulled out of the deal. "Have you been surprised," Weill said when asked about it, "to see all those intelligent people from Lloyd's doing the same thing again in Bermuda?"

Swiss Re, the world's second-largest company in this business (Munich Re remains first), sold off its direct insurance business to others in autumn 1994 to concentrate its resources on reinsurance. If Lloyd's had to be reorganized as groups of small insurance companies, American companies seeking reinsurance of their general corporate liability, professional malpractice, hurricane and earthquake risks, might be inconvenienced, and might have to pay higher premiums, but they probably would not have to abandon these businesses unless they wished to do so.

Still, there might be a good deal of damage done. Insurers pay claims from their reserves, sometimes borrowing from current premium income, and replace the funds from their reinsurance. If the reinsurance company cannot pay, an insurer may find himself with reserves inadequate to meet the standards set by whatever government body licenses and supervises him. At this point, the regulator—in the United States, a state insurance commissioner—may insist that the company raise fresh capital, and failing that may organize a rescue operation involving reductions of payouts on certain policies plus contributions to the defunct's estate from other insurance companies doing business in the state. American insurance companies are counting on reimbursement from Lloyd's for payments that have been or soon will be made to policyholders. If Lloyd's syndicates or their successors at Equitas refuse to pay—and demands that policies be "commuted" are not much more than refusals to pay—a great deal of turmoil may result in the American market.

The cant line among American insurers who see trouble ahead at Lloyd's is that if Lloyd's can't raise the money from the Names, they will do it themselves, pursuing Names individually to make them pay up. But with very few exceptions, Names either don't have enough exposure on individual policies to make it worth a single policyholder's while to sue, or don't have the money to pay off the policyholder who does sue.

Andrew Grossman, the American Name who teaches law on the European continent, has decried what he describes as Lloyd's success in casting the action groups as greedy Names out to cheat innocent policyholders. But it is true that in their anger at Lloyd's, the Names have failed to consider the interests of those who accepted assurances of "ultimate good faith" when they bought the Lloyd's policies from people the Names had accepted as their representatives. If Lloyd's has so far had the support of the governments in its efforts to bleed the Names, it is because the leaders of the governments understand that if the day comes when Lloyd's (or Equitas) admits it cannot pay off the policies at one hundred cents on the dollar, the parcel will have passed into the hands of its ultimate recipient: their taxpayers. Just as the losses are too big to be borne by the Names, the recoveries under the policies are too important to be forgone by the victims of asbestosis, pollution, earthquakes, hurricanes, accidents on land and sea and in the air, malfeasance by directors and officers of corporations and accountants. Political authority would have to distribute the pain.

It would require great luck as well as both intelligence and political will to keep the peace among the many very different claimants from the Lloyd's estate. To date, the participants have retained surprising civility. Apart from Middleton's outburst at one of Tom Benyon's Society of Names conferences, and the clear implication in Rowland's attempt to seize the proceeds of the Gooda Walker suit that if he didn't do so, the Americans would never pay their debts, official Lloyd's has been careful in its statements about how the Americans done us in. And though one hears stories about slow payment of claims from individuals insured by Lloyd's (for damage to big-ticket items: yachts, mansions, racehorses, jewelry), few of the complainers have gone public.

Lloyd's is not the only target of such accusations. Many insurers have drastically slowed their payments on both general liability and disaster claims—after the Oakland fire of 1991 that destroyed so many fine homes in the canyon, the reluctance of insurers to live up to their obligations without a court order became such a scandal that "Alternate Dispute Resolution" panels were set up to handle the cases. But at Lloyd's the change seems to have been systemic. Many more syndicates have been encouraged to leave payment decisions to Lloyd's claims settlement office, and that office, Eugene Anderson says, has increasingly refused to pay claims without at least a threat of lawsuit, and sometimes not until after a trial and court orders confirmed on appeal.

●

Casualty insurance has been a rapidly growing business. Everything costs more and is insured for more. Jumbo aircraft replace puddle jumpers; supertankers plow the seas. The earthquake near

Los Angeles that did $18 billion worth of damage in early 1994 could have struck in the same place twenty years earlier, before the Los Angeles exurbs had ballooned, and scarcely made a blip in the insurers' books. By the year 2000, the demographers estimate that 70 percent of Americans will live within forty miles of a coastline—and even as they disagree about whether or not man has created global warming or ozone holes, the climatologists all predict that the chemicals loosed into the atmosphere in modern society will generate increasingly violent storms. Meanwhile, the second half of the twentieth century in the United States has seen the triumph of a philosophy that holds that there is no such thing as bad luck, that someone should and can *and will* be made to pay for almost anything awful that happens. "To write casualty insurance in the United States," Stephen Merrett said shortly before his resignation from the Council, "requires a belief against all experience that you can write a policy that enables you to remain solvent. It's no comfort to a customer if his insurer goes down the tubes before he can get to him."

Richard Sandor, a chunky American with a wide forehead, is a former University of California economics professor who parlayed an academic interest in financial innovation into a large fortune and a place in the history books. He invented the futures contract on U.S. Treasury bonds, over the last twenty years probably the most heavily traded instrument in the world—and, more remarkably, sold it as an idea to a Chicago Board of Trade executive committee not one member of which had the faintest notion what he was talking about. Later he became research director at the Board of Trade. While in that job, in the 1970s, he wrote the first paper about "catastrophe futures" as a way to bring market disciplines to insurance—the last financial services sector where there is no "price discovery," no way to find out what other purchasers are paying for similar contracts. Nobody nibbled—at Lloyd's, an associate of Sandor's trying to find somebody with whom to discuss the idea was unable to get above the assistant researcher level.

Sandor moved on to be head of the Chicago office of Drexel

Burnham, then a senior executive at Kidder Peabody (leaving both before the roof fell in), and then signed on with Center Re, one of the earliest of the Morgan/Marsh Bermuda companies, now independent of both, to be chairman and CEO of its Centre Trading subsidiary. In 1992, Lester Rosenthal of the Board of Trade, who had been Sandor's advocate twenty years before, showed up in New York to consult with Sandor about launching an insurance contract, and presently the thing had happened.

"The United States," Sandor says in his shining white large corner office on the forty-second floor of New York's Chase Manhattan building (a telescope points through the canyon to the Hudson River, so he can study the fine points of the passing traffic when he wishes), "has $175 billion in capital in 825 reinsurance companies, and there's maybe $15 billion left in Lloyd's—maybe. How can you support $7 trillion of property on $175 billion of capital? A. M. Best [the leading gatherer of insurance statistics] says there's $124 billion of losses in pollution. Northridge [the L.A. earthquake] took out $18 billion. Hurricane Andrew took out $18 billion.

"The risk-bearing ability is no longer present in the insurance business, and may never be present again, for two reasons. One is that the changing social contract means that you cannot run a risk-adjusted portfolio. The other is that economic and demographic developments concentrate population and economic infrastructure in high-risk areas. If you can't socialize the risks and you can't raise the rates, you have to bring in more capital, and the way to do that is to commoditize insurance the way we commoditized mortgages, so people can trade the risks. The technology is there— instead of a portfolio of assets, you have a portfolio of liabilities."

Like the other financial commodities contracts, the insurance future would be based on an index, in this case an index of loss experience month by month over a period of a dozen years. The purchaser of the contract would buy the right to receive a premium, and the obligation to pay losses claimed in that time period (up to $50,000 a contract). Instead of the reinsurance company writing an insurance contract, members of first the trading community and eventually a speculating and perhaps even an investing public would buy a futures contract. ("The trick," says Sandor, "is to make it simple enough so a pension fund is not at an informational disadvantage with the guys who are writing the policies.") These contracts could be tailored to regions, industries, time periods of different durations, according to demand. They could supplement conventional reinsurance—or, in many instances, replace it.

Sandor has been working with the U.S. Department of Agriculture to create a futures contract replacing old-fashioned government crop insurance, which, he says, "suffers from both adverse selection [the farmers most likely to buy it are the worst farmers] and moral hazard [once a farmer has bought insurance he doesn't care whether he farms his land well or not]." The escape is through the creation of an index of normal crop yields in the area where the farmer farms, which relates the insurance he receives to his results by comparison with his neighbors' results.

Asked what income stream could support the recruitment of capital to such markets, Sandor has a quick answer: the revenue would come from what is now paid for brokerage. "Half the stuff brokers sell," he says, "you should sell through QVC [the television home shopping channel]. There is no way a financial industry should have a thirty percent cost for a standardized product. Right now it's like Pirandello—five thousand insurance companies in search of a convention. It may take twenty years, but it's coming." A simpler system is to be offered in New York starting in 1996, when a new exchange will permit insurers to price and trade catastrophe risks in different regions of the United States.

While commoditization is en route, Lloyd's reinsurance business will have a terrible time competing against the new Bermuda companies. A spokesman for Marsh and McLennan admitted that his company was interested in backing Stephen Merrett as a captive to provide reinsurance business without brokerage charges. The acquisitions of Hiscox and Charman by American companies with interests in Bermuda reinsurers illustrate that the process has begun taking giant steps.

Moreover, the Bermuda companies have real advantages. Both as a sales argument to the customer and as a source of revenue, reserves are crucial for a reinsurer. Lenient tax laws in Bermuda permit offshore companies to build reserves, which can then be managed, in most cases, as the insurer wishes. Patient money (the only kind these companies cultivate) can invest in the insurers Morgan and Marsh have launched and watch their capital grow tax-free under the ministrations of Morgan's aggressive asset management.

As noted in Chapter 5, investment in offshore reinsurance vehicles was not foreign to Lloyd's in its glory days, when earnings on revenues could be shielded from the Inland Revenue by purchasing reinsurance abroad. Because this was basically a clandestine activity in London, the practice was abused by Lloyd's insiders, who siphoned off profits that would otherwise have gone to the Names. But the new Bermuda companies formed by the big American banks and brokers are open and aboveboard, most of them now listed corporations, and they have the kind of ratings that draw business that once went to Lloyd's.

There could be a place for a Lloyd's in a world of commodity insurance policies, for many risks will not be so easily trimmed to fit Sandor's Procrustean bed. The Lloyd's that existed before Cromer and before the monstrous expansion of the 1980s could flourish in such an environment, accepting perhaps a net $2 billion of premium income a year, winning higher premiums for the unique expertise of its underwriters and the risk-taking appetite of a close-knit community of Names. Growth was necessary, Rowland's task force insisted, because only a rapidly growing premium income could enable the Names to pay off past losses. With the decision to form NewCo—a concession that the past losses (so much larger than Rowland had estimated) could not be covered by future premiums—the logic of a larger Lloyd's disappeared.

A real hope for the future of Lloyd's is not that its necessarily small syndicates can compete on the world scene for general liability and commercial reinsurance business, but that there is nobody else to meet on reasonable terms what will be a continuing demand for coverage of the one-shot risks—ship sinkings, airplane crashes, kidnappings, twins, bad weather on the movie set, jewel thefts, cancellations by Pavarotti, all the things that can't be commoditized. Syndicates truly restricted to their stated purposes—marine, aviation, motor, casualty risks under British rather than American law—might well flourish even after Bermuda's behemoths and Sandor's markets have moved in on the traditional insurance business.

●

"The alternatives are stark," said David Rowland at the annual general meeting of May 30, 1995, introducing *Reconstruction and Renewal*, his new plan to keep Lloyd's going. One of his senior executives said privately at the end, "If the Names reject this, it's finished."

The heart of the new proposal was an offer to the Names to get them out of their liabilities by reinsuring into the newly created Equitas *everything* in the Lloyd's inventory of open policies up to and including the year 1992. Equitas would be funded by virtually all the reserves held in the syndicates for years before 1992, plus the proceeds of errors-and-omissions insurance benefitting Names who have brought suit against their agents, plus the awards already won in the courts by the action groups, plus a further cash contribution of about $3 billion from the losing Names.

Peter Middleton would try to negotiate a settlement of claims with the Names' action groups between June and October, when members would be asked to give Lloyd's a "mandate" to proceed with the plan. The entire deal would be put to a vote of the membership in spring 1996.

Names are clearly wary. They've won long struggles in courts but have not a pound in their pockets to show for their victories. As Rowland has stated, there is no legal mechanism in place at this time to govern a meltdown of the Society and closure of its syndicates. Rejection leads to the unknown for policyholders and Names alike.

Peter Middleton, employing his customary patience, has held lengthy discussions with leaders of the action groups. Negotiations will probably continue up to the moment when figures are sent to each member for the cost of "finality" on his ballot.

Decisions in court could overtake negotiations. If Names lose important legal battles, their position is very much weaker.

The reverse is also true. A win by the 418 action group would greatly strengthen all the other "long-tail" action groups just as the Gooda Walker Names' success was a powerful precedent for the spiral cases. If the litigating Names prevail in blocking the amendments to the Premium Trust Deeds this fall, cash will go to Names with awards in escrow. Winners will be happy and claimants in other cases will be encouraged to continue litigation.

According to Charlie Sturge of Chatset, Lloyd's could not survive the payout of money to Names from the errors and omissions syndicates. Too much capital would leave the market. Another big if is the progress of the Writs Response case which is scheduled to be heard in English Commercial Court in February. This action still prevents the issuance of writs by the corporation of Lloyd's, while losses from 1992 force further earmarking and drawdowns of the Central Fund.

As a solution to keep Lloyd's alive, *Reconstruction and Renewal* does appear to respond to the demands of Names, as Middleton had indicated to Stockwell at the start of this year. And it pretends to address the concerns of policyholders who have relied on Lloyd's insistence that every valid claim will be paid. Appearances may not match reality in both instances.

For the first time in the litany of Lloyd's "renewal" vehicles, the policyholders may be the worst abused. Equitas is to assume not only the liabilities of run-off syndicates prior to 1986, but in addition all the liabilities from policies written in 1992 and before. In essence, this proposal recognizes that Lloyd's may not be able to squeeze enough money to pay all claims from existing Names. "The future of Lloyd's," the report says, "cannot support an open-ended risk of further exposure to past liabilities."[17] If Lloyd's with its ongoing premium income cannot carry the burden of paying old policies, can Equitas? Lloyd's, as "renewed," would retain its advertising boast that it pays every valid claim, whether or not Equitas paid claims on the old policies.

Putting together its future, Lloyd's will cut the size of the Equitas reserve fund by discounting to present value estimated future payments to its insureds, at an interest rate determined unilaterally by its management "in line with prudent actuarial assumptions." Meanwhile, Lloyd's will assume that because Equitas will not be restricted to short-term investments, the return earned on the reserves will come in at an even higher rate. Thus, the totals needed to fund Equitas can be reduced further by "the anticipated value from these enhanced returns."[18] Many of Lloyd's claimed reserves are in future value rather than present value: Thanks to the "Time and Distance" policies, they have already been discounted. Part of the rest is in reinsurance from weak insurance companies and syndicates, which perhaps should not be credited at face value. And 40 percent of the American reserves, the New York State Insurance Department report reveals, is already in long-term paper.[19] Shortly after Lloyd's cheerful Equitas predictions were published, Heidi Hutter, the American insurance actuary who had signed a three-year contract to get NewCo up and running, and to certify its actuarial solidity, announced she would leave Lloyd's when her contract was completed to become CEO of Swiss Re America. She said her mother was ill and also needed her attention.

To build a "settlement fund" for the Names victimized by monstrous losses caused in part by some of their agents' now proven negligence, Rowland announced a "triple profits release" for spring 1996, for the years 1993 through 1995. This "profits release" will go only to a debt credit for Names; no cash at all: "It will not be possible to pay them to Names at this stage."[20] And for more than half the 1988 Names who are no longer "trading," there is of course nothing. If there ever should be any cash, moreover, one might expect the New York State Insurance Department to grab it to make up some of the $7.8 billion shortfall it has found in Lloyd's American accounts.

The same triple play in spring 1996 will trigger a triple release of profits *commission* for the Names' agents, including those who are being sued by the Names they negligently represented. That triple commission is estimated at about $900 million—and it will be cash for the agents. (Note well that if the deterioration of prior years had been included in the 1993 accounting, instead of separated out into Equitas, the agents probably would not be receiving any profit commission at all for that year.) In return for this beneficence by Lloyd's, and for the Names' signing a release of all their claims against them and anyone else related to their underwriting, the agents will graciously contribute about $300 million to the settlement fund.

Equitas, by reinsuring all Lloyd's owes for the years 1992 and earlier, will give Names "finality"—Lloyd's will excuse them from all additional liabilities to Lloyd's. But the *Renewal* document warns that "It is not within the power of Lloyd's to grant Names an absolute release from their liabilities. There will still be a residual risk for Names in the event of failure by Equitas. In the unlikely event of this happening, Names could once again be exposed to the risk of claims. Names should be aware that the 'finality' offered by Lloyd's as part of their settlement plan does not release Names from their potential exposure." Meanwhile, Lloyd's itself will get out of its Lioncover obligations to pay off the policies illicitly written by Peter Cameron Webb—and its CentreWrite program that funds Estate Protection Plans and the "Hardship Scheme." Note well, again, that the *Renewal* plan calls for the continuing Lloyd's market to pay only $300 million one time only to rid itself forever of losses that ran $400 million in 1994 alone, with much more to come every year.

Six hundred Names are enrolled in Hardship at a cost to the Central Fund of $45 million in 1994. More than two thousand applications are being processed for admission, which promises a hefty increase to sustain them. Names who are dependent upon the support of their Hardship agreements would be among the most vulnerable to a failure of Equitas. If Lloyd's opts out on the Hardship Names, a separate fund should be created, exclusive of any other liabilities, to carry out the terms of their contracts.

Policyholders will retain the right to sue the Names "in the event of failure by Equitas."[21] But they won't be able to sue the Society of Lloyd's for a Lioncover or CentreWrite default, because Lloyd's will be contractually excused from all obligations to Equitas.

Because Equitas mingles all the policies and all the Names, its contract with the reinsured Names will have to say that every Name is liable for any bills Equitas doesn't pay: There will be no more sole traders; each for his own part and not for any other. If Equitas failed, *everyone* with a deep pocket could be liable for the losses, whether or not he had been part of the syndicate that wrote the policy that created the losses. This sort of "finality" could be worse than useless. When the U.S. government's Resolution Trust Corporation was cleaning up the mess in the savings-and-loan industry, the rule of thumb was to pursue any claim that should yield more than $250,000; if the proceeds were likely to be less than that, a lawsuit wouldn't be worth what it would cost. A sole trader a Lloyd's would not have many syndicates in which his share of the underwriting liability was more than $250,000. But as united reinsurers through Equitas, Names would have joint and several liability for everything Equitas failed to pay.

And if it turns out that the triple profits release was optimistic in estimating the cost of the reinsurance to close the 1993–1995 syndicates, which certainly may happen—every previous closed year going back a generation turned out to have been inadequately reinsured at some time in the six following years—the agents will be entitled to go back to the Names who received "debt credit" and tell them they still owe money. One can think of any number of reasons why these Names might not be available for that purpose five or six years later. Under Rowland's plan, the renewed Lloyd's will carry a Central Fund of only $450 million to meet the obligation of Names who don't pay.

To make all this happen, the *Renewal* proposal estimates, to-day's Names will have to contribute more than $3 billion additional cash money to Lloyd's—over and above what they have already lost. "Those Names who decline the offer will not receive these benefits and collection of their outstanding debts will be pursued vigorously."[22] This category would include those who have won their lawsuits against their Names' agents, managing agents, and underwriters, and whose winnings are at this writing still held in escrow until the issue is decided in court, because Lloyd's demands that the money be paid to Lloyd's. If all the money is collected and litigation abandoned according to the provisions of reconstruction and renewal, uncertainty remains. "On the basis of the above projected balance sheet, additional capital is likely to be required from external investors to establish Equitas's required solvency margin."[23]

How well this proposal will be received is still uncertain at this writing. Lloyd's announced its intention to ask members for a "mandate" to proceed on this program in October 1995, obviously in the hope that this indication of approval will convince individual and corporate Names to continue underwriting in 1996, reassure policyholders, encourage business to come to the trading floor, and reduce litigation by action groups. An equally important goal is to retain the publicly silent but uneasy underwriters with ample cash in their reserves. As Rowland said in answer to a question posed to him in early May, "investment bankers are all over the market." It would be surprising to see the rejection of a "mandate," which after all does not cost anybody anything. The vote on specifics, scheduled for spring 1996, would seem more problematic.

There is a large risk for the British government and American state insurance authorities in permitting Lloyd's to continue without close supervision by an external regulator. As the treasury and Civil Service Select Committee of the House of Commons argued in its May 1995 report on Lloyd's, "Until independent and external regulation is put in place, the confidence of the Members of Lloyd's—and to a lesser extent the policyholders—in the regulatory regime will not be achieved."[24] Unfortunately, the conservative government of John Major decided to postpone for at least two years its investigation of regulation at Lloyd's. ("Ministers," *The Financial Times* reported, ". . . dispute that past regulatory failures have damaged the reputation of Lloyd's."[25]) Meanwhile British courts are establishing precedents and American insurance departments are making far-reaching decisions about the issuance of policies by unauthorized insurers in the U.S.

David Rowland has said that for the next two years he will be "too busy" to work with an outside regulator. He had better find the time. The interests involved in the reorganization of Lloyd's are not merely those of the Lloyd's management. The record of recent years gives no reason to believe that without direct government supervision either the policyholders or the Names will receive fair treatment from the insiders at Lloyd's.

"I hope they make it," the then insurance correspondent for *The Financial Times* said to me somewhat shamefacedly in fall 1993, which explained the kindness of the coverage Lloyd's has steadily received in that paper. I hope they make it, too—I remain, after all, however involuntarily, a member of the Society of Lloyd's. But the losses are too great to be finessed by the gimmickry of the new business plans or the reconstructions and renewals. If Lloyd's is to survive in any form, its leaders must accept a continuing obligation to abused Names and endangered policyholders, and must join with them and governments on both sides of the Atlantic to allocate fairly the losses created by the greed, incompetence and negligence that flourished so long in their historic market.

NOTES

1. A Sentimental Business Education

1. Complaint by the Lloyd's Deposit Defence Group to the Commission of the European Communities Against Lloyd's of London, London, 1994, p. 44.
2. George S. Moore, *The Banker's Life*, W. W. Norton, New York, 1987, p. 283.
3. *Report of an Inquiry into Lloyd's Syndicate Participations and the LMX Spiral*, by Sir David Walker, Lloyd's, London, January 1993, pp. 30–31.
4. "John Robson's Speech to the Insurance Institute of London, 18th October 1993," Anton Agency, London, mimeo, p. 3.
5. Ibid., p. 4.
6. "Understanding the Restructured London Insurance Market: Establishing the Key Players and Their Roles," by Seth B. Schafler, *Environmental Claims Journal*, Vol. 6, No. 1, Autumn 1993, pp. 27, 35.
7. *Report on the 1989 and 1990 Underwriting Years of Syndicates 216 and 833/834*, Vol. 1, Lloyd's, London, July 1993, pp. 24–25.
8. *Lloyd's: A Route Forward*, Report of the Task Force, Lloyd's, London, January 1992, p. 56.
9. "Lloyd's Report of Proceedings at the Extraordinary Meeting of Members Held in the Royal Albert Hall on Tuesday, 25 May 1993," mss. transcript, pp. 85–86.
10. *Report of the Gooda Walker Loss Review Committee*, Vol. 1, Lloyd's, London, 1992, p. 106.

11. Moore, *Banker's Life.*
12. "Lloyd's Disputes Suicides Report," by Richard Lapper and Andrew Jack, *Financial Times*, 19/20 February 1994, p. 4.
13. *Briefing*, ALM, London, June 1994, p. 12.
14. "Report of the Proceedings at the General Meeting of Members, the Royal Festival Hall, 22 June 1993," mss. transcript, pp. 62–63.
15. "Collateralizing Reinsurance Recoverables," by Robert M. Hall, in *Solvency Concerns with Foreign Insurers and Reinsurers/Recent Developments/U.S. Reform Efforts*, A Publication of the American Bar Association Section of Business Law, 1994, p. D-7.

2. "A UNIQUE INSTITUTION"

1. *Lloyd's: A Route Forward*, Report of the Task Force, Lloyd's, London, January 1992, p. 25.
2. *Roby* v. *Corporation of Lloyd's*, 796 F. Supp. 103, p. 105.
3. Jonathan Mantle, *For Whom the Bell Tolls*, rev. paper ed., Mandarin, London, 1993, p. 37.
4. Godfrey Hodgson, *Lloyd's of London*, Viking/Penguin, New York, 1984, p. 48.
5. John Plender and Paul Wallace, *The Square Mile: A Guide to the City Revolution*, Hutchinson Business, London, 1986, p. 170.
6. *World-Wide Operations, 1993–94*, The Salvage Association, London, p. 1.
7. "Keeping Underwriters Afloat," by Michael Ellis, *Global Reinsurance*, September 1991.
8. "Challenging the Traditions," by Richard Lapper, *The Financial Times Weekend*, 18/19 June 1994, p. 10.
9. " 'Outsider' Helping to Rescue Lloyd's," by Lisa S. Howard, *National Underwriter*, 1 November 1993, pp. 1, 21.

3. PERSONS

1. Letter from Mrs. J. H. Munn to *One Lime Street*, Lloyd's, London, February 1993, p. 16. She later became somewhat less enthusiastic about Mr. Middleton.
2. "Lloyd's Chief Tells of Drawers Rummage," by Richard Woods, London *Times*, 23 October 1994, p. 3.12.
3. *Report of the Gooda Walker Loss Review Committee*, Vol. 1, Lloyd's, London, 1992, p. iv.
4. See *The Time and Distance Programme of the Gooda Walker Syndicates*, Summary of a Report by Randall Insurance Services, Ltd., to G.W. Run-Off, Ltd., 5 Lloyd's Avenue, London EC3N 3DB, April 1993.
5. "Facing the Music," *One Lime Street*, Lloyd's, London, July 1993, p. 8.
6. *Report on the 1983 Underwriting Year of Syndicate 421*, Lloyd's, London, July 1993, p. 42.

4. Apocalypse Now

1. *Self-Regulation at Lloyd's,* Report of the Fisher Working Party, Lloyd's, London, May 1980, Sec. 3.33, p. 22.
2. *Cromer Report,* Lloyd's, London, 1989 (originally presented 1969), p. 61.
3. *Cromer Report,* Lloyd's, London, pp. 50–51.
4. Godfrey Hodgson, *Lloyd's of London,* Viking/Penguin, New York, 1984, p. 344.
5. *Submission to the Treasury Select Committee on Self Regulation at Lloyd's* by the Lloyd's Names Associations' Working Party, 1 December 1994, p. 20.
6. "Lloyd's Market 1990" DYP Insurance and Reinsurance Research Group Ltd, pp. 6, 31–38, 64, 74, 109, 119, 137, 138, 179, 193, 195, 199.
7. Andrew Tobias, *The Invisible Bankers,* Simon & Schuster, New York, 1982, p. 86.

5. The Beginnings of the Crisis

1. Godfrey Hodgson, *Lloyd's of London,* Viking/Penguin, New York, 1984, pp. 247–48.
2. Jonathan Mantle, *For Whom the Bell Tolls,* rev. paper ed., Mandarin, London, 1993, p. 87.
3. Hansard, 9 July 1993, p. 1722.
4. *Self-Regulation at Lloyd's,* Report of the Fisher Working Party, Lloyd's, London, May 1980, letter of transmission, p. 3.
5. *Self-Regulation at Lloyd's,* pp. vi–ix.
6. Ibid., p. 22.
7. Ibid., p. 43.
8. Ibid., p. 55. It was in this context that Fisher recommended the prohibition of any agreement that restricted the liability of either Names' agents or underwriting agents.
9. Ibid., p. 56.
10. Ibid., p. 58.
11. Ibid., p. 127.
12. Ibid., pp. 138, 139.
13. EGM (Extraordinary General Meeting), 1993, p. 108.
14. Hodgson, *Lloyd's of London,* p. 317.
15. Ian Hay Davison, *A View of the Room: Lloyd's, Change and Disclosure,* Weidenfeld & Nicolson, London, 1987, pp. 53–54.
16. Ibid., p. 50. Emphasis added.
17. Mantle, *For Whom the Bell Tolls,* p. 170.
18. Davison, *View of the Room,* p. 178.
19. "The PCW Settlement Offer" made by Lloyd's, April 1987. Offer 1 Documentation, p. 3. Emphasis in the original.

6. The Rot in the Foundations

1. *Asbestos-Related Occupational Diseases: Hearings on H. 341–31 Before the Subcommittee on Compensation, Health and Safety,* 95th Congress, 2d Sess., 1975, pp. 24–128.
2. "Merrett Syndicate 418/417, 1985 Year of Account," by Richards Butler, *Opinion,* London, 26 October 1992, p. 18.
3. *Report on the 1983 Underwriting Year of Syndicate 421,* Lloyd's, London, July 1993, pp. 21–22.
4. Ibid., p. 25.
5. Ibid., p. 27.
6. Ibid., p. 30.
7. Ibid., p. 31, 32.
8. "Merrett Syndicate 418/417, 1985 Year of Account," p. 40.
9. Ibid., p. 41.
10. Ibid.
11. *Something Quite Excellent,* The Merrett Group, London, 1985, pp. 5, 105–107.
12. *Keene Corporation* v. *Insurance Company of North America,* 667 F.2d 1034.
13. Richards Butler, *Opinion,* p. 8, quoting Merrett's underwriter's statement for 421 in the 1984 Managing Agent's Report to Names.
14. Clive Francis, "Syndicate 418 Chronology of Events," London, 1990, mimeo, p. 1.
15. Richards Butler, *Opinion,* p. 13.
16. *Chatset Guide to Syndicate Run-Offs, 1993,* Chatset, London, November 1993, p. 129.
17. Jonathan Mantle, *For Whom the Bell Tolls,* rev. paper ed., Mandarin, London, 1993, p. 241.
18. Conversation with Mark Connelly and John White Thompson (solicitors with Richards Butler).
19. Francis, "Syndicate 418 Chronology of Events," p. 5.
20. *Merrett Underwriting Agency Management, Ltd.,* 1990 Underwriting Accounts, London, 31 May 1991, pp. 36–37.
21. *Merrett Underwriting Agency Management, Ltd.,* 1991 Underwriting Accounts, London, 31 May 1992, p. 40.
22. Ibid., pp. 14, 15.
23. *Merrett Underwriting Agency Management, Ltd.,* 1992 Underwriting Accounts, Syndicate 418, London, 31 May 1993, p. 12.
24. *Merrett Underwriting Agency Management, Ltd.,* 1993 Underwriting Accounts, Syndicate 418, London, 31 May 1994, pp. 2–3.
25. *Chatset 1993,* p. 2.

7. THE WHIRLPOOL

1. *Report on the 1989 and 1990 Underwriting Years of Syndicates 216 and 833/834*, Vol. 1, Lloyd's, London, July 1993, p. 44.

2. *Angerstein Underwriting Trust PLC*, prospectus, Natwest Markets, London, 1993, p. 10. Salomon Brothers in its 1994 report *Lloyd's and the London Insurance Market—a Pivotal Year* estimates total market costs for Lloyd's (on a basis comparable to the costs of U.S. insurance companies) at 30.6 percent of premiums in 1986 and 40.7 percent in 1990, as against 27 to 29 percent in the United States and the United Kingdom for stand-alone insurance companies.

3. *CLM Insurance Fund PLC: Placing and Offer for Subscription*, Sponsored by Barclays de Zoete Wedd, London, 1993, p. 12.

4. "The Canadian Names Action Against Lloyd's," Investor's Research Corp., 17713 S. Federal Highway, Jupiter, FL 33469, 1993, mimeo, p. 14.

5. *Report of an Inquiry into Lloyd's Syndicate Participations and the LMX Spiral*, by Sir David Walker, Lloyd's, London, January 1993, p. 11.

6. Ibid., p. 21.

7. Archer agencies, 23 May 1991.

8. *Report on the 1989 Underwriting Year of Syndicates 666 and 268*, by Jeremy Casson, Lloyd's, London, 1993, p. 24. Note the splendid British understatement of "the benefits are limited."

9. Ibid.

10. *Report of an Inquiry into Lloyd's Syndicate Participations and the LMX Spiral*, p. 13.

11. Ibid.

12. *Report of the Gooda Walker Loss Review Committee: Syndicate 164— 1989, Syndicate 290—1989 and 1990, Syndicate 298—1988 and 1989, Syndicate 299—1988*, Vol. 1, Lloyd's, London, 1992, p. 20.

13. *Report on the 1989 and 1990 Underwriting Years of Syndicates 216 and 833/834*, Vol. 1, Lloyd's, London, July 1993, p. 13. Percentages calculated by author.

14. *Report of the Gooda Walker Loss Review Committee*, p. 27.

15. Ibid., p. 144.

16. Ibid., p. 146.

17. Ibid., p. 61.

18. *Chatset Guide to Syndicate Run-Offs, 1994*, Chatset, London, November 1993, p. 124.

19. Gooda Walker Action Group letter to members, 13 June 1994, p. 2.

20. Ibid., p. 10.

21. *Deeny* v. *Gooda Walker*, Royal Courts of Justice, 1993 Folio No. 335, p. 31.

22. Ibid., p. 98.

23. Ibid., p. 101.

24. Ibid., p. 39.

25. Ibid., p. 70.
26. Adam Raphael, *Ultimate Risk: The Inside Story of the Lloyd's Catastrophe*, Bantam Press, London, 1994, p. 200.
27. Ibid., pp. 178–79.
28. *Report of an Inquiry into Lloyd's Syndicate Participations and the LMX Spiral*, p. 9.
29. G. S. Christensen and Others, Non-Marine Syndicate 958, *Report and Accounts, 31st December 1993*, London, p. 23.
30. C. F. Palmer and Others, Non-Marine Syndicate 314, *Report and Accounts, 31st December 1993*, Ashley Palmer Syndicates Limited, London, p. 32.
31. M. H. Cockell and Partners, Non-Marine Syndicate 570, *Underwriting Accounts, 1992*, London, p. 22.
32. D. P. Mann, *Syndicate 435 Annual Report, 1993*, London, pp. 7, 27.
33. C. H. Bohling and Others, Marine Syndicate 833/834, *Syndicate Accounts, 31 December 1992*, Devonshire Underwriting Agencies Limited, London, p. 25.
34. Chatset 1993, p. 74.

8. THE COLONIES TO THE RESCUE

1. Letter from Geoffrey C. Hazard, Jr., to Lloyd Cutler, Special Counsel to the President, 11 July 1994, p. 3.
2. Letter from D. G. L. Mott, Director, Roderick Pratt Underwriting Agencies, Ltd., to Judge Stephen Breyer, 7 September 1982.
3. Judge Stephen Breyer, Lloyd's Number 19256X, *1987 Syndicate Commentaries*, Sedgwick Agency, London, 1990, p. 3.
4. Handwritten response to questionnaire from More/Fisher/Brown, solicitors, questionnaire dated May 1992, p. 2.
5. Letter from Judge Stephen Breyer to Mrs. June Armour, Oxford Members Agency, Ltd., 1 September 1988.
6. Agency 1627 F, Sedgwick Lloyd's Underwriting Agents Limited, Lloyd's Solvency Test Members' Agent Report, p. 3.
7. Letter from Judge Stephen Breyer to Mrs. June Armour, 13 December 1993, p. 2.
8. "Breyer's Bad Investment Could Embarrass the High Court," by James K. Glassman, *The Washington Post*, 20 July 1994, sec. F, p. 1.
9. Letter from Douglas Hawes to William Toomey, Esq., 4 March 1988, p. 1.
10. Letter from Douglas Hawes to William E. Morley, 28 September 1987, p. 1.
11. Ibid., p. 9.
12. Ibid., p. 12.
13. Offering memorandum, Lloyd's, London, p. 6.

14. Letter from Douglas Hawes to William Toomey, Esq., 8 January 1988, p. 2.

15. Letter from Douglas Hawes to William Toomey, Esq., 22 February 1988, p. 2.

16. Ibid.

17. In the Matter of: R. W. Sturge, Ltd., Falcon Agencies, Ltd., Tim Coleridge and Nick Wentworth-Stanley, State of Ohio Department of Commerce Division of Securities Order #94-203.

18. Offering memorandum, Lloyd's, London, p. 12.

19. *Roby* v. *Corporation of Lloyd's*, 91 Civ. 7081.

20. *Leslie* v. *Lloyd's*, U.S. District Court for the Southern District of Texas, entered 16 May 1991, Xerox, p. 6.

21. "Leader," *One Lime Street*, Lloyd's, London, November 1994, p. 12.

22. *Kozberg* v. *Alexander and Alexander Services, Inc.*, Case No. BC 071950, First Amended Complaint, 1 March 1993, Los Angeles Superior Court, pp. 25–26.

23. *Wishful Thinking: A World View of Insurance Solvency Regulation*, Report by the Subcommittee on Oversight and Investigations, Committee on Energy and Commerce, U.S. House of Representatives, October 1994, pp. 42–44.

24. *Analog*, Vol. 1, No. 2, 15 October 1993, Rancho Santa Fe, pp. 1–2.

25. Grossman, *Restatement of Legal Defense and Asset Protection Issues*, p. 17, citing *In re Kissel*, 92 B 16589 (Bankr. N. D. Ill. 1992).

26. Ibid., p. 10. Italics in the original.

27. "Hey, Lloyd's, Make Our Day," *Newsweek*, 18 October 1993, p. 59.

28. "Lloyd's Shuts Out Would-Be Names from North America," by Ralph Atkins, *The Financial Times*, July 18, 1995, p. 14.

9. PANIC ON LIME STREET

1. *Market Report*, Sedgwick Lloyd's Underwriting Agents Limited, London, Autumn 1991, p. 3.

2. Adam Raphael, *Ultimate Risk: The Inside Story of the Lloyd's Catastrophe*, Bantam Press, London, 1994, p. 142.

3. Merrett Underwriting Agency Management, Ltd., *1990 Underwriting Accounts*, London, 31 May 1991, p. 55. A small fraction of the result is probably explained by currency fluctuations.

4. *Interim Award Between Stephen Roy Merrett and Michael Turner*, Lloyd's, London, 1988, p. 18.

5. *Chatset Guide to Syndicate Run-Offs, 1993*, Chatset, London, November 1993, p. 77.

6. *One Lime Street*, Lloyd's, London, August 1993, p. 13.

7. Outhwaite Syndicate Report to Names, July 1992, cited in Raphael, *Ultimate Risk*, pp. 146–47.

8. *Lloyd's: A Route Forward*, Report of the Task Force, Lloyd's, London, January 1992, p. 5.

9. Ibid., p. 56.

10. Ibid., p. 107.

11. Ibid., p. 111. Emphasis in the original.

12. Ibid., p. 21.

13. *Chatset 1993*, p. 21.

14. *Value at Lloyd's*, Lloyd's, London, May 1994, p. 19.

15. *Lloyd's: A Route Forward*, p. 158. Emphasis in the original.

16. Ibid., p. 160.

17. *Value at Lloyd's*, p. 5.

18. *Planning for Profit: A Business Plan for Lloyd's of London*, Lloyd's, London, April 1993, p. 3.

19. *Wishful Thinking: A World View of Insurance Solvency Regulation*, Report by the Subcommittee on Oversight and Investigations, Committee on Energy and Commerce, U.S. House of Representatives, October 1994, p. 43.

20. M. H. Cockell and Partners, Non-Marine Syndicate 570, *Underwriting Accounts 1992*, London, p. 2.

21. H. J. Jago and Others, Non-Marine Syndicate 205, *Report and Accounts, 31st December 1993*, p. 3.

22. G. S. Christensen and Others, Non-Marine Syndicate 958, *Report and Accounts, 31st December 1993*, London, p. 7.

23. Joanne Doroshow and Adrian J. Wilkes, *Goliath: Lloyd's of London in the United States*, Center for Study of Responsive Law, Washington, D.C., 1988, p. xi. The internal quote is from the state attorney general's brief.

24. Ibid., pp. 1, 2, 3.

25. *Chatset 1993*, p. 18.

26. "Names rap Lloyd's Figure," by Richard Lapper, 2 September 1994, p. 8.

27. *NEWCO—a Route Forward*, Presentation to the Insurance Institute of London by Heidi E. Hutter, Project Director, Old and Open Years, 12 January 1994, Lloyd's, London, p. 2.

28. M. H. Cockell and Partners, Non-Marine Syndicate 570, *Underwriting Accounts 1992*, p. 2.

29. *Old and Open Years Project Newsletter No. 3*, Lloyd's, London, May 1994, p. 4 (but unpaginated).

30. "Lloyd's: Reconstruction and Renewal," *One Lime Street*, Lloyd's, London, May 1995, p. 42.

10. The Struggles

1. "Report of the Proceedings at the General Meeting of Members, the Royal Festival Hall, 22 June 1993," mss. transcript, p. 32.

2. Ibid., p. 19.

3. "Lloyd's Chief of Finance Is Soon Gone," *The New York Times*, 3 August 1993, sec. D, p. 3.

4. Letter from Judge Stephen Breyer to Ms. Julia Barkworth, Merrett Syndicate 418 Names Association, 11 January 1994, p. 1.

5. "Solvency Sniffing," *The Economist*, 13 August 1994, p. 69.

6. *Proposed Changes to the Premiums Trust Deeds—Consultation Document*, Lloyd's, London, October 1994, p. 7.

7. "Judge Deplores Underwriters' Failure to Assess Full Extent of Risk," by John Mason, *The Financial Times*, 5 October 1994, p. 10.

8. *Note for Names on Amendments to Premiums Trust Deeds*, Lloyd's, March 1995, p. 2

9. Certification of Andrew Alexander Duguid in opposition to Plaintiff's motion to strike the answer of Defendant. *HM Holdings, Inc., U.S. Industries Inc., and Kidde Industries, Inc.* v. *Aetna Casualty & Surety Co., et al.,* Civil Action Docket No. L-11532-94, Superior Court of New Jersey, Law Division, Middlesex County, 5 June 1995, pp. 8–9, 11.

10. *Report on Examination of Lloyd's, London as of December 31, 1993,* New York State Department of Insurance, New York, 11 May 1995, pp. 11–13.

11. *The Society of Lloyd's* v. *John Stewart Clementson,* opinion of the court, November 1994, mimeo; opinion, p. 24, concurring opinion, p. 3.

12. "UK Appeal Court Ruling," *One Lime Street,* Lloyd's, London, November 1994, p. 3.

13. "Still in Troubled Waters," *The Economist,* 10–16 December 1994, p. 87.

11. THE ENDGAMES

1. "London May Cut Catastrophe Brokerage," by Edward Ion, *Lloyd's List,* 15 October 1993.

2. 1993 annual meeting, pp. 43–44. Emphasis added.

3. New York State Insurance Department Regulation No. 41, 11 NYCR 27, effective 1 January 1994, Sec. 27.17, p. 19.

4. Ibid., p. 12.

5. Ibid., p. 15.

6. From Lloyd's American Trust Deed, preprinted in "Collateralizing Reinsurance Recoverables," by Robert M. Hall, in *Solvency Concerns with Foreign Insurers and Reinsurers,* American Bar Association, 1994, p. D-23.

7. Ibid., p. D-8.

8. New York State Insurance Department Report, pp. 20–22.

9. "Selected Issues for Policyholders (Including Ceding Insurers) in Securing Meritorious Claims Being Disputed by Lloyd's or Other Alien Insurers," by G. Larry Engel, in *Solvency Concerns,* p. E-12.

10. Ibid., p. E-29.

11. "Solvency Concerns with Foreign Insurers and Reinsurers," by Allan Gee, in *Solvency Concerns*, p. A-3.
12. Comments on Meetings with Middleton, Lloyd's Names Associations' Working Party, Oxford, 24 January 1995, p. 2.
13. Lloyd's Names Associations' Working Party Newsletter No. 14, September 1994, p. 3.
14. Letter from Richard Hobbs to Lord Alexander of Tunis, 4 May 1995, p. 1.
15. "Trial and Error," by Catrin Griffiths, in *Legal Business*, London, December 1994, p. 70.
16. "2 U.S. Groups Buy Stakes in Syndicates at Lloyd's," *The New York Times*, 1 December 1994, p. D5.
17. *Lloyd's: Reconstruction and Renewal*, London, 1995, p. 28.
18. *Lloyd's: Reconstruction and Renewal*, p. 24.
19. New York State Insurance Department Report, p. 19.
20. Ibid., p. 21.
21. Ibid., p. 4.
22. Ibid., p. 19.
23. *Lloyd's: Reconstruction and Renewal*, p. 41.
24. Lloyd's Names Associations' Working Party Newsletter #18, London, June 1995, pp. 4–5.
25. "MPs Protest at Delay in Reform," by Ralph Atkins and James Blitz, *The Financial Times*, 21 July 1995, p. 6.

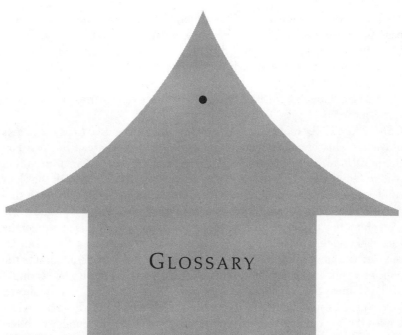

GLOSSARY

AGENT. (1) MANAGING AGENT: a company (usually incorporated) that administers the affairs of one or more syndicates (q.v.). The syndicates, acting for their members, are the actual insurers. The underwriters who place the syndicate's stamp (q.v.) on a policy work for the managing agents, which are not themselves insurers. (2) NAME'S AGENT: a company (again, usually incorporated) that acts at Lloyd's for the "underwriting members" of the Society, called Names (q.v.). Names' agents, also called members' agents, choose the syndicates their Names will support and handle all legal and clerical matters arising out of their clients' membership at Lloyd's.

BINDER: an agreement by an insurance syndicate (or an insurance company, outside the Lloyd's system) to write a policy promising a payment to the insured if certain specified evils befall him. This agreement precedes the creation of the policy itself, requires no advance deposit by the insured, and is a legacy from a time when gentlemen assumed that they were bound by a deal from the time they entered into it, regardless of when the papers were signed. At Lloyd's, it was routine for several months to elapse between the binder and the payment of the first premium on an insurance contract.

BROKER: the intermediary between the insured and the insurer, who negotiates for his client the terms of the insurance policy—the hazards to be covered, the premium to be paid, the deductibles, the maximum payout, the right to renew. The binder may be issued by a broker, if he has been authorized to do so. Brokers are uniquely important at Lloyd's, because they bring in all the business: Lloyd's underwriters do not normally employ insurance agents or operate storefront offices. The brokers handle the money, passing the premiums paid for policies from their clients to the underwriters, and passing the payments on claims from the underwriters to the policyholders. Until the 1990s, because many different Lloyd's syndicates might be involved in any single policy, each taking only a portion of the risk, only the brokers had all the information on Lloyd's policies. Since the early 1980s, most larger Lloyd's brokerage firms have been subsidiaries of American companies.

CENTRAL FUND: money Lloyd's controls that can be used to pay the debts of Names who cannot or will not make good on their share of the losses on the policies for which they accepted premiums. Every dollar of premium paid to Lloyd's is taxed a fraction of a penny to build or replenish the Central Fund, and in 1991 the Council of Lloyd's imposed a large tax on the succeeding three years' premiums to make sure that Lloyd's would have enough money to pay off on the policies of the syndicates. It is to protect the Central Fund that Lloyd's measures the amount of premium a Name can receive by the amount of the funds he has deposited at Lloyd's, and limits the policies a syndicate can write to the "stamp capacity" (q.v., under "stamp") of the Names whose agents have agreed to have them "on" this syndicate. When Lloyd's sues Names to recover losses for which they have not reimbursed their syndicates, the suit is brought by the Central Fund, which has put up the money.

CLAIM: an assertion that the event for which an insurance policy is supposed to provide compensation has occurred, and the insurer now owes money to the insured.

IBNR: an anticipated claim, "incurred but not reported." Estimating future claims is the magical art of the insurance business. It is especially important at Lloyd's because the Lloyd's syndicates are formed anew each year, and the estimate of the claims overhanging on a syndicate's policy determines how much profit the syndicate can claim.

LIONCOVER: the name for the wholly owned insurance company Lloyd's set up within its own framework to pay the losses of the Peter Cameron-Webb (PCW) syndicate that was revealed to have placed its reinsurance contracts with offshore entities controlled by Webb that were liquidated before paying the claims from Webb's Lloyd's syndicates. Because of the overwhelming evidence of fraud, Lloyd's agreed that the Names who had backed these syndicates should not be held liable for their unprotected losses. These losses have been much larger than anticipated, and have placed an annual burden of more than $60 million on the Lloyd's membership, with, apparently, much more to come.

LPSO: Lloyd's Policy Signing Office. Each insurance policy underwritten by a Lloyd's syndicate must be examined and approved (which has always been a formality) by the central office of Lloyd's, which then places the Lloyd's rubber stamp (an anchor) on it to signify that it has become an obligation of a Lloyd's syndicate. Having stamped a policy, Lloyd's in practice guaranteed the payment of valid claims arising from its provisions.

NAME: a member of the Society of Lloyd's. Names are the ultimate underwriters of Lloyd's policies. The term grows out of the fact that in the early days of Lloyd's coffeehouse and for more than a century thereafter, each guarantor of a policy signed the policy himself. The Names' agents arrange with the syndicates for each Name to receive up to a certain maximum amount of premium for the year, which places the Name at risk to pay a certain fraction of any losses that may be incurred by the policies the syndicate writes on his behalf. If their share of the losses is less than the premium they have received, the Names keep the difference as their profit (after the deduction of the costs asserted by their managing and Names' agents and the "profit commissions" these agents take). At the peak (1988) there were more than 32,000 Names at Lloyd's. In 1995, there were less than half as many.

PONZI SCHEME: a pyramid-type swindle, named for a Boston postman, an American term not widely used in England. In a Ponzi scheme, a promoter uses money given him by later "investors" to pay high returns to the first participants, meanwhile skimming a large commission for himself. Eventually, of course, the Ponzi scheme self-destructs, when it runs out of willing new "investors." Insurance policies that pay previous losses out of premiums paid by new insureds to cover the risk of future losses are not unreasonably described as Ponzi schemes.

PREMIUM TRUST FUND: the repository for the premiums Names accept as recompense for assuming the risk of the policies. The premiums deposited in the fund are held in escrow for the Names individually. They cannot be removed from the fund except for the payment of claims and reinsurance until the syndicate has reinsured all its outstanding obligations and has been closed. At that point all money in the fund paid with reference to the expiring year and not needed to pay current or forecast claims or expenses on the maintenance of the Name's account at Lloyd's must be distributed.

REINSURANCE: a policy purchased by an insurance company (or a Lloyd's syndicate) to protect it from losses on its own policies.

RETROCESSION: the reinsurance of a reinsurer.

RISK: the potential losses on an insurance policy; by extension, the policy itself. Underwriters at Lloyd's will refer to "a risk" they have accepted or rejected.

RITC: reinsurance to close. This is the central, informing act of the Lloyd's managing agent. In a system where each year of a syndicate is a separate enterprise, the profits earned on a year's policies will be determined by the decision on how much money will be needed to pay off known claims and IBNR (q.v.) claims. Presumably, that number will be the burden on the successor syndicate that assumes those claims. The premium on the reinsurance to close the dying syndicate will involve, like the premium on a new policy, some calculation of the interest that will be earned on this money in the period before actual payment of the known and latent claims under the policies to be reinsured. The shibboleth is that the RITC must be equitable between the Names on the syndicate that will now be closed and the Names on the new syndicate that assumes the old risks. In the 1980s, obviously, the premiums paid for RITC often were not equitable as between the Names on the old syndicate and the Names on the new one, an injustice mitigated in most cases by the fact that most of the Names on the new syndicate had also been on the old one. Most, but not all.

RUN-OFF: the process of collecting money from Names and paying claims to policyholders on syndicates that for one reason or another cannot negotiate a reinsurance to close. The administration of such run-off syndicates is separate from the writing of insurance and the collecting of premiums, and tends to be very expensive for the Names who are periodically assessed for the losses of the syndicate as the run-off proceeds.

SOLE TRADER: a term of art for an individual who owns and operates an unincorporated business. Any losses that business may have become his personal liability. The owner of a mortgaged home is also a sole trader: The mortgage remains his debt if the home is worth less than what he owes when the time comes for him to sell it. On the other hand, a sole trader is not responsible for anyone else's debts unless he signs that person's note.

STAMP: the acknowledgment, by an inked rubber stamp printed on a piece of paper and countersigned by the underwriter of the syndicate, that the Names on this syndicate have accepted some share of the risk the insured wishes to cover. Each syndicate has its own trademark stamp, and the LPSO (q.v.) has a Lloyd's stamp that concludes the deal. Lloyd's looks at the total exposure in terms of premiums the Names through their agents have agreed to accept in each syndicate, and sets a limit on the amount of insurance that syndicate can write. This limit is the syndicate's STAMP CAPACITY. This limit has not been enforced, nor has Lloyd's imposed significant penalties on managing agents who accept premiums for their Names beyond their stamp capacity.

SYNDICATE: the Lloyd's equivalent of an insurance company. The syndicate acts for its Names as an insurance company would act for its shareholders, but a Lloyd's syndicate has no juridical existence, being merely an association of its Names. Each syndicate covers one calendar year of policy writing. At year's end, another syndicate comes into being. But the accounts of the previous syndicate are not closed for another two years. (This is to change after 1996.) If the syndicate has profits after the calculation of the unpaid claims and the IBNR at the end of the succeeding two years, each Name shares in those profits pro rata to his share of the premium the syndicate has accepted; if the syndicate has losses, each Name is responsible for a pro rata share of the losses. No Name is responsible for the losses of any other Name—each is a sole trader. If one Name fails to pay, the money must be made up by Lloyd's from its Central Fund, or the policyholder receives less than his valid claim.

UNDERWRITING: in the insurance world, the act of assuming responsibility for the payment of claims on an insurance policy. Names are "underwriting members" of Lloyd's. They delegate authority to incur such responsibilities to a managing agent, who employs someone labeled an underwriter to work on the floor at Lloyd's.

INDEX